C000000652

citibank®

全城美食優惠
Great food everywhere.

Powered by Citi.

下載Citibank手機程式
瀏覽身邊最熱優惠
Download Citibank Mobile Application
to search for offers nearby

MICHELIN GUIDE

HONG KONG MACAU 2011

RESTAURANTS

& HOTELS

米芝蓮指南
香港 / 澳門 2011
餐廳及酒店

DEAR READER

We are delighted to present our third edition of the MICHELIN Guide Hong Kong Macau.

The success of our guide has had quite an impact. The quality of the restaurants in Hong Kong and Macau is constantly improving and our teams have made every effort to update the selection in order to fully reflect the richness and diversity of the two cities.

As part of our meticulous and highly confidential evaluation process, Michelin inspectors have spent the year conducting anonymous visits to Hong Kong and Macau restaurants and hotels.

The Michelin inspectors are the eyes and ears of our customers and thus their anonymity is key to ensuring they receive the same treatment as any other guest.

This year, you will notice that new symbols have been created: those restaurants that are new to the guide are indicated by NEW; while restaurants that have been newly promoted are indicated by ℅↗.

You will see that Michelin Stars are not our only awards – look out also for the Bib Gourmand ⊛. These are restaurants where the cooking is still carefully prepared but in a simpler style and, priced at under $300, they represent excellent value for money.

All the restaurants within this guide have been chosen first and foremost for the quality of their cooking.

You'll find comprehensive information on over 200 dining establishments within these pages, ranging from noodle shops to internationally renowned restaurants. The diverse and varied selection bears testament to the rich and buoyant dining scene in Hong Kong and Macau, with both cities now enjoying a worldwide reputation for the breadth and quality of their restaurants.

This guide is renewed and revised each year and we are committed to providing the most up to date information to ensure the success of your dining experience. This is why only this year's edition of the guide to Hong Kong and Macau is worthy of your complete trust.

As well as the restaurants, our team of independent inspectors has also chosen over 50 hotels.

These carefully selected hotels represent the best that Hong Kong and Macau have to offer. All have been chosen for their individuality and personality.

We are always very interested to hear what you, our readers, think. Your opinions and suggestions matter greatly to us and help shape the guide, so please do get in touch.

Email us at michelinguide.hongkong-macau@cn.michelin.com

We wish you the very best in your Hong Kong and Macau hotel and dining experiences.

Bon appétit!

親愛的讀者

很高興向您宣佈:《米芝蓮指南 香港 澳門》第三版(2011年版)隆重登場!

本指南取得的成功,為飲食界帶來了頗大的影響。 香港及澳門地區餐廳質素的不斷提升,我們的團隊盡一切努力地搜羅資訊,令指南內各式各樣的餐廳均經過精挑細選及更新,務求能充份表現兩個城市多姿多彩的美食佳餚。

米芝蓮評審員到訪香港及澳門的餐廳和酒店時不會透露身份,因此評選過程一絲不苟而且高度保密。 他們充當顧客的耳目,保持神秘身份能確保與任何其他顧客都享受相同遇待。

今年,你會留意到新的標記:指南中新增的推介餐廳標有「NEW」、評級有所晉升的餐廳則標為「😊」。

您會發現除了獲得米芝蓮星級評分的餐廳之外,我們也有「米芝蓮車胎人美食」(Bib Gourmand)的推介榜「😀」。 這些餐廳的食物煮法雖然簡單,但一點也不馬虎,而且價錢在$300以下,絕對是價廉物美的起值之選。

米芝蓮指南介紹的餐廳都以高質素的廚藝掛帥,從小小的麵家到享譽全球的餐廳,我們為您帶來超過200間食肆最全面的資料。港澳兩地的餐廳一向以優質和種類繁多而聞名,本指南內各式各樣的餐廳均經過精挑細選,能充份表現兩個城市多姿多彩的美食佳餚。

本指南每年更新修訂,致力提供最新資訊,讓你的覓食旅程更美滿。 故此,今年版的香港及澳門指南絕對值得你去百分百信任。

另外,我們獨立的評審員也揀選了超過50間酒店。 這些酒店全都經過悉心挑選,並以其獨特的個性而取勝,是香港和澳門兩地最出色的酒店。

我們樂意聆聽所有讀者的想法,包括你。 你的意見和提議對我們來說意義重大,並能協助我們令指南做得更好。 請務必與我們聯絡:

電郵:michelinguide.hongkong-macau@cn.michelin.com

祝您在香港和澳門擁有精彩、愉快的住宿和美食體驗!

Bon appétit!

THE MICHELIN GUIDE'S COMMITMENTS

"This volume was created at the turn of the century and will last at least as long".

This foreword to the very first edition of the MICHELIN Guide, written in 1900, has become famous over the years and the Guide has lived up to the prediction. It is read across the world and the key to its popularity is the consistency of its commitment to its readers, which is based on the following promises.

Anonymous inspections:

Our inspectors make regular and anonymous visits to restaurants and hotels to gauge the quality of products and services offered to an ordinary customer. They settle their own bill and may then introduce themselves and ask for more information about the establishment. Our readers' comments are also a valuable source of information, which we can then follow up with another visit of our own.

Independence:

Our choice of establishments is a completely independent one, made for the benefit of our readers alone. The decisions to be taken are discussed around the table by the inspectors and the editor. Inclusion in the Guide is completely free of charge.

Selection and choice:

The Guide offers a selection of the best restaurants and hotels.

This is only possible because all the inspectors rigorously apply the same methods.

Annual updates:

All the practical information, the classifications and awards are revised and updated every single year to give the most reliable information possible. Consistency: The criteria for the classifications are the same in every country covered by the Michelin Guide.

...And our aim:

To do everything possible to make travel, holidays and eating out a pleasure, as part of Michelin's ongoing commitment to improving travel and mobility.

承諾

「這冊書於世紀交替時創辦，
亦將繼續傳承下去。 」

這是 1900 年米芝蓮首冊指南的
前言，多年來享負盛名，並如
預期般一直傳承下去。 指南在
世界各地均大受歡迎，關鍵在
其秉承一貫宗旨，履行對讀者
的承諾。

匿名評審：

我們的評審員以匿名方式定期到
訪餐廳和酒店，以一般顧客的
身份對其產品和服務質素作出評
估。 評審員自行結賬後，有時
可能會介紹自己，並詢問更多
關於餐廳的資料。 讀者的評語
和推薦也是寶貴的資訊來
源，我們隨後會根據讀者的推
薦親身到訪。

獨立性：

餐廳的挑選完全是基於我們獨立
的決定，純以讀者的利益為依
歸。 經評審員和編輯一同討論
後才作出決定，被指南收錄的
餐廳完全不會被收取任何費用。

選擇：

全賴所有評審員都使用相同的嚴謹方法，指南才能提供一系列的最佳餐廳和酒店。

每年更新：

所有實用資訊、分類及評級每年都會修訂和更新，務求為讀者提供最可靠的資料。

…至於我們的目標：

盡全力令旅遊、放假及外出用膳成為一大樂事，實踐米芝蓮一貫優化旅遊和外出的承諾。

一致性：

米芝蓮指南涉及的每個國家都用相同的分類準則。

CONTENTS

目錄

THE MICHELIN GUIDE OVER THE YEARS

Today the MICHELIN Guide and its famous red cover are known around the world. But who really knows the story behind this «travellers' bible» that has served people in many countries for many years? After winning over Europe and the United States, Bibendum – «The Michelin Man» – is now in Asia, and will relate the fantastic adventure that started in France, a long time ago...

The first steps

Everything began one fine day in 1900, when André and Édouard Michelin published a guide to be offered free of charge to motorists. It included information to help these pioneers (barely 3,500 automobiles were on the road) to travel around France: garages, town plans, sights to see, lodgings and restaurants, and so forth. The guide was an instant success and became the indispensable companion of all drivers and travellers, bar none.

On the strength of this success and driven on by the development of the motor car, *the Manufacture française* extended the scope of «the little book

with the red cover» to other European countries beginning in 1904, and a few years later (1908) published an adaptation of the *Guide France* in English.

A star is born

As of 1920, the guide was no longer free, but marketed for sale. Little by little, the practical information gave way to a wider selection of hotels and restaurants. The mysterious, daunting «Michelin inspector» was not in the picture at first. Rather, it was touring clubs and readers that contributed to the discerning selection of establishments.

The goal of officially identifying places «where one dines well» was materialized in 1926 by the *Étoile de Bonne Table* – the first Michelin star – soon to be followed by two and three-star establishments (1931 for the provinces and 1933 for Paris). The guide thus clearly focused on gastronomy and the quest for good restaurants became its real driving force.

In step with the times

During the Second World War, the guide did not appear. The post-war edition of 1945 did not use star ratings, which were applied again as of 1951, when conditions were more settled. Ever more successful, the Guide was to cover all of Western Europe as of the 1960s. In 1982, *Main Cities of Europe* was published in English, marking Michelin's decidedly European dimension.

100 years young...

2000 was a winning year for Michelin: the Guide celebrated its 100th anniversary and The Michelin Man was voted best corporate logo of the century!

More dynamic than ever, the «little red guide» took on new challenges and set off for the United States. The guide New York not only lived up to expectations, but the first edition was awarded the prize for «Best Restaurant Guide in the World». San Francisco followed and this year sees the publication of our first Chicago guide.

In 2007, we published Michelin Tokyo guide which confirmed Tokyo as one of the world's great capitals of fine cuisine. Kyoto and Osaka quickly followed and this year we have added Kamakura, Kobe and Yokohama.

Twenty countries covered in Europe, in addition to guides for US cities, Japan, Hong Kong and Macau: the Michelin Guide confirms its truly international standing.

Just a gleam in the eyes of the founders more than a century ago, The Michelin Man is now an international star to be proud of, carrying the Michelin tradition into the 21st century.

米芝蓮指南的歷史

今時今日，米芝蓮享譽國際，它的紅色封面家傳戶曉。 多年來，這本「旅遊聖經」為很多國家的人提供寶貴資訊，但又有多少人知道它背後的故事呢？

The Michelin Man「米芝蓮車胎人」，在歐洲和美國駐足後，繼而來臨亞洲，將會延續當年在法國展開的探險旅程⋯

旅程的開始

1900年晴朗的一天，André 和 Édouard Michelin 出版了一本指南，免費贈予駕車人士。 當時法國只有約 3,500 部汽車行駛。 指南涵蓋環遊法國的資訊：車房位置、城市地圖、觀光景點、住宿、餐廳等等。 指南的出版取得空前成功，成為所有駕駛者和旅客的必需品。

適逢指南的空前成功和當時汽車業的迅速發展，米芝蓮公司便乘勝追擊，於 1904 年把這本「紅色指南」帶到其他歐洲國家。 1908年，這本「法國指南」更開始以英文出版。

星的誕生

自1920年起，指南開始在市面上發售，不再是免費贈閱。 除了實用資訊外，指南日漸覆蓋更多酒店及餐廳資料。

在神秘的米芝蓮評審員出現之前，餐飲推介與選擇的訊息都是來自旅遊俱樂部和讀者。

直至1926年，米芝蓮首次引入星級評分制度，得到一星（*Étoile de Bonne Table*）的餐廳為最為美味的餐廳；其後，各省份和巴黎更分別於1931年和1933年實行二星及三星評分。 此後指南便集中評選美食，致力搜羅一流餐廳的資訊。

歐洲之旅

指南業務蒸蒸日上，直至1939年戰爭爆發，一切運作暫停。1945年業務回復正常，從1950年起，新一代指南陸續面世：由1952年的西班牙到1994年的瑞士指南，期間更於不同的歐洲國家出版。1982年，米芝蓮出版歐洲主要城市指南（*Main Cities of Europe guide*），確立其歐洲主導地位。

長青一百歲

2000年是米芝蓮的勝利年，不但是指南出版的百週年紀念，The Michelin Man「米芝蓮車胎人」更獲選為世紀最佳公司標誌！這本「紅色小指南」比以往更顯積極，不斷迎接新挑戰，並進軍美國市場。紐約指南非但不負眾望，更於初版被譽為「世界上最佳餐廳指南」。 其後，三藩市指南相繼出版，而今年則可見證第一本芝加哥指南的誕生。

2007年，米芝蓮東京指南隆重面世，確立了東京作為世界美食之都的地位。 其後旋即推出京都及大阪指南，今年更加入鎌倉、神戶和橫濱等城市。

踏入二十一世紀，米芝蓮指南已涵蓋二十三個國家，包括歐洲，美國，日本，以及香港暨澳門，其國際地位實在毋庸置疑。

一個多世紀前，始創人的一絲靈感造就了The Michelin Man「米芝蓮車胎人」的誕生。 今天，「米芝蓮車胎人」是令人引以爲榮的國際巨星，引領米芝蓮於二十一世紀與時並進。

HOW TO USE
THIS RESTAURANT GUIDE
如何使用餐廳指南

Map number / coordinates
地圖號碼 / 座標

New entry in the guide
新增推介

Cuisine type
菜式種類

Name of restaurant
餐廳名稱

Stars for good food
美食星級

✿ to ✿✿✿

**Bib Gourmand
(Inspectors' favourite
for good value)**
(評審員的推介榜)
😋

**Restaurant classification
according to comfort**
餐廳 — 以舒適程度分類

🍴	Simple shop 簡單的食店
✕	Quite comfortable 頗舒適
✕✕	Comfortable 舒適
✕✕✕	Very comfortable 十分舒適
✕✕✕✕	Top class comfort 高級舒適
✕✕✕✕✕	Luxury 豪華

Particularly pleasant if in red
紅色代表上佳

Portuguese/葡式   MAP/地圖 19/B-2

Casa Lisboa   NEW

😋   ✕✕

                                               ⇄60 🕐🍴

Caldo verde, stuffed crab, seafood stews, suckling pig and a reassuringly large selection of bacalhau recipes are just some of the highlights of an appealing menu which sees subtle Macanese influences added to Portuguese dishes. It may be on the 8th floor of the LKF Tower but this cosy room is brightly decorated in a traditional Portuguese style with blue and white azulejos. The national flag is also reflected in the colours of the waitresses' aprons.

傳統葡國腸薯蓉翠菜湯、葡式釀蟹蓋、海鮮雜燴、葡式烤乳豬及多姿多采的馬介休菜式系列，不過是這吸引人的餐牌上部分重點部分，令它的葡國菜流露出絲絲澳門色彩。雖然位於蘭桂坊LKF Tower八樓，但明亮鮮豔的裝潢，以傳統葡萄牙風格配上藍白瓷磚畫（azulejos），給人溫暖而舒適的感覺。侍應圍裙的顏色亦採用葡萄牙國旗顏色。

■ ADDRESS/地址
TEL. 2905 1168
8F, LKF Tower, 55 D'Aguilar Street, Central
中環德己立街55號 LKF Tower 8樓
www.ad-caterers.com

■ ANNUAL AND WEEKLY CLOSING
休息日期
Closed 4 days Lunar New Year and Sunday
農曆新年4天及週日休息

● OPENING HOURS, LAST ORDER
營業時間, 最後點菜時間
Lunch/午膳 12:00-15:00 L.O.14:30
Dinner/晚膳 18:30-24:00 L.O.23:00

● PRICE/價錢
Lunch/午膳   set/套餐 $138
             à la carte/點菜 $220-420
Dinner/晚膳 à la carte/點菜 $220-420

76

Cantonese/粵菜　　　　　　　　　　　　　MAP/地圖　17/B-2

Celebrity Cuisine
名人坊

✿ ✿　　　　　　　　　　　　　　　　　　✕✕

⇦16 ◔⊪

Limited capacity and a host of regulars mean that booking ahead is vital at this very discreet restaurant concealed within the Lan Kwai Fong hotel. Those regulars come for authentic Cantonese cuisine that is also delicate and sophisticated. The menu may be quite short but there are usually plenty of specials; highlights include chicken with Huadiao rice wine, ox tongue and, one of the chef's own creations, 'bird's nest in chicken wing'.

餐廳座位有限，但常客眾多，故此提早預約是必須的。這隱藏在蘭桂坊酒店內的餐廳看似不甚出眾但內有乾坤，這裡最大的賣點就是廣東菜，既精緻又獨具特色。餐牌雖則頗短，但提供大量特選菜式，包括花雕焗飛天雞及紅燒牛脷。其中，由主廚創作的是燕窩釀鳳翼。

■ ADDRESS/地址
TEL. 3650 0066
1F, Lan Kwai Fong Hotel,
3 Kau U Fong, Central
中環九如坊3號蘭桂坊酒店1樓

■ ANNUAL AND WEEKLY CLOSING
休息日期
Closed 3 days Lunar New Year
農曆新年休息3天

■ OPENING HOURS, LAST ORDER
營業時間, 最後點菜時間
Lunch/午膳 12:00-14:30 (L.O.)
Dinner/晚膳 18:00-23:00 (L.O.)

■ PRICE/價錢
Lunch/午膳　à la carte/點菜 $200-600
Dinner/晚膳　à la carte/點菜 $300-800

Restaurant promoted
to a Bib Gourmand
or Star
評級有所晉升的餐廳

Restaurant symbols
餐廳標誌

Ⓢ	Cash only 只收現金
♿	Wheelchair access 輪椅適用
🛖	Terrace dining 陽台用餐
⋖	With a view 有景觀
🗝	Valet parking 代客泊車
🅿	Car park 停車場
⇦25	Private room with maximum capacity 私人房間及容納人數
⋤	Counter 櫃檯式
◔⊪	Reservations required 需訂座
◔⊬	Reservations not accepted 不可訂座
🍇	Interesting wine list 供應優良的酒類

HOW TO USE
THIS HOTEL GUIDE
如何使用酒店指南

Map number / coordinates
地圖號碼 / 座標

New entry in the guide
新增推介

Name of hotel
酒店名稱

Hotel classification according to comfort
酒店 — 根據舒適程度分類

🏠 Quite comfortable
頗舒適

🏠🏠 Comfortable
舒適

🏠🏠🏠 Very comfortable
十分舒適

🏠🏠🏠🏠 Top class comfort
高級舒適

🏠🏠🏠🏠🏠 Luxury
豪華

Particularly pleasant if in red
紅色代表上佳

● MAP/地圖 27/B-1

East NEW
東隅

Describes itself as a 'lifestyle business hotel' where even the water feature by the entrance tells you it's a little different. It has it all: an uncluttered lobby, a chic bar, relaxed dining, even a paperless check-in (you sign a screen); plus a stunning rooftop terrace bar named 'Sugar', as this was once a sugar factory. Bedrooms are minimalist and use plenty of glass and wood to create a warm, tasteful feel. Corner rooms have great views.

294

RESTAURANTS/ 餐廳

Recommended/推薦	Also/其他
	Feast

Restaurant information
餐廳資料

Hotel symbols
酒店標誌

標榜為一家悠閒式商務酒店，東隅入口處的水飾已顯出一點兒與別不同。整潔的大堂，時尚的酒吧，氣氛輕鬆的餐廳，甚至電子入住登記（你可在輕觸式螢幕上簽名），加上一個可觀看維港迷人景色的天台露台酒吧"Sugar"一名字靈感源自酒店前身為糖廠，絕對切合你所需。客房佈置採用簡約風格，利用大量玻璃與木材來塑造溫暖而具品味的感覺。位處轉角的客房景觀尤佳。

■ ADDRESS/地址
TEL. 3968 3968
FAX. 3968 3933
29 Taikoo Shing Road, Island East
港島東太古城道29號
www.east-hongkong.com

■ ROOMS AND SUITES/客房及套房
Rooms/客房 =345

■ PRICE/價錢

👤	$ 1,200-2,000
👥	$ 1,200-2,000
Suites/套房	$ 3,500-6,000
☕	$ 140

295

Symbol		
♿	Wheelchair access	輪椅適用
⋖	With a view	有景觀
🅿🔑	Valet parking	代客泊車
🅿	Car park	室外停車場
🚗	Garage	室內停車場
🚭	Non smoking bedrooms	非吸煙臥室
🏃	Conference rooms	會議室
🏊 🏊	Outdoor/Indoor Swimming pool	室外／室內游泳池
Spa	Spa	水療
🏋	Exercise room	健身室
🎰	Casino	娛樂場

HONG KONG
香港

THE ART OF IMPROVISATION

RESTAURANTS
餐廳

STARRED RESTAURANTS

Within this selection, we have highlighted a number of restaurants for their particularly good cooking. When awarding one, two or three Michelin Stars there are a number of factors we consider: the quality and compatibility of the ingredients, the technical skill and flair that goes into their preparation, the clarity and combination of flavours, the value for money and above all, the taste. Equally important is the ability to produce excellent cooking not once but time and time again. Our inspectors make as many visits as necessary, so that you can be sure of the quality and consistency.

A two or three star restaurant has to offer something very special that separates it from the rest. Three stars – our highest award – are given to the very best.

Cuisines in any style of restaurant and of any nationality are eligible for a star. The decoration, service and comfort levels have no bearing on the award.

星級餐廳

在這系列的選擇裡，我們特意指出菜式上佳的餐廳。 給予一、二或三粒米芝蓮星時，我們考慮到以下因素：材料的質素和相容性、烹調技巧和特色、氣味濃度和組合、價錢是否相宜，以及味道。同樣重要的是能夠持續提供美食。 我們的評審員會因應需要而多次到訪，所以讀者可肯定食物品質和一致性。

二或三星餐廳必有獨特之處，比其他餐廳更出眾。最高評級-三星-只會給予最好的餐廳。

不論餐廳的風格如何，供應哪個國家的菜式，都可獲星級。 餐廳陳設、服務及舒適程度亦不會影響評級。

Exceptional cuisine, worth a special journey.
出類拔萃的菜餚，值得專程到訪。

One always eats here extremely well, sometimes superbly. Distinctive dishes are precisely executed, using superlative ingredients.

食客可在這裡享用美味的菜餚，有時令人更讚不絕口。獨特的菜式以最高級的材料精密地烹調。

Caprice		XXXX	French 法式	75
Lung King Heen 龍景軒		XXXX	Cantonese 粵菜	173
Sun Tung Lok 新同樂	NEW	XXXX	Chinese 中式	222

Excellent cuisine, worth a detour.
傑出美食，值得繞道前往。

Skilfully and carefully crafted dishes of outstanding quality.

有技巧地精心烹調菜餚，品質優秀。

Amber			XXXX	French contemporary 時尚法式	67
Celebrity Cuisine 名人坊	ㄜ		XX	Cantonese 粵菜	77
Cuisine Cuisine at The Mira 國金軒 (The Mira)	NEW		XXX	Cantonese 粵菜	94
8½ Otto e Mezzo	NEW		XXX	Italian contemporary 時尚意式	105
L'Atelier de Joël Robuchon			XX	French contemporary 時尚法式	151
Ming Court 明閣			XXX	Cantonese 粵菜	181
Pierre	ㄜ		XXXX	French contemporary 時尚法式	199
T'ang Court 唐閣			XXXX	Cantonese 粵菜	233
Tim's Kitchen 桃花源小廚			XXX	Cantonese 粵菜	250

NEW : New entry in the guide/ 新增推介
ㄜ : Restaurant promoted to a Bib Gourmand or Star/ 評級有所晉升的餐廳

A very good restaurant in its category.
同類別中出眾的餐廳。

A place offering cuisine prepared to a consistently high standard.
持續高水準菜式的地方。

Bo Innovation		XXX	Fusion 多國菜	71
Café Gray Deluxe	NEW	XX	European contemporary 時尚歐陸式	73
Cépage		XXX	French contemporary 時尚法式	79
Chilli Fagara 麻辣燙	⁹⁄	X	Sichuan 川菜	83
Din Tai Fung (Causeway Bay) 鼎泰豐 (銅鑼灣)	NEW	X	Shanghainese 上海菜	97
Din Tai Fung (Tsim Sha Tsui) 鼎泰豐 (尖沙咀)		X	Shanghainese 上海菜	98
Dynasty (Wan Chai) 滿福樓 (灣仔)		XXX	Cantonese 粵菜	104
Farm House 農圃		XX	Cantonese 粵菜	107
Fook Lam Moon (Kowloon) 福臨門 (九龍)		XXX	Cantonese 粵菜	109
Fook Lam Moon (Wan Chai) 福臨門 (灣仔)		XXX	Cantonese 粵菜	110
Forum 富臨		XX	Cantonese 粵菜	111
Fu Ho (Tsim Sha Tsui) 富豪 (尖沙咀)	NEW	XXX	Cantonese 粵菜	112
Fung Lum 楓林小館	⁹⁄	XX	Cantonese 粵菜	113
Golden Leaf 金葉庭		XXX	Cantonese 粵菜	120
Golden Valley 駿景軒	⁹⁄	XXX	Cantonese and Sichuan 粵菜及川菜	121
Hin Ho Curry (Shau Kei Wan) 恆河咖喱屋 (筲箕灣)	NEW	◔	Indian 印度菜	129
Ho Hung Kee 何洪記	⁹⁄	◔	Noodles and Congee 粥麵	130
Hoi King Heen 海景軒	NEW	XXX	Cantonese 粵菜	131
Hong Zhou 杭州酒家		XX	Hang Zhou 杭州菜	134
Hung's Delicacies 阿鴻小吃		◔	Chiu Chow 潮洲菜	139
Island Tang 港島廳		XXX	Cantonese 粵菜	144
Kin's Kitchen 留家廚房	⁹⁄	X	Cantonese 粵菜	149
Lei Bistro 利小館	NEW	X	Chinese 中式	153

BIB GOURMAND

This symbol indicates our inspector's favourites for good value. Restaurants offering good quality cooking for $ 300 or less (price of a 3 course meal excluding drinks).

這標誌表示評審員認為價錢合理而美味的餐廳。300 元或以下便可享用優質美食（三道菜式的價錢，不包括飲料）。

Bombay Dreams	NEW	✗✗	Indian 印度菜	72
Café Siam		✗	Thai 泰式	74
Casa Lisboa	NEW	✗✗	Portuguese 葡式	76
Che's 車氏粵菜軒		✗✗	Cantonese 粵菜	80
Cheung Kee 祥記飯店		✗	Pekingese 京菜	82
Chuen Cheung Kui (Causeway Bay) 泉章居（銅鑼灣）	NEW	✗	Hakkanese 客家菜	86
Chuen Cheung Kui (Mong Kok) 泉章居（旺角）	NEW	✗	Hakkanese 客家菜	87
Crystal Jade La Mian Xiao Long Bao (Kowloon Bay) 翡翠拉麵小籠包（九龍灣）		⅋	Chinese 中式	90
Crystal Jade La Mian Xiao Long Bao (TST) 翡翠拉麵小籠包（尖沙咀）		✗	Chinese 中式	91
Crystal Jade La Mian Xiao Long Bao (Wan Chai) 翡翠拉麵小籠包（灣仔）		✗	Chinese 中式	92
Da Ping Huo 大平伙		✗	Sichuan 川菜	95
Dong Lai Shun 東來順	⅋	✗✗	Chinese 中式	100
Fofo by el Willy	NEW	✗	Spanish (Tapas) 西班牙菜(小菜)	108
Fu Sing (Causeway Bay) 富聲（銅鑼灣）	NEW	✗✗	Cantonese 粵菜	115

NEW : New entry in the guide/ 新增推介
⅋ : Restaurant promoted to a Bib Gourmand or Star/ 評級有所晉升的餐廳

RESTAURANTS BY AREA
餐廳 — 以地區分類

Hong Kong Island/香港島

Admiralty/金鍾

Café Gray Deluxe	NEW	❀	XX	European contemporary 時尚歐陸式 73
Domani			XX	Italian 意式 99
Golden Leaf 金葉庭		❀	XxX	Cantonese 粵菜 120
Lobster Bar and Grill 龍蝦吧			XX	Seafood 海鮮 168
Man Ho 萬豪殿			XX	Cantonese 粵菜 179
Nicholini's 意寧谷			XxX	Italian contemporary 時尚意式 187
Peking Garden (Admiralty) 北京樓 (金鍾)			XX	Pekingese 京菜 194
Petrus 珀翠		❀	XxXX	French 法式 198
Roka			XX	Japanese contemporary 時尚日式 203
Summer Palace 夏宮		❀	XxX	Cantonese 粵菜 220
Thai Basil			X	Thai 泰式 238
Yè Shanghai (Admiralty) 夜上海 (金鍾)			XxX	Shanghainese 上海菜 274

Causeway Bay/銅鑼灣

Chuen Cheung Kui (Causeway Bay) 泉章居 (銅鑼灣)	NEW	⊕	X	Hakkanese 客家菜 86
Din Tai Fung (Causeway Bay) 鼎泰豐 (銅鑼灣)	NEW	❀	X	Shanghainese 上海菜 97
Fan Tang 飯堂	NEW		XxX	Chinese 中式 106
Farm House 農圃		❀	XX	Cantonese 粵菜 107
Forum 富臨		❀	XX	Cantonese 粵菜 111
Fu Sing (Causeway Bay) 富聲 (銅鑼灣)	NEW	⊕	XX	Cantonese 粵菜 115
Ho Hung Kee 何洪記	✤	❀	凵	Noodles and Congee 粥麵 130

NEW : New entry in the guide/ 新增推介
✤ : Restaurant promoted to a Bib Gourmand or Star/ 評級有所晉升的餐廳

Central/中環

Sai Wan Ho/西灣河

Hin Ho Curry (Sai Wan Ho)
恆河咖喱屋 (西灣河)　NEW　🐟　🍚　Indian 印度菜　128

Shau Kei Wan/筲箕灣

Hin Ho Curry (Shau Kei Wan)
恆河咖喱屋 (筲箕灣)　NEW　🐟　🍚　Indian 印度菜　129

On Lee 安利　NEW　🍚　Noodles 麵食　192

Sheung Wan/上環

Lin Heung Kui 蓮香居　🐟　🍚　Cantonese 粵菜　164

Sang Kee Congee & Noodles (Sheung Wan)
生記清湯牛腩麵家 (上環) NEW　🍚　Noodles and Congee 粥麵　207

Sun Yuen Hing Kee
新園興記　NEW　🐟　🍚　Cantonese Roast Meats 燒味　223

Tim's Kitchen 桃花源小廚　🐟🐟　XXX　Cantonese 粵菜　250

Wagyu Kaiseki Den　🐟　XXX　Japanese 日式　258

Tai Koo Shing/太古城

Peking Garden (Tai Koo Shing)
北京樓 (太古城)　XXX　Pekingese 京菜　197

Tin Hau/天后

Kin's Kitchen 留家廚房　🍜　🐟　X　Cantonese 粵菜　149

Wan Chai/灣仔

Bo Innovation　🐟　XXX　Fusion 多國菜　71

Cépage　🐟　XXX　French contemporary 時尚法式　79

Che's 車氏粵菜軒　🐟　XX　Cantonese 粵菜　80

Cheung Kee 祥記飯店　🐟　X　Pekingese 京菜　82

Crystal Jade La Mian Xiao Long Bao (Wan Chai)
翡翠拉麵小籠包 (灣仔)　🐟　X　Chinese 中式　92

Dynasty (Wan Chai)
滿福樓 (灣仔)　🐟　XXX　Cantonese 粵菜　104

Fook Lam Moon (Wan Chai)
福臨門 (灣仔)　🐟　XXX　Cantonese 粵菜　110

Kowloon/九龍

Hung Hom/紅磡

Jordan/佐敦

Choi Lung 彩龍	NEW	🍜	Congee 粥品		85
Lo Chiu (Jordan) 老趙 (佐敦)	NEW	🍜	Vietnamese 越南菜		169
Nice Congee Shop 和味生滾粥店	NEW	🍜	Congee 粥品		186
Tam's Yunnan Noodles (Jordan Road) 譚仔雲南米線 (佐敦道)		🍜	Noodles 麵食		231
Xin Dan Ji 新斗記		X	Seafood 海鮮		267
Yat Tung Heen (Jordan) 逸東軒 (佐敦)		XX	Cantonese 粵菜		271

Kowloon Bay/九龍灣

Crystal Jade La Mian Xiao Long Bao (Kowloon Bay) 翡翠拉麵小籠包 (九龍灣)	⊛	🍜	Chinese 中式		90
Lei Garden (Kowloon Bay) 利苑酒家 (九龍灣)	🍲 ⊛	XX	Cantonese 粵菜		156
Shanghai Xiao Nan Guo (Kowloon Bay) 上海小南國 (九龍灣)		XX	Shanghainese 上海菜		210
Siu Shun Village Cuisine 肇順名匯河鮮專門店		X	Shun Tak 順德菜		213
Tasty (Kowloon Bay) 正斗粥麵專家 (九龍灣) NEW	⊛	🍜	Noodles and Congee 粥麵		237

Kwun Tong/觀塘

Lei Garden (Kwun Tong) 利苑酒家 (觀塘)	XX	Cantonese 粵菜		157

Mong Kok/旺角

Chuen Cheung Kui (Mong Kok) 泉章居 (旺角)	NEW	⊛ X	Hakkanese 客家菜		87
Fung Shing (Mong Kok) 鳳城 (旺角)	NEW	X	Cantonese 粵菜		114
Good Hope Noodles 好旺角麵家		🍜	Noodles and Congee 粥麵		122
Lei Garden (Mong Kok) 利苑酒家 (旺角)		⊛ XX	Cantonese 粵菜		158

RESTAURANTS BY CUISINE TYPE
餐廳 — 以菜式分類

Cantonese/粵菜

NEW　: New entry in the guide/ 新增推介

♺　: Restaurant promoted to a Bib Gourmand or Star/ 評級有所晉升的餐廳

Cantonese and Sichuan/粵菜及川菜

Cantonese Roast Meats/燒味

Chinese /中式

Crystal Jade La Mian Xiao Long Bao (Kowloon Bay) 翡翠拉麵小籠包 (九龍灣)			⊕	🍴	Kowloon Bay 九龍灣	90
Crystal Jade La Mian Xiao Long Bao (TST) 翡翠拉麵小籠包 (尖沙咀)			⊕	🍴	Tsim Sha Tsui 尖沙咀	91
Crystal Jade La Mian Xiao Long Bao (Wan Chai) 翡翠拉麵小籠包 (灣仔)			⊕	🍴	Wan Chai 灣仔	92
Dong Lai Shun 東來順	🍃		⊕	🍴🍴	Tsim Sha Tsui 尖沙咀	100
Fan Tang 飯堂	NEW			🍴🍴🍴	Causeway Bay 銅鑼灣	106
Kimberley Chinese Restaurant 君怡閣	NEW		⊕	🍴🍴🍴	Tsim Sha Tsui 尖沙咀	148
Kwan Cheuk Heen 君綽軒	NEW			🍴🍴🍴	North Point 北角	150
Lei Bistro 利小館	NEW	✿		🍴	Causeway Bay 銅鑼灣	153
Queen's Palace 帝后殿			⊕	🍴🍴	Wan Chai 灣仔	200
Shanghai Garden 紫玉蘭				🍴🍴🍴	Central 中環	209
Sun Tung Lok 新同樂	NEW	✿✿✿		🍴🍴🍴🍴	Tsim Sha Tsui 尖沙咀	222
The Chinese Restaurant 凱悅軒	NEW			🍴🍴🍴	Tsim Sha Tsui 尖沙咀	241
Xi Yan Sweets 囍宴 甜 · 藝				🍴	Wan Chai 灣仔	268
Yellow Door Kitchen 黃色門廚房	🍃		⊕	🍴	Central 中環	273
Yung Kee Siu Choi Wong 容記小菜王			⊕	🍴	Sham Shui Po 深水埗	279

Chinese contemporary/時尚中式

Hutong 胡同		🍴🍴	Tsim Sha Tsui 尖沙咀	140
Nanhai No.1 南海一號 NEW	✿	🍴🍴	Tsim Sha Tsui 尖沙咀	183

Chiu Chow/潮洲菜

Chiu Chow Garden (Tsuen Wan) 潮江春 (荃灣)		🍴🍴	West New Territories 新界西部	84
Hung's Delicacies 阿鴻小吃	✿	🍴	North Point 北角	139

Congee/粥品

Choi Lung 彩龍	NEW	🍴	Jordan 佐敦	85
Nice Congee Shop 和味生滾粥店	NEW	🍴	Jordan 佐敦	186
Trusty Congee King 靠得住	NEW	🍴	Wan Chai 灣仔	252

Dim Sum/點心

Dim Sum 譽滿坊			X	Happy Valley 跑馬地	96
One Dim Sum 一點心	NEW	✿	⌁	Mong Kok 旺角	190
Tim Ho Wan (Mong Kok) 添好運 (旺角)		✿	⌁	Mong Kok 旺角	248
Tim Ho Wan (Sham Shui Po) 添好運 (深水埗)	NEW	✿	⌁	Sham Shui Po 深水埗	249

Dumplings/餃子

Dumpling Yuan (Central) 餃子園 (中環)	NEW		⌁	Central 中環	103
Wang Fu 王府	NEW	⌂	⌁	Central 中環	259

European/歐陸式

Hugo's 希戈	NEW		XX	Tsim Sha Tsui 尖沙咀	136

European contemporary/時尚歐陸式

Café Gray Deluxe	NEW	✿	XX	Admiralty 金鐘	73
Le 188°	NEW		XX	North Point 北角	163
Mandarin Grill + Bar 文華扒房+酒吧		✿	XXX	Central 中環	178
Watermark			XX	Central 中環	261

French/法式

Agnès b. Le Pain Grillé (Central)			XX	Central 中環	66
Caprice		✿✿✿	XXXX	Central 中環	75
Gaddi's 吉地士			XXXX	Tsim Sha Tsui 尖沙咀	117
On Lot 10		⌂	X	Central 中環	193
Petrus 珀翠		✿	XXXX	Admiralty 金鐘	198
Spoon by Alain Ducasse		✿	XX	Tsim Sha Tsui 尖沙咀	216
The Press Room			X	Central 中環	245

French contemporary/時尚法式

Amber		✿✿	XXX	Central 中環	67
Cépage		✿	XXX	Wan Chai 灣仔	79
Harvey Nichols			XX	Central 中環	126
L'Atelier de Joël Robuchon		✿✿	XX	Central 中環	151
Pierre		✿✿	XXX	Central 中環	199
St. George	NEW		XXX	Tsim Sha Tsui 尖沙咀	219
Whisk	NEW		XX	Tsim Sha Tsui 尖沙咀	262

Fusion/多國菜

Hakkanese/客家菜

Hang Zhou/杭州菜

Hunanese/湖南菜

Indian/印度菜

Indonesian/印尼菜

International/國際菜

Italian/意式

Malaysian/馬拉菜

Noodles/麵食

Noodles and Congee/粥麵

Tasty (Kowloon Bay) 正斗粥麵專家 (九龍灣) NEW	◉	ᵁ⊔	Kowloon Bay 九龍灣	237
Tsim Chai Kee (Queen's Road) 沾仔記 (皇后大道中)		ᵁ⊔	Central 中環	253
Tsim Chai Kee (Wellington Street) 沾仔記 (威靈頓街)		ᵁ⊔	Central 中環	254

Pekingese/京菜

Cheung Kee 祥記飯店	◉	⅄	Wan Chai 灣仔	82
Peking Garden (Admiralty) 北京樓 (金鐘)		⅄⅄	Admiralty 金鐘	194
Peking Garden (Central) 北京樓 (中環)		⅄⅄⅄	Central 中環	195
Peking Garden (Kowloon) 北京樓 (九龍)		⅄⅄	Tsim Sha Tsui 尖沙咀	196
Peking Garden (Tai Koo Shing) 北京樓 (太古城)		⅄⅄⅄	Tai Koo Shing 太古城	197

Portuguese/葡式

Casa Lisboa NEW	◉	⅄⅄	Central 中環	76

Seafood/海鮮

Chuen Kee Seafood 全記海鮮菜館		⅄	East New Territories 新界東部	88
Dragon Inn 容龍 NEW		⅄⅄	West New Territories 新界西部	101
Hing Kee 避風塘興記		⅄	Tsim Sha Tsui 尖沙咀	127
Lobster Bar and Grill 龍蝦吧		⅄⅄	Admiralty 金鐘	168
Xin Dan Ji 新斗記		⅄	Jordan 佐敦	267

Shanghainese/上海菜

Din Tai Fung (Causeway Bay) 鼎泰豐 (銅鑼灣) NEW	⊛	⅄	Causeway Bay 銅鑼灣	97
Din Tai Fung (Tsim Sha Tsui) 鼎泰豐 (尖沙咀)	⊛	⅄	Tsim Sha Tsui 尖沙咀	98
Liu Yuan Pavilion 留園雅敘		⅄⅄	Wan Chai 灣仔	166
Shanghai Xiao Nan Guo (Kowloon Bay) 上海小南國 (九龍灣)		⅄⅄	Kowloon Bay 九龍灣	210
Snow Garden (Causeway Bay) 雪園 (銅鑼灣)		⅄⅄	Causeway Bay 銅鑼灣	214
Wu Kong (Causeway Bay) 滬江 (銅鑼灣)	◉	⅄⅄	Causeway Bay 銅鑼灣	266

PARTICULARLY PLEASANT RESTAURANTS
上佳的餐廳

NEW : New entry in the guide/ 新增推介
⌣ : Restaurant promoted to a Bib Gourmand or Star/ 評級有所晉升的餐廳

RESTAURANTS
WITH PRIVATE ROOMS
具備私人房間的餐廳

Agnès b. Le Pain Grillé (Central)			✗✗	capacity 14	66
Amber		✿✿	✗✗✗✗	capacity 16	67
Aspasia			✗✗✗	capacity 18	69
Bo Innovation		✿	✗✗✗	capacity 12	71
Café Gray Deluxe	NEW	✿	✗✗	capacity 12	73
Caprice		✿✿✿	✗✗✗✗✗	capacity 12	75
Casa Lisboa	NEW	⌂	✗✗	capacity 60	76
Celebrity Cuisine 名人坊	⌣	✿✿	✗✗	capacity 16	77
Celestial Court 天寶閣			✗✗	capacity 25	78
Cépage		✿	✗✗✗	capacity 14	79
Che's 車氏粵菜軒		⌂	✗✗	capacity 35	80
Chiu Chow Garden (Tsuen Wan) 潮江春 (荃灣)		✗✗		capacity 70	84
Chuen Cheung Kui (Causeway Bay) 泉章居 (銅鑼灣)	NEW	⌂	✗	capacity 36	86
Crystal Jade La Mian Xiao Long Bao (Kowloon Bay) 翡翠拉麵小籠包 (九龍灣)		⌂	✗	capacity 14	90
Crystal Jade La Mian Xiao Long Bao (TST) 翡翠拉麵小籠包 (尖沙咀)		⌂	✗	capacity 14	91
Crystal Jade La Mian Xiao Long Bao (Wan Chai) 翡翠拉麵小籠包 (灣仔)		⌂	✗	capacity 24	92
Cuisine Cuisine at The Mira 國金軒 (The Mira)	NEW	✿✿	✗✗✗	capacity 12	94
Din Tai Fung (Causeway Bay) 鼎泰豐 (銅鑼灣)	NEW	✿	✗	capacity 14	97
Din Tai Fung (Tsim Sha Tsui) 鼎泰豐 (尖沙咀)		✿	✗	capacity 12	98
Dong Lai Shun 東來順	⌣	⌂	✗✗	capacity 20	100
Dragon Inn 容龍	NEW		✗✗	capacity 48	101

NEW : New entry in the guide/ 新增推介
⌣ : Restaurant promoted to a Bib Gourmand or Star/ 評級有所晉升的餐廳

Dragon King (Yau Ma Tei) 龍皇 (油麻地)	NEW	✗✗	capacity 20	102
Dynasty (Wan Chai) 滿福樓 (灣仔)	❀	✗✗✗	capacity 24	104
8½ Otto e Mezzo	NEW ❀❀	✗✗✗	capacity 30	105
Fan Tang 飯堂	NEW	✗✗✗	capacity 30	106
Farm House 農圃	❀	✗✗	capacity 20	107
Fook Lam Moon (Kowloon) 福臨門 (九龍)	❀	✗✗✗	capacity 100	109
Fook Lam Moon (Wan Chai) 福臨門 (灣仔)	❀	✗✗✗	capacity 100	110
Forum 富臨	❀	✗✗	capacity 40	111
Fu Ho (Tsim Sha Tsui) 富豪 (尖沙咀)	NEW ❀	✗✗✗	capacity 36	112
Fung Lum 楓林小館	❧ ❀	✗✗	capacity 40	113
Fu Sing (Causeway Bay) 富聲 (銅鑼灣)	NEW ⊕	✗✗	capacity 32	115
Fu Sing (Wan Chai) 富聲 (灣仔)	❧ ⊕	✗✗	capacity 20	116
Gaddi's 吉地士		✗✗✗✗	capacity 16	117
Gaylord 爵樂	NEW	✗✗	capacity 20	118
Golden Bauhinia 金紫荊		✗✗	capacity 14	119
Golden Leaf 金葉庭	❀	✗✗✗	capacity 12	120
Golden Valley 駿景軒	❧ ❀	✗✗✗	capacity 24	121
Grissini		✗✗✗	capacity 24	123
Hoi King Heen 海景軒	NEW ❀	✗✗✗	capacity 40	131
Hoi Yat Heen 海逸軒		✗✗✗	capacity 12	132
H One		✗✗✗	capacity 26	133
Hong Zhou 杭州酒家	❀	✗✗	capacity 30	134
Hugo's 希戈	NEW	✗✗✗	capacity 12	136
Hunan Garden (Causeway Bay) 洞庭樓 (銅鑼灣)		✗✗✗	capacity 16	137
Hunan Garden (Central) 洞庭樓 (中環)		✗✗✗	capacity 16	138
Hutong 胡同		✗✗	capacity 40	140
Inagiku (IFC) 稻菊 (國際金融中心)		✗✗	capacity 40	141

NEW : New entry in the guide/ 新增推介
🍴 : Restaurant promoted to a Bib Gourmand or Star/ 評級有所晉升的餐廳

RESTAURANTS WITH A VIEW
有景觀的餐廳

Agnès b. Le Pain Grillé (Central)

🍴🍴

🚌14 ⏰🍴 🍇

Located within the celebrated fashion store, Agnès b. and decorated to resemble a private, yet luxurious, French country home from the 19C. It's divided into three rooms: Paris, Antibes, and Lyon; each with its own character and personality. Chic it most certainly is, to match its elegant clientele. Not surprisingly, the menu is French, with a Mediterranean bias. The impressive wine list features over 100 champagnes.

餐廳位於Agnès b.時裝店內，裝潢模仿十九世紀私人奢華法國田園家居。餐廳分為三個空間：Paris、Antibes和Lyon；每個都具有獨特個性風格。餐廳的時尚風格毋庸置疑，配合其高貴客源。菜單一如所料，是帶有地中海風格的法國菜。酒牌上更有超過100種香檳可供選擇。

■ ADDRESS/地址

TEL. 2805 0798

Shop 3096-3097, Podium Level 3,
IFC Mall, 8 Finance Street, Central
中環金融街8號國際金融中心商場3樓
3096-3097號舖
www.agnesb-lepaingrille.com

■ ANNUAL AND WEEKLY CLOSING
　休息日期
Closed Lunar New Year
年初一休息

■ OPENING HOURS, LAST ORDER
　營業時間，最後點菜時間
Lunch/午膳　12:00-15:00 (L.O.)
Dinner/晚膳　19:00-22:30 (L.O.)

■ PRICE/價錢
Lunch/午膳　set/套餐　　　　$228-318
　　　　　　à la carte/點菜　$300-650
Dinner/晚膳　à la carte/點菜　$300-650

Amber

❁ ❁ XXXX

♿ ☞ 🖼16 ☎🍴 🎴

The hanging ceiling sculpture, which features over 3,500 copper tubes, is the most striking element of Adam Tihany's bold restaurant design. Service is detailed and courteous without ever being stuffy or starchy. But it is the adventurous and creative French cuisine, using superb ingredients, which attracts diners to these plush surroundings. The sommeliers can be relied upon for sound recommendations from the comprehensive wine list.

從天花懸垂下來，以超過3,500條銅管做成的雕像，是Adam Tihany 前衛餐廳設計的最觸目元素。服務禮貌週到而不會令客人有咄咄逼人、吃不消的感覺。不過，採用優質材料烹調，大膽而富創意的法國菜才是真正將客人吸引到這豪華的環境。你可信任品酒師的可靠建議，從齊全的酒單挑選合適的選擇。

■ ADDRESS/地址

TEL. 2132 0066

7F, The Landmark Mandarin Oriental Hotel, 15 Queen's Road, Central

中環皇后大道中15號置地文華東方酒店7樓

www.mandarinoriental.com/landmark

■ ANNUAL AND WEEKLY CLOSING
　　休息日期

Closed Sunday

週日休息

■ OPENING HOURS, LAST ORDER
　　營業時間，最後點菜時間

Lunch/午膳 12:00-14:30 (L.O.)

Dinner/晚膳 18:30-22:30 (L.O.)

■ PRICE/價錢

Lunch/午膳	set/套餐	$518-1,588
	à la carte/點菜	$850-1,500
Dinner/晚膳	set/套餐	$688-1,588
	à la carte/點菜	$850-1,500

Angelini

The young chef is extremely passionate about the dishes he produces and, while other regions are represented, it is the cooking of Campania that gets the upper hand. Specialities include artisanal spaghetti with garlic confit and cherry tomatoes, steamed red snapper with black mussels and anchovies, and country-style veal chop with shallots and porcini mushrooms. A window seat is a must as the views are spectacular.

年輕的主廚對他所創作的菜式抱著驚人的熱情。雖然有來自各地的不同佳餚，但最受青睞的還是坎帕尼亞菜。招牌菜包括香蒜意大利粉，蒸紅鯛配黑青口香蒜及銀魚柳醬，及鄉村風味牛仔扒配牛肝菌。請務必選擇靠窗的座位，以欣賞出色的景觀。

■ ADDRESS/地址

TEL. 2733 8750

Mezzanine Level, Kowloon Shangri-La Hotel, 64 Mody Road, East Tsim Sha Tsui, Kowloon
九龍尖東麼地道64號
九龍香格里拉酒店閣樓
www.shangri-la.com

■ OPENING HOURS, LAST ORDER
　營業時間，最後點菜時間
Lunch/午膳 12:00-15:00 (L.O.)
Dinner/晚膳 18:30-22:30 (L.O.)

■ PRICE/價錢

Lunch/午膳	set/套餐	$238
	à la carte/點菜	$400-1,000
Dinner/晚膳	set/套餐	$980
	à la carte/點菜	$400-1,000

Aspasia

Named after the Greek beauty renowned for her cosmopolitan style and good taste, this restaurant aims to project a similar image. There is subtle Louis XV styling here, mixed with bold animal designs and original artwork on the walls. The cuisine, though, is resolutely Italian with a roll-call of antipasti, pastas and both fish and meat dishes. Their jazz band, Dada, perform on the floor above.

店名是Aspasia古希臘一位代表創新、帶領潮流的女士名字，亦符合這家餐廳希望帶出的感覺。餐廳裝潢帶有路易十五風格，混合牆上強烈的動物圖案及原創藝術。餐飲方面則貫徹義大利風格，頭盤、義大利麵、魚及肉的主菜。餐廳的爵士樂隊Dada於上層演出。

■ ADDRESS/地址

TEL. 3763 8800

1F, The Luxe Manor Hotel,
39 Kimberley Road, Tsim Sha Tsui,
Kowloon
九龍尖沙咀金巴利道39號
帝樂文娜公館1樓
www.aspasia.com.hk

■ OPENING HOURS, LAST ORDER
　營業時間，最後點菜時間
Lunch/午膳 12:00-15:00 (L.O.)
Dinner/晚膳 18:30-23:00 (L.O.)

■ PRICE/價錢

Lunch/午膳	set/套餐	$318
	à la carte/點菜	$500-800
Dinner/晚膳	set/套餐	$788
	à la carte/點菜	$500-800

BLT Steak

In this instance those initials stand for Bistro Laurent Tourondel, a New York celebrity chef. His restaurant specialises in prime beef from the US and Australia, all USDA certified and naturally aged. Choose your cut – perhaps a Porterhouse or a rib-eye – a sauce and sides. There are a few lighter options for those intimidated by a 16oz New York strip. Its terrace overlooking The Star ferry quay and Victoria Harbour is a 'prime' spot.

BLT 取紐約名廚 (Bistro) Laurent Tourondel之名，餐廳以來自美國及澳洲頂級牛排為主，全部通過美國農產部認證，自然生長。你可選擇喜歡食用的部份，從大脊骨牛排到肉眼排任君選擇，並配上自選醬汁及配菜。你亦可選擇較輕盈的16oz紐約無骨西冷扒。其平台花園是「搶手」熱點，可觀賞天星碼頭及維多利亞港景致。

■ ADDRESS/地址

TEL. 2730 3508
Shop G62, GF, Ocean Terminal,
Harbour City, Tsim Sha Tsui, Kowloon
九龍尖沙咀海運大廈海港城地下G62號舖
www.diningconcepts.com.hk

■ OPENING HOURS, LAST ORDER
營業時間，最後點菜時間
12:00-23:00 (L.O.)

■ PRICE/價錢
Lunch/午膳   set/套餐 $ 168
                à la carte/點菜 $ 300-660
Dinner/晚膳   à la carte/點菜 $ 450-700

Bo Innovation

Bo Innovation and owner-chef Alvin Leung's cooking seem to inspire plenty of conflicting opinions: some love it; others just can't see what all the fuss is about. It is certainly true that the dishes, from whichever set menu you choose, are highly original, extremely creative, sometimes puzzling and occasionally unexpected. Eat in the contemporary dining room with its tiny open kitchen or on the terrace. Entry is via a lift on Ship Street.

Bo Innovation與餐廳老闆兼廚師梁經倫 (Alvin) 的菜式似乎得到許多有矛盾的意見,有些人很喜歡;有些則覺得完全不能理解。但絕對可以肯定的,是這裡的菜式,不論你選擇哪一款套餐,都是百分百原創、充滿新意 。 有時候令人驚奇,甚至意想不到。可選擇在連著小型開放式廚房,設計時尚的餐廳或露台用膳。在船街乘搭升降機即可到達。

■ ADDRESS/地址
TEL. 2850 8371
2F, J Residence, 18 Ship Street, Wan Chai
灣仔船街18號嘉薈軒2樓
www.boinnovation.com

■ ANNUAL AND WEEKLY CLOSING
休息日期
Closed 3 days Lunar New Year, Sunday and lunch Saturday and Public Holidays
農曆新年3天、週日、週六午膳及公眾假期午膳休息

■ OPENING HOURS, LAST ORDER
營業時間,最後點菜時間
Lunch/午膳 12:00-14:00 (L.O.)
Dinner/晚膳 19:00-22:00 (L.O.)

■ PRICE/價錢
Lunch/午膳	set/套餐	$228-750
Dinner/晚膳	set/套餐	$680-1,580

Bombay Dreams   NEW

While most regions of India are represented on the menu, the kitchen's strengths lie with the specialities from the more northerly parts of the country. At lunchtime, the well-stocked buffet proves to be quite a draw, especially on Sundays. The authentic cooking, together with the sensible pricing, means that booking is recommended. The room is comfortable and the staff do their best to ensure that their guests are enjoying themselves.

儘管餐牌上囊括了印度各地的菜式，這裡的招牌菜多源自印度北部。午市自助餐菜式豐富，是個不俗的選擇，尤其在星期天。由於出品水準高，加上價錢合理，最好預訂座位。餐廳環境舒適，工作人員亦盡其所能，確保客人賓至如歸。

■ ADDRESS/地址
TEL. 2971 0001
1F, 75-77 Wyndham Street, Central
中環雲咸街75-77號1樓
www.diningconcepts.com.hk

■ OPENING HOURS, LAST ORDER
營業時間，最後點菜時間
Lunch/午膳 12:00-15:00 L.O.14:45
Dinner/晚膳 18:00-23:00 L.O.22:30

■ PRICE/價錢
Lunch/午膳　set/套餐　　$ 108
Dinner/晚膳　set/套餐　　$ 190-248
　　　　　à la carte/點菜 $ 200-300

Café Gray Deluxe   NEW

Café Gray Deluxe is a suitably cool restaurant to have on the 49th floor of the fashionable Upper House hotel. There's a terrific, lively bar – a reminder perhaps of Gary Kunz's New York background – the views are spectacular and the service fluent and good-looking. When it comes to cooking, the mark of a good kitchen is to take recognisable, everyday dishes, such as European classics like risotto and coq au vin, and make them extraordinary.

Café Gray Deluxe是一家位處時尚的Upper House酒店49樓的型格餐廳，餐廳裏充滿活力的酒吧讓大家想起主廚Gary Kunz的紐約背景。用餐的同時又可所賞維港的超凡景緻，服務亦極為周到。說到菜式，一家出色餐廳的必殺技就是能將平平無奇的家常菜，例如意大利燴飯、紅酒燴雞等傳統歐洲菜，變成色香味俱全的不平凡菜式。

■ ADDRESS/地址
TEL. 3968 1106
49F, The Upper House Hotel, Pacific Place, 88 Queensway, Admiralty
香港金鐘道88號太古廣場奕居49樓
www.cafegrayhk.com

■ OPENING HOURS, LAST ORDER
   營業時間，最後點菜時間
Lunch/午膳 12:00-14:30 (L.O.)
Dinner/晚膳 17:30-21:30 (L.O.)
■ PRICE/價錢
Lunch/午膳   set/套餐 $345
             à la carte/點菜 $400-700
Dinner/晚膳 à la carte/點菜 $400-700

Café Siam

Staff cope efficiently with the lunchtime crowds descending daily on this no-nonsense Thai operation. But still get here early, sit upstairs by the window and order yourself a lemongrass ginger ale while you decide what to eat. The strong elements of the authentic menu are the curries and the seafood dishes such as the stir-fried spicy pepper prawns. If you're pressed for time then the carefully prepared pad thai will leave you satisfied.

在每天繁忙的午膳時間，侍應都能有效率地處理大批顧客。但若能早點到達，便可選擇樓上靠窗的座位，先點一杯香茅薑茶，再慢慢考慮點甚麼菜。主打菜式包括各種咖哩和海鮮，例如招牌炒大蝦。若你時間不多，那麼精心炮製的泰式炒金邊粉包蛋亦能讓你滿意。

■ ADDRESS/地址
TEL. 2851 4803
40-42 Lyndhurst Terrace, Central
中環擺花街40-42號
www.cafesiam.com.hk

■ OPENING HOURS, LAST ORDER
營業時間，最後點菜時間
12:00-22:30 (L.O.)

■ PRICE/價錢

Lunch/午膳	set/套餐	$88
	à la carte/點菜	$200-350
Dinner/晚膳	set/套餐	$168
	à la carte/點菜	$200-350

Caprice

The chandeliers and coloured walkway into this striking restaurant add instant glamour and heighten expectations. As well as the wonderful harbour views, the room's main feature is the large, raised, open kitchen which is framed by a jewelled canopy. From here, the sizeable brigade of chefs produce accomplished French cuisine using luxury ingredients. Be sure to sample the impressive selection of cheeses. Service is meticulous and charming.

璀璨的吊燈及色彩繽紛的走廊帶領你走進這動人心弦的餐廳，即時帶來豪華的感覺，令你的期望也相應提高。除了美妙絕倫的維港景緻，以水晶珠簾圍繞著的大型開放式廚房也令人賞心悅目。在這裡，陣容鼎盛的廚師團隊以豪華食材炮製法國美食。記得試試出色的特選芝士系列。服務一絲不苟，令人醉心。

■ ADDRESS/地址

TEL. 3196 8860

6F, Four Seasons Hotel, 8 Finance Street, Central
中環金融街8號四季酒店平臺6樓
www.fourseasons.com/hongkong

■ OPENING HOURS, LAST ORDER
營業時間，最後點菜時間
Lunch/午膳 12:00-14:30 (L.O.)
Dinner/晚膳 18:00-22:30 (L.O.)

■ PRICE/價錢

Lunch/午膳	set/套餐	$420
	à la carte/點菜	$800-1,100
Dinner/晚膳	set/套餐	$880-1,280
	à la carte/點菜	$800-1,100

Casa Lisboa   NEW

🚗60   🔔

Caldo verde, stuffed crab, seafood stews, suckling pig and a reassuringly large selection of bacalhau recipes are just some of the highlights of an appealing menu which sees subtle Macanese influences added to Portuguese dishes. It may be on the 8th floor of the LKF Tower but this cosy room is brightly decorated in a traditional Portuguese style with blue and white azulejos. The national flag is also reflected in the colours of the waitresses' aprons.

傳統葡國腸薯蓉翠蔬湯、葡式釀蟹蓋、海鮮雜燴、葡式烤乳豬及多姿多采的馬介休菜式系列，不過是這吸引人的餐牌上部分重點部分，令它的葡國菜流露出絲絲澳門色彩。雖然位於蘭桂坊LKF Tower八樓，但明亮鮮豔的裝潢，以傳統葡萄牙風格配上藍白瓷磚畫（azulejos），給人溫暖而舒適的感覺。侍應圍裙的顏色亦採用葡萄牙國旗顏色。

■ ADDRESS/地址
TEL. 2905 1168
8F, LKF Tower, 55 D'Aguilar Street, Central
中環德己立街55號 LKF Tower 8樓
www.ad-caterers.com

■ ANNUAL AND WEEKLY CLOSING
    休息日期
Closed 4 days Lunar New Year and Sunday
農曆新年4天及週日休息

■ OPENING HOURS, LAST ORDER
    營業時間，最後點菜時間
Lunch/午膳 12:00-15:00 L.O.14:30
Dinner/晚膳 18:30-24:00 L.O.23:00

■ PRICE/價錢
Lunch/午膳   set/套餐 $138
                à la carte/點菜 $220-420
Dinner/晚膳 à la carte/點菜 $220-420

Celebrity Cuisine
名人坊

✿ ✿ 　　　　　　　　　　　　　　　　　　　✗✗

🍽 16 📞🍴

Limited capacity and a host of regulars mean that booking ahead is vital at this very discreet restaurant concealed within the Lan Kwai Fong hotel. Those regulars come for authentic Cantonese cuisine that is also delicate and sophisticated. The menu may be quite short but there are usually plenty of specials; highlights include chicken with Huadiao rice wine, ox tongue and, one of the chef's own creations, 'bird's nest in chicken wing'.

餐廳座位有限，但常客眾多，故此提早預約是必須的。這隱藏在蘭桂坊酒店內的餐廳看似不甚出眾但內有乾坤。這裡最大的賣點就是廣東菜，既精緻又獨具特色。餐牌雖則頗短，但提供大量特選菜式，包括花雕焗飛天雞及紅燒牛脷。其中，由主廚創作的是燕窩釀鳳翼。

■ ADDRESS/地址

TEL. 3650 0066
1F, Lan Kwai Fong Hotel,
3 Kau U Fong, Central
中環九如坊3號蘭桂坊酒店1樓

■ ANNUAL AND WEEKLY CLOSING
　休息日期
Closed 3 days Lunar New Year
農曆新年休息3天

■ OPENING HOURS, LAST ORDER
　營業時間，最後點菜時間
Lunch/午膳　12:00-14:30 (L.O.)
Dinner/晚膳　18:00-23:00 (L.O.)

■ PRICE/價錢
Lunch/午膳　à la carte/點菜 $200-600
Dinner/晚膳　à la carte/點菜 $300-800

Celestial Court
天寶閣

♟♟

♿ ☞ 🚗25 🍽

Red and green tones, silks and wood adorn this spacious, traditional dining room within the Sheraton Hotel. Despite its size, scores of regulars mean that queuing for a table is sometimes required. A large selection of Cantonese and Chinese specialities include braised bean-curd sheet rolls filled with mushrooms and assorted vegetables, steamed boneless chicken with Yunnan ham and assorted seasonal creations. Service comes courtesy of an experienced team.

紅與綠的色調、絲綢與木材裝飾著喜來登酒店內這寬敞、傳統的中菜廳。眾多的常客令這間面積不小的中菜廳偶然也需要排隊輪候。餐牌選擇甚多，包括許多廣東和其他中國地方的佳餚，如鴛鴦素千層、金華玉樹雞和時令菜式。禮貌週到的服務團隊經驗十分豐富。

■ ADDRESS/地址
TEL. 2369 1111
2F, Sheraton Hotel, 20 Nathan Road, Tsim Sha Tsui, Kowloon
九龍尖沙咀彌敦道20號喜來登酒店2樓
www.sheraton.com/hongkong

■ OPENING HOURS, LAST ORDER
營業時間，最後點菜時間
Lunch/午膳 11:30-15:00 (L.O.)
Dinner/晚膳 18:00-23:30 (L.O.)

■ PRICE/價錢
Lunch/午膳   set/套餐 $262
       à la carte/點菜 $350-900
Dinner/晚膳 à la carte/點菜 $350-900

Cépage

Three floors of stylish design offer the chic diner something special: sophistication but also a relaxed atmosphere. The cuisine is contemporary French but with Asian touches and uses fine ingredients from around the world: fish is mostly from Japan; caviar from China and langoustine arrives from New Zealand. The wine list is one of the most impressive in Hong Kong. The restaurant is from the same stable as Les Amis in Singapore.

樓高三層的時尚設計為新潮食客提供不一樣的選擇：餐飲風格現代，有新派法國菜及義大利菜，以世界各地的精美食材炮製，魚類大多來自日本、魚子醬來自中國、langoustine小龍蝦則來自紐西蘭。酒牌提供的選擇之多，更是全港數一數二。這正是新加坡得獎餐廳集團Les Amis開設的特色餐廳。

■ ADDRESS/地址

TEL. 2861 3130
23 Wing Fung Street, Wan Chai
灣仔永豐街23號
www.lesamis.com.sg

■ OPENING HOURS, LAST ORDER
　營業時間，最後點菜時間
Lunch/午膳　12:00-14:30　L.O.14:00
Dinner/晚膳　19:00-22:30　L.O.22:15

■ PRICE/價錢
Lunch/午膳　set/套餐　　　　　$390-720
　　　　　　à la carte/點菜　$750-1,200
Dinner/晚膳　set/套餐　　　　$580-1,550
　　　　　　à la carte/點菜　$750-1,200

Che's
車氏粵菜軒

🛋35 📞🍴

This unremarkable-looking little restaurant is very popular with the local businessmen who come here in their droves for the house speciality: crispy pork buns. But there are lots of other reasons to visit: the dim sum at lunch, the extensive menu of classic dishes, simpler offerings such as congee or braised clay pot dishes and the chilled mango to end. The service is prompt and efficient: another reason why it's so popular at lunchtimes.

這家小餐館可能並不起眼，但其實在本地商界人士間卻享負盛名，對其馳名脆皮叉燒包趨之若鶩。除此之外，午市點心、選擇豐富的經典名菜、簡單菜式如粥或瓦罉煲仔菜，加上一道冰凍芒果便是個完美結束。服務快速且有效率：這也是令餐廳在午餐時分座無虛席的原因。

■ ADDRESS/地址

TEL. 2528 1123
4F, 54-62 Lockhart Road, Wan Chai
灣仔駱克道54-62號4樓

■ OPENING HOURS, LAST ORDER
  營業時間，最後點菜時間
Lunch/午膳 11:30-15:00 L.O.14:15
Dinner/晚膳 18:00-22:15 (L.O.)

  ■ PRICE/價錢
Lunch/午膳   set/套餐 $550-900
              à la carte/點菜 $150-700
Dinner/晚膳 set/套餐 $550-900
              à la carte/點菜 $150-700

Chesa
瑞樵閣

For over forty years, the cuisine of Switzerland has found a charming niche here. An imposing wood door leads you into an intimate Swiss-style chalet with wooden objects left, right and centre. Traditional Swiss dishes sit alongside the cheese specialities: fondue Vaudoise (traditional fondue) or raclette du Valais (hot melted cheese with potatoes, pickled onions and gherkins). For dessert: chocolate fondue or Swiss chocolate mousse.

瑞士美食在香港穩佔一席位超過四十年。壯觀的木門帶領你到親切的瑞士農舍，裡面四處都有木製的裝飾。傳統瑞士菜式與特選芝士系列互相輝映：沃州芝士火鍋（傳統芝士火鍋）或瓦萊州烤芝士（熱熔的芝士配馬鈴薯、醃洋蔥及青瓜）。至於甜品，巧克力火鍋或瑞士巧克力慕絲是兩大必吃！

■ ADDRESS/地址
TEL. 2920 2888
1F, The Peninsula Hotel, Salisbury Road, Tsim Sha Tsui, Kowloon
九龍尖沙咀梳士巴利道半島酒店1樓
www.peninsula.com

■ OPENING HOURS, LAST ORDER
營業時間，最後點菜時間
Lunch/午膳 12:00-14:30 (L.O.)
Dinner/晚膳 18:30-22:30 (L.O.)

■ PRICE/價錢
Lunch/午膳   set/套餐 $280
             à la carte/點菜 $500-700
Dinner/晚膳   à la carte/點菜 $500-700

Cheung Kee
祥記飯店

Things almost seem to spill out onto the colourful street at this compact establishment spread over two small rooms. As they've been going since 1948 and have quite a local following, you'd better book to ensure a place. The extremely good-value menu features honest and earthy dishes that include seafood, casseroles and chicken. But it's the Peking duck that remains the must-have dish. Keep some room for the banana fritters too.

這家設有兩間餐室設備俱全的餐館食客如雲，擁擠情況有如把人客擠瀉於多彩多姿的街道上。這家自1948年創業的老店一向有不少忠實食客，如欲前往，最好先行預約，以免向隅。菜餚價錢超值，菜式樸實地道，包括海鮮、砂鍋、雞，而北京填鴨更是不可不吃的招牌菜。注意別吃太飽，留點胃口嚐嚐高力豆沙！

■ ADDRESS/地址
TEL. 2529 0707
1F, 75 Lockhart Road, Wan Chai
灣仔駱克道75號1樓

■ OPENING HOURS, LAST ORDER
營業時間，最後點菜時間
12:00-23:30 (L.O.)

■ PRICE/價錢
à la carte/點菜 $ 170-280

Chilli Fagara
麻辣燙

Chillies are a passion here! The window's filled with them, as well as orange flames, which act as a forewarning! Rich red walls create an intimate atmosphere. The heat is turned up as you progress from mild 'natural' dishes through to the likes of red hot chilli prawn – which is only for the very brave. Caramelized banana and chrysanthemum tea cool things down at the end. A sweet ambience prevails as the small team ensures all runs smoothly.

這裡充滿辣椒的激情！窗口充滿著辣椒，而橙色的火焰就像是預警！濃豔的紅牆營造親切的氣氛，當你從溫和的「普通」菜式吃到辣椒蝦之類的菜餚時，便會渾身發熱！當然，只有夠膽的人才會一嚐後者。最後可用拔絲香蕉及菊花茶涼快下來。為數不多的員工，和諧的團隊合作，令餐廳運作順暢，更顯溫馨。

■ ADDRESS/地址

TEL. 2893 3330
Shop E, GF, 51A Graham Street,
Soho, Central
中環嘉咸街51A地下舖
www.chillifagara.com

■ ANNUAL AND WEEKLY CLOSING
　休息日期
Closed 8 days Lunar New Year
農曆新年休息8天

■ OPENING HOURS, LAST ORDER
　營業時間，最後點菜時間
Lunch/午膳 11:30-15:00 L.O.14:00
Dinner/晚膳 17:00-23:30 L.O.23:00

■ PRICE/價錢
Lunch/午膳　set/套餐　　$78
Dinner/晚膳　à la carte/點菜 $220-400

Chiu Chow Garden (Tsuen Wan)
潮江春 (荃灣)

✗✗

🍽 70

You will find this Maxim group restaurant busy during peak hours as it is situated in a shopping centre which is conveniently integrated into Tsuen Wan station. Instead of ordering from the main menu, opt for the little sheets of colourful paper which offer a range of dim sum and small dishes at great prices. Some of the most popular dishes include soyed sliced goose, deep-fried sliced pomfret with salad dip and sautéed kale with salted pork.

你會發現這家美心集團屬下的酒家在繁忙時間擠滿食客，因為她所處的商場直通港鐵荃灣站。與其從餐牌點菜，倒不如在不同顏色的點心紙上選擇經濟美味的點心和小食。部分受歡迎菜式包括澄海鹵水鵝片、潮州沙律鯧魚片和潮州鹹肉炒芥蘭。

■ ADDRESS/地址

TEL. 2498 3381
Shop 10-12, 2F, Luk Yeung Galleria,
22-66 Wai Tsuen Road, Tsuen Wan,
New Territories
新界荃灣蕙荃路22-66號綠楊坊2樓
10-12號舖
www.maxims.com.hk

■ OPENING HOURS, LAST ORDER
　營業時間，最後點菜時間
Lunch/午膳 08:00-16:30 L.O.16:15
Dinner/晚膳 18:00-23:30 L.O.23:15

■ PRICE/價錢
Lunch/午膳　à la carte/點菜 $120-700
Dinner/晚膳　à la carte/點菜 $200-700

Choi Lung NEW
彩龍

Located in a lively pedestrianised street occupied by a food market. Father, mother and daughter are all involved in this simple little shop; just three round tables and a tiny kitchen – that's it! But the congee choice is extensive: beef, fish slices, chicken, pork blood, pork liver and belly, not forgetting the famous dried vegetable congee. Also popular are the steamed rice rolls with barbecue pork.

粥店位於熱鬧行人路旁的露天街市內；這小店由父親、母親與女兒一家三口一同經營，只有三張小圓桌與一個窄小的廚房——就這麼多！然而，這裡的粥品選擇繁多：牛肉、魚片、雞、豬紅、豬膶、豬腩等，菜乾粥更是特別有名，叉燒腸粉也很受歡迎。

■ ADDRESS/地址
TEL. 2388 9335
7 Reclamation Street, Jordan, Kowloon
九龍佐敦新填地街7號

■ ANNUAL AND WEEKLY CLOSING
休息日期
Closed 1 week Lunar New Year
農曆新年休息7天

■ OPENING HOURS, LAST ORDER
營業時間，最後點菜時間
06:00-19:30

■ PRICE/價錢
à la carte/點菜　　　　$ 20-40

Chuen Cheung Kui (Causeway Bay) NEW
泉章居 (銅鑼灣)

Its Causeway Bay Plaza location means that this isn't the easiest place to find but customers have been coming in droves for over 25 years so there must be a reason. It's a family business, based around excellent value Hakkanese cuisine, and they employ chefs from this region to ensure authenticity. Of course there's salt baked chicken, but the stewed pork with preserved vegetables and the tofu are good too. There's further seating upstairs.

位於銅鑼灣廣場的泉章居位置不易找。然而，超過25年來，一直有大量顧客慕名而來，必有其吸引之處。餐館是家族式經營，以超值的客家菜為主，更特地從客家地區聘請主廚，以確保菜式正宗。鹽焗雞是必然之選，但梅菜扣肉和豆腐亦相當美味。樓上另設雅座。

■ ADDRESS/地址
TEL. 2577 3833
7-8F, Causeway Bay Plaza I,
489 Hennessy Road, Causeway Bay
銅鑼灣軒尼詩道489號
銅鑼灣廣場第一期7-8樓

■ OPENING HOURS, LAST ORDER
營業時間，最後點菜時間
11:00-00:00 L.O.23:40

■ PRICE/價錢
à la carte/點菜 $ 100-330

Chuen Cheung Kui (Mong Kok)   NEW
泉章居 (旺角)

Highlights of the menu of this first floor restaurant, which overlooks the street below, are those dishes based largely on traditional Hakkanese recipes, such as chicken baked in salt or stewed pork with preserved vegetables. In the afternoon, the smaller ground floor room is used for the serving of simpler, rice-based dishes. The restaurant has been owned by the same family since the 1960s and relocated to its current location in 2004.

餐館的一樓，可看到街景。精選菜式以傳統客家菜為主，為人樂道的如鹽焗雞和梅菜扣肉。面積較小的地下，在下午時分主要供應烹調較簡單的「碟頭飯」。菜館自1960年代起一直由同一家族經營，直至2004年才遷至現址。

■ ADDRESS/地址
TEL. 2396 0672
Lisa House, 33 Nelson Street,
Mong Kok, Kowloon
九龍旺角奶路臣街33號依利大廈

■ ANNUAL AND WEEKLY CLOSING
　休息日期
Closed 4 days Lunar New Year
農曆新年休息4天

■ OPENING HOURS, LAST ORDER
　營業時間，最後點菜時間
11:00-23:15 (L.O.)

■ PRICE/價錢
à la carte/點菜 $ 100-330

Chuen Kee Seafood
全記海鮮菜館

Two family-run restaurants overlook a pleasant harbour to distant islands; choose the one with the rooftop terrace and the quayside plastic seats. An extraordinary range of seafood is available from adjacent fishmongers: cuttlefish, bivalve, crab and lobster, mollusc, shrimps, prawns... Go to the tank, select your meal, and minutes later it appears in front of you, steamed, poached, or wok fried. Then settle back and watch the boats go by.

這兩家餐廳是家族生意，位置優越，可觀賞海港及離島。天台陽台那一家，以及碼頭邊的塑膠座位備受推介。這裡海鮮種類繁多，包括墨魚、貝殼、蟹、龍蝦、賴尿蝦、大蝦小蝦等等。你可以到魚缸挑選你的海鮮，蒸、燉、炒也好，幾分鐘後便會奉到餐桌上，成為你的食物。然後你便可輕鬆地細賞船艇來來往往。

■ ADDRESS/地址
TEL. 2791 1195
53 Hoi Pong Street, Sai Kung
西貢海傍街53號

■ OPENING HOURS, LAST ORDER
　營業時間，最後點菜時間
11:00-23:00 L.O. 22:30

■ PRICE/價錢
set/套餐　　　　　　　$ 174
à la carte/點菜　　　　$ 130-300

City Hall Maxim's Palace NEW
大會堂美心皇宮

City Hall not only hosts a concert hall, theatre and exhibition room but also this huge dining room, well known for its dim sum. Renovated and renewed, it's nicely decorated in a 19C European style. Bookings are not accepted at lunch so be prepared to queue for the traditional but tasty dim sum, to be chosen directly from the carts. At dinner the menu focuses on Cantonese dishes, such as prawn in egg white custard and roasted crispy chicken.

大會堂不只設有音樂廳、劇院和展覽廳，更設有這家以點心聞名的大型酒家。最近這裡重新裝修，以十九世紀歐洲風格示人。午市不設訂座服務，因此，要嘗試這裡傳統、美味，而且可以直接在手推車點菜挑選的點心，恐怕免不了輪候一番。晚市菜牌以廣東菜為主，例如蛋白蝦仁與脆皮燒雞。

■ ADDRESS/地址
TEL. 2521 1303
2F, Low Block, City Hall, Central
中區大會堂低座2樓
www.maxims.com.hk

■ ANNUAL AND WEEKLY CLOSING
　休息日期
Closed Lunar New Year
年初一休息

■ OPENING HOURS, LAST ORDER
　營業時間，最後點菜時間
Lunch/午膳 11:00-15:00 (L.O.)
Dinner/晚膳 17:30-23:30 (L.O.)

■ PRICE/價錢
Lunch/午膳　à la carte/點菜 $150-250
Dinner/晚膳　à la carte/點菜 $200-800

Crystal Jade La Mian Xiao Long Bao (Kowloon Bay)
翡翠拉麵小籠包（九龍灣）

♿ 🍴14

This simple shop is slightly smaller than the other establishments in the group, which was founded in Singapore in 1991. The many customers come here largely for their La Mian noodles, which are served in a number of different styles: perhaps with chicken and preserved vegetables or minced meat and mushroom in a spicy sauce. The menu also features a variety of different regional specialities and dim sum is served all day.

集團1991年於新加坡創辦。與其他分店相比，此店顯得略小。許多顧客都是為了這裡多款不同拉麵而來：嫩雞煨麵或者炸醬麵都是不錯的選擇。菜單上亦有各種地道小吃與點心，全日供應。

■ ADDRESS/地址

TEL. 2305 9990
Shop 520, 5F, Telford Plaza II, Kowloon Bay
九龍灣德福廣場第2期5樓520號舖

■ ANNUAL AND WEEKLY CLOSING
　休息日期
Closed 2 days Lunar New Year
農曆新年休息2天

■ OPENING HOURS, LAST ORDER
　營業時間，最後點菜時間
11:00-23:00 (L.O.)

■ PRICE/價錢
à la carte/點菜　　　　　$ 100-200

Crystal Jade La Mian Xiao Long Bao (TST)
翡翠拉麵小籠包 (尖沙咀)

Could this be Harbour City Mall's most popular eatery? Very probably. It's a modern cafeteria that buzzes all day - if your party is less than four strong, you'll be eating communally with strangers. The food – a mix of Northern Chinese and Sichuan, prepared in a sizzling semi-open kitchen – is very fresh, aromatic and tasty. Signature dishes include steamed pork dumpling with warm soup, or la Mian hand-made noodles with shrimp and cashew nuts.

這裡是海港城裡最受歡迎的食肆嗎？很可能是。這是家整天繁忙的餐廳，如果同行少於四人，你們很可能要和人併桌而坐。食物混合了中國北方菜式和四川菜，在熱烘烘的半開放式廚房烹調，非常新鮮，既香又美味。招牌菜包括上海小籠包、四川擔擔拉麵。

■ ADDRESS/地址
TEL. 2622 2699
Shop 3328, 3F, Gateway Arcade, Harbour City, Canton Road, Tsim Sha Tsui, Kowloon
九龍尖沙咀廣東道海港城
港威商場3樓3328號舖

■ ANNUAL AND WEEKLY CLOSING
  休息日期
Closed 2 days Lunar New Year
農曆新年休息2天

■ OPENING HOURS, LAST ORDER
  營業時間，最後點菜時間
11:00-23:00 L.O. 22:30

■ PRICE/價錢
à la carte/點菜 $ 100-200

Crystal Jade La Mian Xiao Long Bao (Wan Chai)
翡翠拉麵小籠包 (灣仔)

🛒24 🚇

Has quickly established a reputation for its Shanghai dumplings and noodles. This modern, slightly retro looking diner, with its plush booths, has light flooding through it. The place positively buzzes with atmosphere and there is a distinct air of satisfaction from its customers. Look out for smoked duck with tea leaves and fried Shanghai rice cake. Being a pre-eminent member of this group, they also specialise in double-boiled soups.

上海小籠包與麵食很快就為餐廳打響名堂。餐廳裝潢在現代中帶點懷舊，設有絲絨卡座，雖然位於三樓依然吸引不少食客。餐廳氣氛熱鬧，從中清楚感受到顧客的滿足。值得一試的有樟茶鴨及上海炒年糕。作為集團的新星，炖湯亦是餐廳的主打。

■ ADDRESS/地址

TEL. 2573 8844

Shop 310, 3F, Tai Yau Plaza, Wan Chai
灣仔大有廣場3樓310號舖

■ ANNUAL AND WEEKLY CLOSING
　休息日期
Closed 2 days Lunar New Year
農曆新年休息2天

■ OPENING HOURS, LAST ORDER
　營業時間，最後點菜時間
11:00-22:30 (L.O.)

■ PRICE/價錢
à la carte/點菜　　　　$ 100-300

Cucina

If members of your party can't decide whether they want Chinese or Italian then they can always come to Cucina, which offers a curiously diverse menu covering both cuisines. So some can order lobster cioppino while others enjoy barbecued Peking duck. In addition to the à la carte menu, there is also a lunch buffet and brunch on Sunday. Throw in some great views and stylish surroundings and you have all bases covered.

如果同行友人在中菜和意大利菜之間不知如何取捨，你們大可選擇馬哥孛羅香港酒店內同時提供兩種菜系的Cucina餐廳。有些人可以點番茄湯配龍蝦，有些則可享用北京烤填鴨。除了散餐牌外，星期日更設有早午合併自助餐。加上美麗海景和時尚裝潢，就萬無一失了。

■ ADDRESS/地址
TEL. 2113 0808
6F, Marco Polo Hotel, Harbour City,
Canton Road, Tsim Sha Tsui, Kowloon
九龍尖沙咀廣東道海港城馬哥孛羅酒店6樓
www.cucinahk.com

■ OPENING HOURS, LAST ORDER
營業時間，最後點菜時間
Lunch/午膳 12:00-15:00 L.O. 14:30
Dinner/晚膳 18:00-23:00 L.O. 22:30

■ PRICE/價錢
Lunch/午膳   set/套餐 $198-238
            à la carte/點菜 $400-1,200
Dinner/晚膳 à la carte/點菜 $400-1,200

Cuisine Cuisine at The Mira   NEW
國金軒 (The Mira)

❀ ❀   ✗✗✗

           ♿   ☞   🎫12   ✿

When you come across a stylish and contemporary dining room such as this one, located on the 3rd floor of the fashionable Mira hotel, with its eye-catching chandeliers, intimate spaces and modern furniture, you can be fairly certain that the Cantonese food will also come with a few modern twists. Signature dishes include honey-glazed barbecue pork, pan-fried cod fillet with pomelo sauce and rack of lamb with cumin.

位於時尚的The Mira酒店三樓，這家餐廳時髦而充滿現代感，配上引人注目的吊燈、私人空間、摩登家具，你幾乎可以肯定這裡的廣東菜也會加上一些現代變化。招牌菜包括蜜餞叉燒皇、柚子汁燒鱈魚與孜然燒羊架。

■ ADDRESS/地址
TEL. 2315 5222
3F, The Mira Hotel, 118 Nathan Road, Tsim Sha Tsui, Kowloon
九龍尖沙咀彌敦道118號The Mira 3樓
www.themirahotel.com

■ OPENING HOURS, LAST ORDER
   營業時間，最後點菜時間
Lunch/午膳 11:30-14:30 (L.O.)
Dinner/晚膳 18:00-22:30 (L.O.)

■ PRICE/價錢
Lunch/午膳   à la carte/點菜 $ 200-1,000
Dinner/晚膳 à la carte/點菜 $ 250-1,000

Da Ping Huo
大平伙

This charming, hidden restaurant is ideal for those wanting something a little different. It is run by a couple from Sichuan: he is an artist and his wife is a singer. Here she cooks a nightly 12 course menu, using authentic and family-style Sichuan recipes while he welcomes the guests into the modern and elegant restaurant which he created himself. And at the end of the meal, she'll even sing for her customers.

這家獨具魅力卻鮮為人知的餐廳讓追求與眾不同的人士有多一個選擇。餐廳由一對來自四川的夫婦經營：丈夫是藝術家，太太則是歌手。太太負責烹調十二道菜的晚餐，以正宗四川家庭菜譜炮製，丈夫則負責在他親自設計，既現代又優雅的餐廳內招待賓客。酒足飯飽之際，太太甚至會為人客高歌一兩首民謠。

■ ADDRESS/地址
TEL. 2559 1317
LG, Hilltop Plaza, 49 Hollywood Road, Central
中環荷李活道49號鴻豐商業中心地下低層

■ ANNUAL AND WEEKLY CLOSING
　休息日期
Closed 1 week Lunar New Year, Easter, mid-August, Christmas and Sunday
農曆新年7天、復活節、8月中、聖誕節及週日休息

■ OPENING HOURS, LAST ORDER
　營業時間，最後點菜時間
Dinner/晚膳 18:30-24:00 L.O.23:30

■ PRICE/價錢
set/套餐 $ 280

Dim Sum
譽滿坊

Get here early to beat the loyal Happy Valley following. There's a cosy and homely charm here defined by closely set tables: peek across at nearby diners to see what they've ordered. Start with the steamed dumplings, Leong Har Gao and Siu Mai. Top three dim sums in the luxury section are Yu Chee Gao, abalone Siu Mai and Koon Yin Gao. Also worth trying are Loong Har Tong (lobster bisque) and Goon Tong Gao (soup with giant Chinese dumpling).

早一點抵埗,在跑馬地的信眾到來前搶先入座。這裡餐桌排列緊密,既舒適又有在家中的感覺:你可以偷偷看鄰座的食客點了甚麼。先試燕液蝦餃、竹笙龍蝦餃和鮑翅燒賣,而比較昂貴的有最受歡迎的三大點心─鮮蝦魚翅餃、BB鮑燒賣和官燕鮮蝦餃。此外,竹笙龍蝦湯和鮑翅灌湯餃亦值得一試。

■ ADDRESS/地址

TEL. 2834 8893

63 Shing Woo Road, Happy Valley
跑馬地成和道63號

■ ANNUAL AND WEEKLY CLOSING
    休息日期   .
Closed Lunar New Year
年初一休息

■ OPENING HOURS, LAST ORDER
    營業時間,最後點菜時間
Lunch/午膳 11:00-16:30 L.O.16:00
Dinner/晚膳 18:00-22:30 L.O.22:00

■ PRICE/價錢
Lunch/午膳 à la carte/點菜 $100-250
Dinner/晚膳 à la carte/點菜 $180-300

Din Tai Fung (Causeway Bay)
鼎泰豐 (銅鑼灣) NEW

🖼 14

It was inevitable that the success of the Tsim Sha Tsui branch would lead to the opening of another. This new addition is more modern but also larger which hopefully means shorter queues. The menu is a mix of Shanghainese and Taiwanese, with dumplings a highlight; popular dishes are the double-boiled chicken soup and braised beef brisket noodle soup. First-timers will find the instructions on eating the renowned Xiao Lang Bao helpful.

尖沙嘴分店的成功，促成了下一間分店的開幕。位於銅鑼灣的新分店不但更摩登，而且佔地更大，可望縮短等候時間。菜牌包括上海菜與台灣菜，小籠包更是重點所在。熱賣菜式有原盅雞湯與紅燒牛肉湯麵。飯店更為初次光顧的客人提供進食馳名小籠包的説明以供參考，非常周到。

■ ADDRESS/地址
TEL. 3160 8998
Shop 3-9, GF, 68 Yee Woo Street, Causeway Bay
銅鑼灣怡和街68號地下3-9號舖
www.dintaifung.com.hk

■ OPENING HOURS, LAST ORDER
營業時間，最後點菜時間
11:30-22:00 (L.O.)
■ PRICE/價錢
à la carte/點菜 $ 90-160

Din Tai Fung (Tsim Sha Tsui)
鼎泰豐 (尖沙咀)

🚋12

Mr Yang opened up his dumpling shop in Taiwan back in 1958 and focused on delivering service, price and quality; there are now branches in all major Asian cities. Fresh, handmade Shanghai dumplings are their speciality and they are extremely good; the steamed pork ones being especially tasty. Queues are the norm here, but don't worry: a team of 130 smart and efficient staff serve at least 1000 people a day and take it all in their stride.

楊先生在1958年於台灣開辦其第一家小籠包店，特別注重服務、價格及品質；如今，已在所有主要亞洲城市開辦分店。新鮮手包的上海小籠包是餐廳主打，令人食指大動；蒸豬肉餡更是美味。店前總擠滿排隊等候的人，但不用擔心：由130名員工組成精明有效率的服務團隊，每天服務最少一千名客人，令人賓至如歸。

■ ADDRESS/地址

TEL. 2730 6928
Shop 130 & Restaurant C, 3F, Silvercord, 30 Canton Road, Tsim Sha Tsui, Kowloon
九龍尖沙咀廣東道30號
新港中心3樓C130號舖
www.dintaifung.com.hk

■ ANNUAL AND WEEKLY CLOSING
　休息日期
Closed 3 days Lunar New Year
農曆新年休息3天

■ OPENING HOURS, LAST ORDER
　營業時間，最後點菜時間
11:30-22:30 (L.O.)

■ PRICE/價錢
à la carte/點菜　　　　　$ 90-160

Domani

The talented Italian chef puts his own interpretation on classic combinations and in doing so creates some of the more original Italian cooking found in Hong Kong, with seafood being the speciality. The room, within a glass structure on Pacific Place offering good views and natural light, is elegantly furnished, with an open kitchen and a wave patterned ceiling. The wine list is comprehensive and there is an appealing weekly lunch menu.

才華洋溢的義籍廚師以自創風格詮釋傳統組合，並透過此法成功打造全港最原汁原味的義大利菜之一，以海鮮菜式為招牌菜。房間在太古廣場的玻璃部份當中，提供絕佳景觀及自然光，且經過精緻裝潢，附有開放式廚房及波浪形天花。酒牌提供不少選擇，每週午市套餐亦相當吸引。

■ ADDRESS/地址

TEL. 2111 1197
Shop 406, Level 4, Pacific Place,
88 Queensway, Admiralty
香港金鐘道88號太古廣場4樓406號舖
www.domani.hk

■ OPENING HOURS, LAST ORDER
　營業時間，最後點菜時間
Lunch/午膳 12:00-15:00 (L.O.)
Dinner/晚膳 19:00-23:00 (L.O.)

■ PRICE/價錢
Lunch/午膳   set/套餐 $310-350
　　　　　　 à la carte/點菜 $400-780
Dinner/晚膳 set/套餐 $980
　　　　　　 à la carte/點菜 $400-780

Dong Lai Shun
東來順

The first Dong Lai Shun was founded in 1903 in Peking, and has been successfully transplanted to the basement of the Royal Garden hotel. Its décor is contemporary with distinct Asian nuances, such as panels and paintings; there's a water feature which creates a relaxing atmosphere. The mix of Beijing and Huaiyang recipes includes hot pot, Peking duck and 'shuan yang rou': paper thin slices of Mongolian black-headed mutton.

於1903年在北京創辦的東來順，其後成功遷移到帝苑酒店地庫層。餐廳的裝修揉合了現代和傳統格調；　鮮明細緻的亞洲特色，從牆板和壁畫便可略窺一二。這裡的人工噴泉更營造了輕鬆的氣氛。食物方面，餐廳的北京和淮陽菜共冶一爐，包括火鍋、北京填鴨，以及「涮羊肉」：採用蒙古黑頭白羊的上乘部分，肉質薄如紙，軟如棉。

■ ADDRESS/地址

TEL. 2733 2020
B2F, The Royal Garden Hotel,
69 Mody Road, East Tsim Sha Tsui,
Kowloon
九龍尖東麼地道69號帝苑酒店地庫2樓
www.rghk.com.hk

■ OPENING HOURS, LAST ORDER
　營業時間，最後點菜時間
Lunch/午膳 11:30-14:30 (L.O.)
Dinner/晚膳 18:00-22:30 (L.O.)

■ PRICE/價錢
Lunch/午膳　set/套餐　　　$88-314
　　　　　　à la carte/點菜 $180-1,300
Dinner/晚膳 set/套餐　　　$228-314
　　　　　　à la carte/點菜 $220-1,300

Dragon Inn   NEW
容龍

There aren't many in this area who haven't heard of The Dragon Inn as it's been here in one form or another since 1939 and, with such great views to the sea across tropical gardens, it's not surprising. But it's the seafood most come for – some don't even look at the main menu, but just pick dishes from the seafood speciality list. Baked baby lobster with cheese or baked oysters with port are favourites. Ask for a window table when booking.

容龍海鮮酒家的大名在本區幾乎無人不曉。自1939年開業，不少遊人都喜愛到那裏享受一望無際的海景，同時欣賞它的熱帶花園，受歡迎可謂意料中事。但最吸引客人的是這裡的海鮮。有些人根本不翻看主菜牌，而是直接從海鮮單挑選。芝士焗龍蝦與砵酒焗生蠔都是必然之選。預訂時可選擇靠窗座位。

■ ADDRESS/地址
TEL. 2450 6366
Castle Peak Road, Miles 19,
Tuen Mun, New Territories
新界屯門青山19咪

■ ANNUAL AND WEEKLY CLOSING
　休息日期
Closed 2 days Lunar New Year
農曆新年休息2天

■ OPENING HOURS, LAST ORDER
　營業時間，最後點菜時間
11:00-23:00 (L.O.)

■ PRICE/價錢
à la carte/點菜 $ 150-400

Dragon King (Yau Ma Tei) NEW
龍皇 (油麻地)

Many will know Chef Wong Wing Chee from his regular TV cookery programmes but those who want a more first-hand experience of his skills should come here to the original branch of his small restaurant group. The menu features Cantonese cooking with a pronounced seafood bias, such as king crab prepared three ways and shrimps and crab with egg white. The restaurant is divided between two modern, soberly decorated rooms, with the smaller one downstairs.

相信各位對主廚黃永幟的電視節目都毫不陌生，但若你想親身嘗試他的廚藝，就該到他旗下飲食集團的這家總店。菜式以粵菜為主，尤其喜愛以特色海鮮為主食材，例如皇帝蟹三味與芙蓉蟹。酒家分為兩個裝潢簡潔而摩登的部分，較小的一間在樓下。

■ ADDRESS/地址
TEL. 2771 5821
41-43 Pitt Street,
Yau Ma Tei, Kowloon
九龍油麻地碧街41-43號
www.dragonking.com.hk

■ OPENING HOURS, LAST ORDER
營業時間，最後點菜時間
11:00-23:00 (L.O.)

■ PRICE/價錢
à la carte/點菜　　　　　　$ 180-550

Dumpling Yuan (Central)   NEW
餃子園（中環）

You might wonder why there are only ladies working here – it's because they take their dumplings very seriously and don't consider men to have the required patience or the delicate touch needed to make good dumplings. What is certain is that their Shanghainese varieties are good. We recommend the pork with cabbage and the mutton with green onions; steamed of course. If it's full here then try their branch across the road.

你也許會奇怪為何這裡只有女性員工，因為此店非常重視他們的餃子，他們不認為男性具備做出色餃子必須的條件—足夠耐性與纖細觸覺。這裡的上海菜非常出色。推薦鮮肉白菜餃與北蔥羊肉餃。滿座時，可選擇馬路對面的分店。

■ ADDRESS/地址
TEL. 2525 9018
69 Wellington Street, Central
中環威靈頓街69號

■ ANNUAL AND WEEKLY CLOSING
　休息日期
Closed 3 days Lunar New Year
農曆新年休息3天

■ OPENING HOURS, LAST ORDER
　營業時間，最後點菜時間
11:00-23:00 (L.O.)

■ PRICE/價錢
à la carte/點菜 $ 40-100

Dynasty (Wan Chai)
滿福樓 (灣仔)

The flying fairy motif is on everything but is used to good effect to highlight the Cantonese menu's signature dishes, which are well worth trying: traditional plates of barbecue pork, roast pigeon, and steamed crab claw, along with family-style dishes of boiled rice in clay pots with chicken and salted fish. Desserts are done particularly well. Dine beside the convincing-looking palm trees, here on the third floor of the hotel.

天外飛仙的主題無處不在，用以點出粵菜菜單中值得一試的招牌菜更為適合：古法叉燒拼盤、燒乳鴿、蒸蟹鉗，還有住家風味的鹹魚雞粒煲仔飯。甜品特別出色。雖然身處酒店三樓，你仍可在幾可亂真的棕櫚樹旁用餐。

■ ADDRESS/地址

TEL. 2584 6971

3F, Renaissance Harbour View Hotel,
1 Harbour Road, Wan Chai
灣仔港灣道1號萬麗海景酒店3樓
www.renaissancehotels.com/HKGHV

■ OPENING HOURS, LAST ORDER
    營業時間，最後點菜時間
Lunch/午膳 12:00-15:00 (L.O.)
Dinner/晚膳 18:30-23:00 (L.O.)

■ PRICE/價錢
set/套餐 $ 690-880
à la carte/點菜 $ 450-850

8½ Otto e Mezzo   NEW

❀ ❀

XX X

⌷ 30 ☎¶ ౘ

Fellini's film about the search for inspiration is behind the name of chef-owner Umberto Bombana's bright, bold, restaurant, which opened in early 2010. It is an exquisitely framed and thoughtfully lit space, with a chic, urbane feel. The Italian cooking is equally sophisticated; the homemade pasta dishes and Tajima beef specialities are not to be missed. The 'ageing cellar' for the hams and cheeses is an attractive feature.

費里尼那齣有關尋找靈感的電影，正是主廚兼老闆Umberto Bombana為這家裝修色彩鮮豔大膽的餐廳命名的來源。餐廳開業於2010年初，不論裝潢還是照明都經過深思熟慮，帶有都市時尚感。餐廳的意大利菜式同樣精美；自製意大利麵與田島牛特製菜式都是必然之選。火腿與芝士的發酵窖亦甚為吸引。

■ ADDRESS/地址

TEL. 2537 8859

Shop 202, 2F, Alexandra House,
18 Chater Road, Central
中環遮打道18號歷山大廈2樓202號舖
www.otto-e-mezzo.com

■ ANNUAL AND WEEKLY CLOSING
　　休息日期
Closed Sunday
週日休息

■ OPENING HOURS, LAST ORDER
　　營業時間，最後點菜時間
Lunch/午膳 12:00-15:00
Dinner/晚膳 18:00-23:00

■ PRICE/價錢

Lunch/午膳	set/套餐	$330
	à la carte/點菜	$650-810
Dinner/晚膳	set/套餐	$880-1,280
	à la carte/點菜	$650-810

Fan Tang NEW
飯堂

Press the buzzer, the façade slides open and you enter a different world. Seven large and exquisitely laid tables are surrounded by mirrors, fine art and rich drapes. The private dining rooms upstairs are even more opulent. The Chinese cooking uses mostly Cantonese and Sichuan influences but there are also some subtle touches of originality. Look out for stir-fry chicken with chillies and the deep-fried yellow croaker with chilli and pepper.

只要你按下門鐘,店門立刻為你而開,帶領你進入一個與別不同的世界。鏡子、藝術品與帷簾圍繞著七張大桌,非常雅致。樓上的貴賓房更為富麗堂皇。這裡的中國菜主要以粵菜與川菜為主,但也帶有原創味道。辣子雞與椒鹽小黃魚都值得一試。

■ ADDRESS/地址

TEL. 2890 3339

93-95 Leighton Road, Causeway Bay
銅鑼灣禮頓道93-95號

■ ANNUAL AND WEEKLY CLOSING
　　休息日期
Closed 3 days Lunar New Year
農曆新年休息3天

■ OPENING HOURS, LAST ORDER
　　營業時間,最後點菜時間
Lunch/午膳 12:00-15:00 L.O.14:30
Dinner/晚膳 18:30-23:00 L.O. 22:00

■ PRICE/價錢
Lunch/午膳　à la carte/點菜 $180-300
Dinner/晚膳　à la carte/點菜 $450-1,500

Farm House
農圃

In a sleek business building, this contemporary-style dining room has private rooms leading off it as well as an eye-catching aquarium running the length of one entire wall. The Cantonese menu uses exceedingly fresh ingredients and includes such specialities as deep-fried chicken wing with stuffed glutinous rice and steamed minced pork with preserved duck egg and squid. The serving team are very courteous and professional.

這家裝潢富現代感的飯店位處線條流麗的商業大廈中，一進門便可見數間貴賓房和一個伸延整道牆的巨型水族箱，非常引人注目。農圃的粵菜選用特級新鮮材料炮製而成，著名菜式有古法釀雞翼和咸蛋土魷蒸肉餅。員工非常專業有禮。

■ ADDRESS/地址

TEL. 2881 1331

1F, Phase 1, Ming An Plaza,
8 Sunning Road, Causeway Bay
銅鑼灣新寧道8號民安廣場1期1樓
www.farmhouse.com.hk

■ OPENING HOURS, LAST ORDER
　　營業時間，最後點菜時間
Lunch/午膳 11:00-15:00 L.O. 14:45
Dinner/晚膳 18:00-24:00 L.O. 23:00

■ PRICE/價錢

Lunch/午膳	set/套餐	$250-980
	à la carte/點菜	$220-1,150
Dinner/晚膳	set/套餐	$480-980
	à la carte/點菜	$220-1,150

Fofo by el Willy　NEW

Fofo means 'chubby' and, judging by the look on the faces of the plump pig and penguin figures dotted around the room, therein lies contentment. But, for the rest of us, three dishes plus some rice per person should suffice. The appealing tapas ranges from the popular suckling pig, which is slow-roasted overnight, to more modern creations that may even use a little Asian flavour. The terrific roof-top terrace has its own separate menu.

Fofo是「圓胖」的意思。從餐館內的小豬與企鵝裝飾臉上滿足的表情看來，我們不難理解餐廳名字的意思。不過對一般食客而言，三道菜加上每人吃點白飯經已足夠。讓人垂涎三尺的西班牙小菜從大受歡迎以慢火通宵烤製的脆及乳豬，到創新的菜式，甚至帶點亞洲風味的，應有盡有。別有特色的天台花園另設不同的餐牌。

■ ADDRESS/地址

TEL. 2900 2009
20F, M88 2-8 Wellington Street, Central
中環威靈頓街2-8號M88 20樓
www.fofo.hk

■ ANNUAL AND WEEKLY CLOSING
　休息日期
Closed Sunday
週日休息

■ OPENING HOURS, LAST ORDER
　營業時間，最後點菜時間
Lunch/午膳　12:00-14:30
Dinner/晚膳　18:00-22:30

■ PRICE/價錢
Lunch/午膳　set/套餐　　　　　$ 188
　　　　　　à la carte/點菜　$ 290-670
Dinner/晚膳　à la carte/點菜　$ 290-670

Cantonese/粵菜　　　　　　　　　　　　　　MAP/地圖　14/C-1

Fook Lam Moon (Kowloon)
福臨門（九龍）

⚀ ✥ 🖐 📺100 📞🍽

This Kowloon branch may have fewer business people among its customers than the one in Wan Chai but it shares the same principles: fresh, seasonal ingredients treated with the utmost care. The result is that this refined Cantonese cooking has been attracting a loyal following since the restaurant opened in 1972. Specialities include aged abalone braised in stock with oyster sauce and baked crab shell with onions and fresh crab meat.

與灣仔店相比，光顧九龍分店的商務人士可能較少，但兩店都秉承同一宗旨：以新鮮、時令材料精心炮製。這種優良的粵菜烹調方法備受美食愛好者的欣賞，難怪自1972年開業迄今吸引不少忠實捧場客。不防試一試特別推薦的蠔皇原隻乾鮑及釀焗鮮蟹蓋。

■ ADDRESS/地址
TEL. 2366 0286
53-59 Kimberley Road,
Tsim Sha Tsui, Kowloon
九龍尖沙咀金巴利道53-59號
www.fooklammoon-grp.com

■ ANNUAL AND WEEKLY CLOSING
　休息日期
Closed 2 days Lunar New Year
農曆年新休息2天

■ OPENING HOURS, LAST ORDER
　營業時間，最後點菜時間
Lunch/午膳　11:30-14:30 (L.O.)
Dinner/晚膳　18:00-22:30 (L.O.)

■ PRICE/價錢
à la carte/點菜　　　　$ 370-2,000

Fook Lam Moon (Wan Chai)
福臨門 (灣仔)

♿ ☞ 🍽100 🍽

Meaning 'good fortune arriving at your door', Fook Lam Moon is a luxurious restaurant now being run with considerable passion by the third generation of the same family. The decoration is based around a colour scheme of gold, silver and bronze which seems appropriate as there are so many luxury items on the menu. The respect for the ingredients is palpable and signature dishes include baked stuff crab shell and roast suckling pig.

「福臨門」意指「好運來到你家門」,是一家豪華的高級酒家,現在由創業家族的第三代經營。店內以金、銀、銅色系裝潢,映襯著菜單上的珍饈百味。食材明顯經過精心處理,招牌菜包括釀焗鮮蟹蓋與大紅片皮乳豬。

■ ADDRESS/地址

TEL. 2866 0663
35-45 Johnston Road, Wan Chai
灣仔莊士敦道35-45號
www.fooklammoon-grp.com

■ ANNUAL AND WEEKLY CLOSING
　休息日期
Closed 2 days Lunar New Year
農曆新年休息2天

■ OPENING HOURS, LAST ORDER
　營業時間,最後點菜時間
Lunch/午膳 11:30-14:30 (L.O.)
Dinner/晚膳 18:00-22:30 (L.O.)

■ PRICE/價錢
Lunch/午膳　à la carte/點菜 $ 250-1,000
Dinner/晚膳　à la carte/點菜 $ 750-2,750

Forum
富臨

You cannot fail to notice the pictures of owner-chef Yeung Koon Yat. For over thirty years he's been attracting everyone from world leaders to locals to his Forum restaurant, thanks largely to his celebrated speciality: abalone. His fried bird's nest is noteworthy too but it is for the abalone cooked in a clay pot that many come. The restaurant is spread over three floors, with seating for around 150.

你肯定會留意到世界御廚楊貫一的照片。三十多年來，光顧他的客人從世界領導人到本地食客包羅萬有，這大概應歸功於他的拿手名菜：阿一鮑魚。大部分客人都為其砂鍋鮑魚慕名而來，而皇冠燕盞也相當不俗。飯店佔地三層，可容納約一百五十人。

■ ADDRESS/地址
TEL. 2891 2555
485 Lockhart Road, Causeway Bay
銅鑼灣駱克道485號

■ OPENING HOURS, LAST ORDER
營業時間，最後點菜時間
Lunch/午膳 11:00-15:00 (L.O.)
Dinner/晚膳 18:00-23:00 (L.O.)

■ PRICE/價錢
à la carte/點菜　　　　　$ 380-2,580

Fu Ho (Tsim Sha Tsui)   NEW
富豪 (尖沙咀)

❀

🍴🍴🍴

🚪36 📞🍴

Wood panelling, comfortable red armchairs and deep-pile carpets add to the warm, smart, yet relaxing, feel of this Cantonese restaurant. It has been attracting diners to its location on a hidden floor of the Miramar shopping centre for over a decade, thanks to its authentic cooking. Among the specialities that appeal to its scores of regulars are braised superior dried fish maw, bird's nest with almond cream and fried rice 'Ah Yung'.

木鑲板、舒適的紅色扶手椅、長絨地毯給這家粵菜酒家帶來溫暖、醒目而放鬆的感覺。十多年來，這裡憑著正宗的佳餚打響名堂，雖然位於美麗華商場不太起眼的一層，這裡依然吸引無數饕客。招牌菜有超特厚花膠、杏汁官燕、阿翁炒飯。

■ ADDRESS/地址

TEL. 2736 2228

4F, Miramar Shopping Centre,
132 Nathan Road, Tsim Sha Tsui,
Kowloon

九龍尖沙咀彌敦道132號美麗華商場4樓

■ OPENING HOURS, LAST ORDER
　營業時間, 最後點菜時間
11:00-24:00 L.O.22:30

■ PRICE/價錢

Lunch/午膳	set/套餐	$368-1,980
	à la carte/點菜	$250-2,500
Dinner/晚膳	set/套餐	$438-1,980
	à la carte/點菜	$250-2,500

Fung Lum
楓林小館

Located opposite Tai Wai station and known for its striking façade, this is the original Fung Lum; the famed replica in Los Angeles was a hit in the 1980s. The recipes remain untarnished to this day, with the seafood being highly recommended, particularly the baked shrimps with salt and lobster and the baked crab with black beans. Regulars believe the pigeon is a must. If ordering several dishes, ask for them to be paced accordingly.

位於大圍火車站對面的楓林小館正面的設計讓人印象深刻；這是原汁原味的楓林；洛杉磯著名的複製品在一九八零年代曾一度讓人瘋靡。今天菜單依然毫不遜色，尤其推薦海鮮，如鹽焗蝦及豉汁焗蟹。常客相信不能缺少一道乳鴿。如果點了好幾道菜，可交由店員編排次序。

■ ADDRESS/地址

TEL. 2692 1175
45-47 Tsuen Nam Road, Tai Wai,
Sha Tin, New Territories
新界沙田大圍村南道45-47號

■ ANNUAL AND WEEKLY CLOSING
　休息日期
Closed 4 days Lunar New Year
農曆新年休息4天

■ OPENING HOURS, LAST ORDER
　營業時間，最後點菜時間
Lunch/午膳 11:00-15:00 (L.O.)
Dinner/晚膳 18:00-22:30 L.O. 22:00

■ PRICE/價錢
à la carte/點菜　　　$ 150-500

Fung Shing (Mong Kok) NEW
鳳城 (旺角)

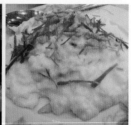

It is the region of Shun Tak that the owner-chef looks to for inspiration for his tasty Cantonese cooking. Look out for dishes such as stir-fried milk with white eggs and crab meat. This family business has been going since 1954, having initially been based in Causeway Bay; their story, together with some recipes, has been published in a book. Divided into two simple rooms, the restaurant is always busy, so it's well worth booking in advance.

主廚兼老闆從順德菜中尋找烹調美味廣東菜的靈感。大良炒鮮奶值得一試。這個家族生意始於1954年，初期位於銅鑼灣。他們的故事與部分食譜已輯錄成書出版。酒家分為兩個大廳。由於這裡客似雲來，建議預早訂座。

■ ADDRESS/地址
TEL. 2381 5261
1-2F, 749 Nathan Road,
Mong Kok, Kowloon
九龍旺角彌敦道749號1-2樓

■ ANNUAL AND WEEKLY CLOSING
  休息日期
Closed 4 days Lunar New Year
農曆新年休息4天

■ OPENING HOURS, LAST ORDER
  營業時間，最後點菜時間
Lunch/午膳 09:00-15:00 (L.O.)
Dinner/晚膳 18:00-22:30 (L.O.)

■ PRICE/價錢
Lunch/午膳 à la carte/點菜 $140-350
Dinner/晚膳 à la carte/點菜 $180-350

Fu Sing (Causeway Bay)   NEW
富聲 (銅鑼灣)

🗋 32 📞🍽

With its contemporary interior, friendly and attentive service and accessible location, it is little wonder that this second Fu Sing restaurant has proved so successful. The dim sum selection is comprehensive and the prices are suitably appealing to allow for much over-ordering. Specialities include steamed crab in Chinese wine and soy sauce chicken in Fu Sing style. Two private dining rooms are also available.

富現代感的裝潢，親切又細心的服務，加上地點方便，難怪這間富聲第二分店會如此成功。點心選擇豐富，價錢合理，客人總忍不住多點幾道菜！招牌菜包括富聲花雕蒸蟹和鮑汁豉油雞。設有兩間貴賓廳。

■ ADDRESS/地址

TEL. 2504 4228
1F, 68 Yee Wo Street, Causeway Bay
銅鑼灣怡和街68號1樓

■ OPENING HOURS, LAST ORDER
　營業時間, 最後點菜時間
Lunch/午膳 11:00-15:00 L.O.14:30
Dinner/晚膳 18:00-23:00 L.O.22:30

■ PRICE/價錢
set/套餐 $ 228-1,480
à la carte/點菜 $ 135-1,380

Fu Sing (Wan Chai)
富聲

🖥20 📞

Taking the lift up in this stylish modern building will bring you out directly into the plush, spacious restaurant with its smart carpeting and wall plates. The service is very attentive and the cooking is equally precise with its broad range of Cantonese dishes. Among the recommendations are stewed abalone and goose web as well as braised cow tail in red wine. Plenty of fresh juices are available and there's a fine collection of cognacs.

進入設計時尚、富現代感的大樓後,升降機帶你直達富麗堂皇、佔地寬廣的餐廳,牆紙和地毯的鋪設均見心思。服務非常周到,烹調方法亦獨具特色,備有一系列粵菜可供選擇。推介菜式包括炆鮑魚鵝掌和紅酒燉牛尾。除了各種鮮榨果汁,店內亦提供精選法國干邑白蘭地。

■ ADDRESS/地址

TEL. 2893 0881
1F, 353 Lockhart Road,
Sunshine Plaza, Wan Chai
灣仔駱克道353號三湘大廈1樓

■ OPENING HOURS, LAST ORDER
　營業時間,最後點菜時間
Lunch/午膳 11:00-15:00 (L.O.)
Dinner/晚膳 18:00-23:00 (L.O.)

■ PRICE/價錢
Lunch/午膳　set/套餐　　　$250-680
　　　　　à la carte/點菜 $160-550
Dinner/晚膳　set/套餐　　　$320-680
　　　　　à la carte/點菜 $160-550

Gaddi's
吉地士

XXXXX

☞♟ ⛶16 🕐🍴 🎱

Gaddi's is something of an institution in the city. A private lift whisks you to this legend which celebrates over fifty years of fine dining. Live music and old-style British formality accompany the classical French cuisine. If you want to make an evening of it you should try the tasting menu. Gaddi's harks back to a bygone age where the act of dining is taken very seriously and, as such, gentlemen are required to wear a jacket.

吉地士可說是城內有名的食府。私人電梯迅速把你把帶到這個超過五十年的優質餐飲傳奇之地。現場音樂和古老英國禮節配襯著經典法國菜。如果想享受美好的晚餐，便要品嚐吉地士的tasting menu。餐廳保留著一種昔日的典雅，餐飲的真正意義得以尊重。男士們，謹記帶上一件西裝外套。

■ ADDRESS/地址

TEL. 2920 2888
1F, The Peninsula Hotel,
Salisbury Road, Tsim Sha Tsui,
Kowloon
九龍尖沙咀梳士巴利道半島酒店1樓
www.peninsula.com

■ OPENING HOURS, LAST ORDER
　營業時間，最後點菜時間
Lunch/午膳　12:00-14:30 (L.O.)
Dinner/晚膳　19:00-22:30 (L.O.)

■ PRICE/價錢
Lunch/午膳　set/套餐　　　$428
　　　　　　à la carte/點菜　$1,000-1,700
Dinner/晚膳　set/套餐　　　$1,388
　　　　　　à la carte/點菜　$1,000-1,700

Gaylord   NEW
爵樂

It's easy to see why Gaylord has been pulling in regulars for nearly 40 years: prices are good, especially those of the lunch buffet, staff are enthusiastic and the à la carte menu offers an appealing mix of dishes. Tender boneless lamb in an onion and red pepper sauce and prawns in aromatic spices are signature dishes. The restaurant is warmly decorated; ask for one of the five booths. A live band plays ghazal music every night from 7.30pm.

不難想到爵樂在將近四十年來為何吸引無數常客：價錢合理，尤其是自助午餐；員工的服務殷勤；「à la carte」餐牌上也提供一系列誘人美食可供搭配。香草羊肉和洋蔥香汁鮮蝦是他們的招牌菜。餐廳裝潢溫馨，設有五個廂座，不妨要求坐到其中一個。每晚7:30更有樂隊現場演奏ghazal音樂。

■ ADDRESS/地址
TEL. 2376 1001
1F, Ashley Centre Building,
23-25 Ashley Road, Tsim Sha Tsui,
Kowloon
九龍尖沙咀亞士厘道23-25號
雅士利中心1樓
www.chiram.com.hk

■ OPENING HOURS, LAST ORDER
　營業時間，最後點菜時間
Lunch/午膳　12:00-14:45 L.O.14:30
Dinner/晚膳　18:00-22:45 (L.O.)

■ PRICE/價錢
Lunch/午膳　set/套餐　　　　$108-128
　　　　　à la carte/點菜　$200-350
Dinner/晚膳　à la carte/點菜 $200-350

Golden Bauhinia
金紫荊

XX

    👤 P 🍽14

Conveniently located for visitors to the Hong Kong Convention and Exhibition Centre (and not far from the ferry pier either), this large dining room may be monochrome in tone but it is ideally positioned for admiring the Bauhinia sculpture. Specialities include steamed bean curd with shrimp and scallop in fish soup, and sautéed prawns with honey beans and fungus. Great care is taken with the service.

前往香港會議展覽中心的人士可輕易找到這家餐廳，離碼頭亦是咫尺之遙。偌大的餐廳配色可能較為單一，但欣賞金紫荊雕像則是一流位置。特色小菜包括：海皇魚湯浸豆腐及蜜豆愉耳炒蝦球。服務非常細心。

■ ADDRESS/地址

TEL. 2582 7728

Hong Kong Convention and Exhibition Centre, Golden Bauhinia Square, Expo Drive East, Wan Chai
灣仔博覽道金紫荊廣場
香港會議展覽中心地下

■ OPENING HOURS, LAST ORDER
　營業時間，最後點菜時間
Lunch/午膳　12:00-14:45 (L.O.)
Dinner/晚膳　18:30-22:45 (L.O.)

■ PRICE/價錢
Lunch/午膳　à la carte/點菜 $ 150-800
Dinner/晚膳　à la carte/點菜 $ 250-800

Golden Leaf
金葉庭

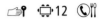

The extremely popular Golden Leaf is elegantly dressed with panels, sculptured wood, antique art pieces and chandeliers. It is to this cosy oriental environment that customers come to enjoy the chef's recommendations, such as the steamed, fresh crab claw with minced ginger and rice wine or the poached chicken with chicken essence. A bargain set lunch menu and an appealing selection of dim sum are also available.

非常受歡迎的金葉庭以高雅屏風、木雕、古董藝術品及吊燈裝飾。客人都愛身處此溫暖而具東方特色的環境，享受廚師推介的菜式，如蒸薑米酒鮮蟹鉗，或是貴妃雞。此外，亦有午飯特惠套餐及一系列吸引點心可供選擇。

■ ADDRESS/地址
TEL. 2521 3838
5F, Conrad Hotel, Pacific Place,
88 Queensway, Admiralty
香港金鐘道88號太古廣場港麗酒店5樓
www.conradhotels.com

■ OPENING HOURS, LAST ORDER
營業時間，最後點菜時間
Lunch/午膳 11:30-15:00 (L.O.)
Dinner/晚膳 18:00-23:00 (L.O.)

■ PRICE/價錢
Lunch/午膳   set/套餐 $388-528
             à la carte/點菜 $350-1,000
Dinner/晚膳 set/套餐 $528-628
             à la carte/點菜 $350-1,000

Golden Valley
駿景軒

♿   🖐️   🍽️24   📞🍴

Not only is The Emperor hotel fortunate to be close to the famous race course, it also has this fine traditional restaurant. They serve classic Cantonese and Sichuan cuisine, the menu equally divided between the two varieties. It's a regular haunt of many a famous face and avid race-goer, all of whom enjoy the archetypal surroundings. From delicate dim sum to fiery hotpots, the choice is exhaustive.

英皇駿景酒店座落於跑馬地，鄰近著名馬場。除了坐擁極佳的地理位置外，酒店更設有駿景軒這家精緻的傳統中菜廳。餐廳提供傳統粵菜及川菜，選擇平均。不少名流及馬場常客經常現身，享受保留傳統的環境。從精美點心到火鍋，選擇層出不窮。

■ ADDRESS/地址

TEL. 2961 3330
1F, The Emperor Hotel, 1 Wang Tak Street, Happy Valley
跑馬地宏德街1號英皇駿景酒店1樓
www.emperorhotel.com.hk

■ OPENING HOURS, LAST ORDER
營業時間，最後點菜時間
Lunch/午膳 11:00-16:30 (L.O.)
Dinner/晚膳 18:00-22:30 (L.O.)

■ PRICE/價錢
à la carte/點菜 $ 160-450

Good Hope Noodles
好旺角麵家

Choosing what you want to eat here is easy – just watch the chefs preparing food in the two tiny kitchens – wontons and noodles in one, congee in the other - as you wait for a table. Whether having the beef, pork knuckles or wonton noodles, you'll find it all very fresh and tasty, which explains its popularity with those locals who have been coming here for years. Two generations of owners keep the place looking clean and bright.

要決定吃什麼非常容易——在等待座位時看看廚師在兩個小廚房裡如何烹調食物吧。無論是牛肉、豬手或雲吞麵，你都可以在這裡嚐到最新鮮、最美味的麵食，這也解釋了為什麼這餐廳多年來如此受常客歡迎。兩代店主致力保持店面清潔明亮。

■ ADDRESS/地址
TEL. 2393 9036
146 Sai Yeung Choi Street,
Mong Kok, Kowloon
九龍旺角西洋菜街146號

■ ANNUAL AND WEEKLY CLOSING
　　休息日期
Closed Lunar New Year
年初一休息

■ OPENING HOURS, LAST ORDER
　　營業時間，最後點菜時間
11:00-03:00 (L.O.)

■ PRICE/價錢
à la carte/點菜　　　　$ 22-70

Grissini

XXX

♿ ‹ ☞ **P** 🖵24 ☎️🍴

If you fancy a romantic dinner with views to match, then this smart Italian restaurant with its candlelit tables is just the job. The range of authentic dishes captures the length and breadth of Italy's regions and manages to be both traditional and imaginative. Equal space is given to pasta, risotto, meat and fish. You'll find it hard restricting yourself to just one of the exquisite grissini that lend the place its name.

假如你嚮往在醉人夜景下享受燭光晚餐，這家時尚的餐廳定是必然之選。真材實料的菜式囊括意大利不同地域的尊長，兼具傳統特色和創意。意大利麵，意大利燴飯，肉類和魚類菜式均有不少選擇。這店的名詞來自意大利一種長條麵包，也是餐廳裡忍不住要吃的美食。

■ ADDRESS/地址

TEL. 2584 7722

Grand Hyatt Hotel,
1 Harbour Road, Wan Chai
灣仔港灣道1號君悅酒店
www.hongkong.grand.hyatt.com

■ ANNUAL AND WEEKLY CLOSING
　休息日期
Closed Saturday lunch
週六午膳休息

■ OPENING HOURS, LAST ORDER
　營業時間，最後點菜時間
Lunch/午膳 12:00-14:30 (L.O.)
Dinner/晚膳 19:00-22:30 (L.O.)

■ PRICE/價錢

Lunch/午膳	set/套餐	$315-345
	à la carte/點菜	$670-950
Dinner/晚膳	set/套餐	$700-1,100
	à la carte/點菜	$670-950

Hakka Yé Yé
客家爺爺

The food of the Hakka people is very much sophisticated peasant cookery, relying largely on pork and chicken. Specialities here include braised pork belly with preserved vegetables and Emperor chicken. The small contemporary room is simply furnished but the charming team go out of their way to explain the distinctive characteristics of their authentic and reasonably-priced regional cuisine.

客家菜的特色是農家菜，大部分食材選用豬肉和雞肉。這裡的推介菜式包括西施梅菜扣肉和霸爺雞。地方小巧裝潢現代精緻，親切友善的員工用獨有方式介紹原汁原味的客家菜，且價錢合理。

■ ADDRESS/地址
TEL. 2537 7060
2F, Parekh House, 63 Wyndham Street, Central
中環雲咸街63號巴力大廈2樓
www.yeyegroup.com

■ ANNUAL AND WEEKLY CLOSING
　休息日期
Closed Sunday and Public Holidays
週日及公眾假期休息

■ OPENING HOURS, LAST ORDER
　營業時間，最後點菜時間
Lunch/午膳 12:00-14:15 (L.O.)
Dinner/晚膳 18:30-22:15 (L.O.)

■ PRICE/價錢
Lunch/午膳　set/套餐　　$92
　　　　　à la carte/點菜 $160-250
Dinner/晚膳　à la carte/點菜 $160-250

Harbour Grill

The décor here is elegant and comfortable and suits a romantic evening just as well as a more formal business occasion. The international menu shows ambition, placing French classics alongside grilled dishes that could include Wagyu beef, whole Italian sea bass or Welsh lamb rack. Other specialities include scallops seared with pork belly, lobster bisque and dark chocolate cake. An extensive wine list has been well chosen.

這裡的裝潢優雅舒適，既適合浪漫約會，也可用於較正式的商業場合。菜單上來自世界各地的佳餚顯示了餐廳的野心，如將傳統法國菜配合燒烤菜式，包括和牛、全條意大利海鱸或威爾斯羊架。其他招牌菜包括烤帶子配豬腩、龍蝦濃湯與黑巧克力蛋糕。酒單經過精心挑選，選擇甚豐。

■ ADDRESS/地址

TEL. 2996 8433

GF, Harbour Grand Kowloon Hotel,
20 Tak Fung Street, Whampoa Garden,
Hung Hom, Kowloon
九龍紅磡黃埔花園德豐街20號
九龍海逸君綽酒店地下
www.harbour-grand.com

■ OPENING HOURS, LAST ORDER
　營業時間，最後點菜時間
Lunch/午膳 12:00-14:00 (L.O.)
Dinner/晚膳 18:00-22:00 (L.O.)

■ PRICE/價錢
Lunch/午膳 　set/套餐 　　$220
　　　　　　 à la carte/點菜 $450-950
Dinner/晚膳 à la carte/點菜 $450-950

Harvey Nichols

It's not just the shopping that's chic here: the fourth floor restaurant is design-led, with a harlequin style ceiling and floor, the colours illuminated by shifting beams of light; and black leather seating with comfortable imitation snakeskin armchairs. Service is confident and affable. And the food? The light but satisfying French cuisine comes with some subtle contemporary twists. Afternoon tea is also served.

這裡入時的不僅是購物。這家位於四樓的餐廳設計新穎,天花及地板採用了丑角服裝的風格,移動的燈光照亮顏色。餐廳內有黑色皮革座位及舒適的仿蛇皮扶手椅。服務周到妥貼。至於食物又如何?是帶有些許現代創新元素的法國佳餚,份量不多、卻讓人滿足。設有下午茶餐。

■ ADDRESS/地址

TEL. 3695 3389
4F, The Landmark, 15 Queen's Road Central, Central
中環皇后大道中15號置地廣場4樓

■ ANNUAL AND WEEKLY CLOSING
  休息日期
Closed Lunar New Year and Sunday
年初一及週日休息

■ OPENING HOURS, LAST ORDER
  營業時間,最後點菜時間
Lunch/午膳 12:00-14:30 (L.O.)
Dinner/晚膳 19:00-22:30 (L.O.)

■ PRICE/價錢
Lunch/午膳   set/套餐 $340
Dinner/晚膳 set/套餐 $428
            à la carte/點菜 $470-570

Hing Kee
避風塘興記

Originated from Causeway Bay two generations ago, the family moved their business to Tsim Sha Tsui, where they've made a name for themselves with their Boat People style cuisine; further testimony comes from the celebrity signatures lining the walls. Elder sister heads the serving team; younger brother takes charge in the kitchen. They are famous for their stir-fry crabs with black beans and chilli, roast duck and rice noodles in soup and congee.

兩代前已於銅鑼灣開業，家族將餐廳移往尖沙嘴，建立了避風塘特色菜的名聲，牆上貼滿明星簽名，更見證此店美味。招牌菜包括避風塘炒蟹、燒鴨湯河及艇仔粥。

■ ADDRESS/地址
TEL. 2722 0022
1F, Bowa House, 180 Nathan Road, Tsim Sha Tsui, Kowloon
九龍尖沙咀彌敦道180號
寶華商業大廈1樓

■ ANNUAL AND WEEKLY CLOSING
　　休息日期
Closed 2 days Lunar New Year
農曆新年休息2天

■ OPENING HOURS, LAST ORDER
　　營業時間，最後點菜時間
Dinner/晚膳 18:00-05:00 (L.O.)

■ PRICE/價錢
à la carte/點菜 $ 300-800

Hin Ho Curry (Sai Wan Ho)   NEW
恆河咖喱屋 (西灣河)

The original, found not that far from here, proved so successful that this second branch was opened back in 1997. The young Indian chef is passionate about his craft and standout dishes from his extensive menu include massala mutton and the baby pork leg tandoori. Fish, from the tank by the entrance, is handled particularly well. Service is young and enthusiastic; lunchtimes fill very quickly so it's worth coming a little later.

由於離這裡不遠的本店極為成功，因此這家第二分店便在1997年誕生。年輕的印度主廚對他創作的菜式充滿熱誠。豐富的餐牌中特別出色的菜式有瑪沙拉羊肉與印式烤豬仔脾。從入口處魚缸取來的魚做的菜式也特別美味。這裡的侍應年輕又朝氣勃勃；午餐時間很快就滿座，建議稍遲才去。

■ ADDRESS/地址

TEL. 2967 8348

90 Shau Kei Wan Road, Sai Wan Ho
西灣河筲箕灣道90號
www.hinhocurry.com/hk

■ ANNUAL AND WEEKLY CLOSING
    休息日期

Closed 4 days Lunar New Year
農曆新年休息4天

■ OPENING HOURS, LAST ORDER
    營業時間，最後點菜時間
Lunch/午膳 11:00-15:00 L.O.14:45
Dinner/晚膳 18:00-23:00 L.O.22:45

■ PRICE/價錢

Lunch/午膳	set/套餐	$40-110
	à la carte/點菜	$80-150
Dinner/晚膳	set/套餐	$75-110
	à la carte/點菜	$80-150

Hin Ho Curry (Shau Kei Wan) NEW
恆河咖喱屋（筲箕灣）

As soon as you see the tandoor in the front window you know you're in for an authentic experience. The chefs are from Nepal and trained in Delhi so the cuisine has a north Indian bias; Masala lamb chop bhuna and Indian crab curry are good choices. If you can't decide then the Nawabi Bhojan or 'Royal Fare' menu offers a great selection of classic dishes. The Indian lights add a little exoticism to this former noodle shop.

從櫥窗看到印度式烤爐，就知道這裡必能品嚐正宗印度菜。主廚是尼泊爾人，在德里學師，因此這裡的菜式都帶有北印度風味。瑪沙拉炒羊鞍扒與印式咖喱蟹，都是不錯的選擇。若你覺得難以取捨，「印度帝皇餐」套餐也有大量的傳統印度菜以供選擇。店裡以印度燈飾做裝飾，為這家前身是麵店的菜館帶來一絲異國風情。

■ ADDRESS/地址

TEL. 2560 1268

Shop 11, East Way Tower,
59-99 Main Street East, Shau Kei Wan
筲箕灣東大街59-99號東威大廈11號舖
www.hinhocurry.com/hk

■ OPENING HOURS, LAST ORDER
營業時間，最後點菜時間
Lunch/午膳 11:00-15:00 L.O.14:45
Dinner/晚膳 18:00-23:00 L.O.22:45

■ PRICE/價錢

Lunch/午膳	set/套餐	$40-110
	à la carte/點菜	$80-150
Dinner/晚膳	set/套餐	$75-110
	à la carte/點菜	$80-150

Ho Hung Kee
何洪記

The owner's parents opened the business in Wan Chai in 1946 and the restaurant's been here, near Times Square, since 1974; so Mr Ho advisedly calls it the Original Noodle Shop! His wife claims the noodles won her over before she'd even met her husband. On both sides of the entrance, two little cooking stations entice you in with their aromas. Exceptional shrimp wonton boasts a decades-old recipe, while congee with fish is also of legendary status.

東主父母於1946年在灣仔開設此家餐廳。自1974年以來，餐廳一直座落於現時位置，毗鄰時代廣場。因此，何先生特意稱它為「傳統麵店」！他太太聲稱還未與丈夫第一次見面，麵就已經贏得芳心。入口兩邊都有廚師以食物香味引誘你。著名的鮮蝦雲吞以幾十年的祖傳食譜烹調，而魚粥亦是令人讚不絕口的菜式。

■ ADDRESS/地址

TEL. 2577 6558
2 Sharp Street, Causeway Bay
銅鑼灣雲東街2號

■ OPENING HOURS, LAST ORDER
營業時間，最後點菜時間
11:30-23:30 (L.O.)

■ PRICE/價錢
Lunch/午膳   à la carte/點菜 $ 26-38
Dinner/晚膳   à la carte/點菜 $ 33-99

Hoi King Heen　NEW
海景軒

✿　　　　　　　　　　　　　　　　　XXX

♿　☞　🅿　▢ 40

As if to compensate for its hotel basement location, the restaurant is elegantly decorated with wood panelling and warm colours; the private dining rooms are also particularly charming. The authentic Cantonese cooking draws plenty of regulars from beyond the hotel, thanks to signature dishes such as steamed garoupa rolls with Yunnan ham; steamed crab claw with egg white and the Fortune chicken – which needs to be ordered in advance.

海景軒以暖色系與木鑲板裝潢，格調高雅，彷彿是彌補位置上的不足之處——位於酒店地庫，貴賓房裝潢更特別雅致。出色的正宗廣東烹調，如其中一款招牌菜龍皇白玉卷，吸引許多酒店以外的常客。花雕蛋白蒸鮮蟹鉗、順德富貴雞必須預訂。

■ ADDRESS/地址
TEL. 2731 2883
B2F, Intercontinental Grand Stanford Hotel, 70 Mody Road, East Tsin Sha Tsui, Kowloon
九龍尖東麼地道70號海景嘉福酒店B2樓
www.hongkong.intercontinental.com

■ OPENING HOURS, LAST ORDER
　營業時間，最後點菜時間
Lunch/午膳　11:30-14:30 (L.O.)
Dinner/晚膳　18:30-22:30 (L.O.)

■ PRICE/價錢
Lunch/午膳　set/套餐　　$ 148-198
　　　　　　　à la carte/點菜 $ 260-1,300
Dinner/晚膳　à la carte/點菜 $ 260-1,300

Hoi Yat Heen
海逸軒

This large restaurant has great harbour views and so too do the two private rooms. With live music every night, it serves carefully prepared Cantonese cooking which has been given a contemporary twist. Specialities include oven-baked crab meat with shredded onion on the crab shell; sautéed sliced pork with pear and black vinegar, and steamed egg white and bird's nest with pumpkin broth. The very diligent manager heads up an attentive team.

這家餐廳不論主廳與貴賓房，都能俯瞰美麗的維港景色。每晚有現場音樂演奏，配搭大廚精美菜式，為廣東菜添上一絲現代感。特色菜包括：金牌焗釀蟹蓋、桂花梨黑醋脆柳及金湯芙蓉燴燕窩。勤快的經理帶領著出色的服務團隊，為客人提供賓至如歸的服務。

■ ADDRESS/地址

TEL. 2996 8459

2F, Harbour Grand Kowloon Hotel, 20 Tak Fung Street, Whampoa Garden, Hung Hom, Kowloon

九龍紅磡德豐街20號
九龍海逸君綽酒店2樓
www.harbour-grand.com

■ OPENING HOURS, LAST ORDER
營業時間，最後點菜時間
Lunch/午膳 11:30-15:00 (L.O.)
Dinner/晚膳 18:00-23:00 (L.O.)

■ PRICE/價錢

Lunch/午膳	set/套餐	$198-1,688
	à la carte/點菜	$300-1,000
Dinner/晚膳	set/套餐	$998-1,688
	à la carte/點菜	$300-1,000

H One

Away from the bustle and the crowds of IFC sits H One – a comfortable and discreet Italian restaurant with good food and courteous service. The menu features classics from most parts of Italy, offering something for everyone and for all sizes of appetite. The wine list is an impressive tome, with much of its contents visible in the wine room. Be sure to ask for a table in the main room where the harbour views are spectacular.

遠離IFC(國際金融中心商場)的繁囂，舒適而隱蔽的意大利餐廳 H One ——為顧客提供美味的食物與周到的服務。菜單包括來自意大利 各地的經典菜式，並提供適合不同顧客的份量。這裡的酒單提供極豐富 的選擇，大部分都能在藏酒室看到。推薦主廳的座位，海景一流。

■ ADDRESS/地址

TEL. 2805 0638

Shop 4008, Podium Level 4, IFC Mall,
8 Finance Street, Central
中環金融街8號
國際金融中心商場4樓4008號舖
www.h-one.com.hk

■ ANNUAL AND WEEKLY CLOSING
　休息日期
Closed Lunar New Year
年初一休息

■ OPENING HOURS, LAST ORDER
　營業時間，最後點菜時間
Lunch/午膳　12:00-14:30 (L.O.)
Dinner/晚膳　18:30-22:30 (L.O.)

■ PRICE/價錢
Lunch/午膳　set/套餐　　　　$278-298
　　　　　　à la carte/點菜　$450-850
Dinner/晚膳　à la carte/點菜　$450-850

Hong Zhou
杭州酒家

The owner-chef has his fresh ingredients delivered directly from Hong Zhou every afternoon and you can certainly tell when you bite into those delicious fried river prawns with Longjing tea leaves; the braised pork belly is also worth trying. The chef inherited his obvious passion for food and the delicate cuisine of Hong Zhou from his father (who is also a famous chef in town) and strives to keep his cooking authentic.

餐廳主廚兼老闆堅持每天下午由杭州運來新鮮食材。你不難察覺這點：嚐嚐鮮美的龍井河蝦仁吧，東坡肉同樣值得一試。廚師從其父親身上遺傳了對飲食及杭州美食的熱愛（其父同為城中名廚），並努力維持正宗煮法。

■ ADDRESS/地址

TEL. 2591 1898

1F, Chinachem Johnston Plaza, 178-186 Johnston Road, Wan Chai
灣仔莊士敦道178-186號
華懋莊士敦廣場1樓

■ ANNUAL AND WEEKLY CLOSING
休息日期
Closed 2 days Lunar New Year
農曆新年休息2天

■ OPENING HOURS, LAST ORDER
營業時間，最後點菜時間
Lunch/午膳 11:30-14:30 L.O. 14:15
Dinner/晚膳 17:30-22:30 L.O. 22:15

■ PRICE/價錢
Lunch/午膳 à la carte/點菜 $120-200
Dinner/晚膳 à la carte/點菜 $200-1,800

Ho To Tai   NEW
好到底

Divided into two cosy and simple dining areas, with the first floor being the more animated of the two and from where diners can see through into the equally small kitchen. This noodle shop is still run by the family who opened it back in 1949; they also have their own noodle factory a few blocks away. The most popular dishes are the wonton noodles, dried prawn noodles and dumplings stuffed with fish skin.

店內分為兩個簡單而舒適的用餐區。兩層當中，以一樓較為熱鬧，食客可看見小小的廚房裡員工忙碌的情形。這家麵店自1949年開業以來一直由同一家族經營，他們更在附近自設製麵工場。最受歡迎的菜式有雲吞麵、蝦子撈麵與特製水餃。

■ ADDRESS/地址
TEL. 2476 2495
67 Fau Tsoi Street, Yuen Long,
New Territories
新界元朗阜財街67號

■ ANNUAL AND WEEKLY CLOSING
　休息日期
Closed 10 days Lunar New Year
農曆新年休息10天

■ OPENING HOURS, LAST ORDER
　營業時間，最後點菜時間
08:00-20:00 (L.O.)

■ PRICE/價錢
à la carte/點菜　　　　$ 16-35

Hugo's NEW
希戈

The original Hugo's was founded back in 1969 but this new version remains true to its origins by offering the charms of a bygone age. That means there's everything from suits of armour to silver Christofle trolleys being wheeled around the room. The chef and his team prepares traditional European style cuisine with pronounced French influences. Expect the likes of escargots, lobster bisque, steak au poivre and soufflés.

希戈本店創立於1969年，新店延續其懷舊感覺，忠於原店的氣氛。這意味著店裡的一切——全套的銀鎧甲、Christofle品牌的頭盤餐車，全都原汁原味重現眼前。主廚與他的團隊為客人準備有明顯法國特色的傳統歐洲菜。你可在這裡找到法國焗田螺、龍蝦湯、法式黑胡椒牛柳扑與梳乎厘一類的菜式。

■ ADDRESS/地址

TEL. 2311 1234

4F, Hyatt Regency Tsim Sha Tsui,
18 Hanoi Road, Tsim Sha Tsui, Kowloon
九龍尖沙咀河內道18號
凱悅酒店·尖沙咀4樓
www.hongkong.tsimshatsui.hyatt.com

■ ANNUAL AND WEEKLY CLOSING
　　休息日期
Closed lunch Saturday and Sunday
週六、日午膳休息

OPENING HOURS, LAST ORDER
　　營業時間，最後點菜時間
Lunch/午膳 12:00-14:30 (L.O.)
Dinner/晚膳 18:30-22:30 (L.O.)

■ PRICE/價錢

Lunch/午膳	set/套餐	$275-375
	à la carte/點菜	$580-1,050
Dinner/晚膳	set/套餐	$828-888
	à la carte/點菜	$580-1,050

Hunan Garden (Causeway Bay)
洞庭樓（銅鑼灣）

♿ ⛄16 ☎️🍽

As you walk in on the 13th floor, you will be welcomed by courteous staff near a channel of running water complete with live fish. This leads into a spacious contemporary room with bright chandeliers and painted wood panels on the walls. The Hunan-style cooking uses well-sourced, fresh local ingredients. Specialities include sautéed prawns with fermented beans and chilli and fish fillets with fried minced bean.

甫踏進十三樓，你就會看見水流源源不絕的活魚水槽。繼續往前走，便進入了寬敞時尚的進餐區。璀璨的吊燈點綴加上牆身的漆木板，交織成獨特的風格。粵菜選料皆採用本地新鮮食材，午飯時段設有一系列的點心，供購物及商務客人選擇。特別推薦有四季豆豉香辣蝦及豆酥魚。

■ ADDRESS/地址

TEL. 2506 9288
Shop 1302, 13F, Food Forum,
Times Square,1 Matheson Street,
Causeway Bay
銅鑼灣勿地臣街1號時代廣場
食通天13樓1302號舖
www.maxims.com.hk

■ OPENING HOURS, LAST ORDER
　營業時間，最後點菜時間
Lunch/午膳 11:30-14:30 (L.O.)
Dinner/晚膳 18:00-23:00 (L.O.)

■ PRICE/價錢
à la carte/點菜　　　　$ 300-850

Hunan Garden (Central)
洞庭樓 (中環)

🍴16

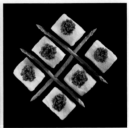

If you think the main room is big, then look to your right and you'll see even more space, and it's all decorated in vivid tones of pink and green. Despite the size, the service is attentive and well organised, with staff more than happy to make suggestions. The menu covers a number of regions but the highlights are the Hunanese specialities. Look out for fillet of fish with minced yellow bean or sautéed diced chicken with peanut and chilli.

如果你覺得主餐廳很大，看看你的右手面吧——你會發現更大空間，全都以鮮豔粉紅和翠綠色彩裝飾。雖然餐廳佔地廣闊，但服務卻依然細心，而且非常有系統，服務員亦非常樂意提供建議。餐廳提供數個不同菜系的菜式，但主要以湖南菜為主。洞庭豆酥鮮魚、京城宮爆雞丁值得一試。

■ ADDRESS/地址
TEL. 2868 2880
3F, The Forum, Exchange Square, Central
中環交易廣場富臨閣3樓
www.maxims.com.hk

■ OPENING HOURS, LAST ORDER
營業時間，最後點菜時間
Lunch/午膳 11:30-14:45 (L.O.)
Dinner/晚膳 17:30-23:00 (L.O.)

■ PRICE/價錢
set/套餐　　　　　　　$ 488
à la carte/點菜　　　$ 210-540

Hung's Delicacies
阿鴻小吃

The news of Mr Lai's success has spread far and wide so now there's always a queue of people outside either wanting a table or ordering a take-away from his charming wife. In fact so many people are keen to come, he's taken on more chefs to cope and the menu is now also in English! The quality of the Cantonese and Chiu Chow dishes remains high, whether that's the marinated pork belly or the braised assorted vegetables in red tofu sauce.

黎先生的成功廣為人知,現在慕名而來的人客往往要大排長龍——不論是堂食,還是向魅力十足的黎太太購買外賣。為了應付眾多人客,黎先生雇用了更多廚師,菜單更設有英文版!這裡的粵菜與潮州菜仍然保持高水準,鹵水豬腩肉、南乳粗齋都十分出色。

■ ADDRESS/地址
TEL. 2570 1108
Shop 4, GF, Ngan Fai Building,
84-94 Wharf Road, North Point
北角和富道84-94號銀輝大廈地下4號舖

■ ANNUAL AND WEEKLY CLOSING
　休息日期
Closed 1 week Lunar New Year,
Monday and Tuesday
農曆新年7天, 週一及週二休息

■ OPENING HOURS, LAST ORDER
　營業時間,最後點菜時間
14:00-22:00 (L.O.)

■ PRICE/價錢
à la carte/點菜　　　　　　$ 100-150

Hutong
胡同

♿   ≼   40   ☎🍴

Come here for dinner to really experience one of Kowloon's hippest establishments. The subtle lighting, the huge array of bird cages and the beautiful carved wood panels make it all so atmospheric that one almost forgets the stunning harbour views. The cuisine is also a little different: it puts a modern twist on Cantonese classics and presents them in a stylish way – try the Hutong signature dishes to see it at its best.

來到胡同享受晚餐，你可置身九龍區的時尚尖端。柔和燈光、一列列的鳥籠和精雕細琢的木層板，營造強烈的氣氛，幾乎令人忘卻醉人海港景緻。菜色方面也極具驚喜：為傳統廣東菜進行現代大變身，以時尚風格呈現——嚐嚐胡同盡心設計的出色招牌菜吧。

■ ADDRESS/地址

TEL. 3428 8342

28F, One Peking Road, Tsim Sha Tsui, Kowloon

九龍尖沙咀北京道1號28樓

www.aqua.com.hk

■ OPENING HOURS, LAST ORDER

營業時間，最後點菜時間

Lunch/午膳 12:00-15:00 L.O. 14:30

Dinner/晚膳 18:00-24:00 L.O. 23:00

■ PRICE/價錢

à la carte/點菜 $ 350-800

Inagiku (IFC)
稻菊（國際金融中心）

Adjacent to the Four Seasons Hotel in the IFC Mall, this is a delightfully uncluttered contemporary installation with illuminated flooring and large plate glass windows affording fine views. There are separate sushi, teppanyaki and tempura counters and a whole series of special set menus. This is traditional Japanese cooking, successfully adapted to suit the local market.

鄰靠中環國際金融中心商場四季酒店，餐廳設計極具時尚風格。射燈地板配上大型落地玻璃，怡人景觀盡收眼底。餐廳設有壽司、鐵板燒及天婦羅吧，更提供一系列的特選套餐。這可算是傳統日式料理進軍本地市場的成功例子。

■ ADDRESS/地址
TEL. 2805 0600
4F, Four Seasons Hotel,
8 Finance Street, Central
中環金融街8號四季酒店4樓
www.fourseasons.com/hongkong

■ OPENING HOURS, LAST ORDER
營業時間，最後點菜時間
Lunch/午膳 11:30-14:30 (L.O.)
Dinner/晚膳 18:00-22:30 (L.O.)

■ PRICE/價錢
Lunch/午膳   set/套餐 $280-680
           à la carte/點菜 $350-1,200
Dinner/晚膳   set/套餐 $580-1,680
           à la carte/點菜 $350-1,200

Inagiku (Tsim Sha Tsui)
稻菊 (尖沙咀)

Inagiku has a strong pedigree: the first was established over a century ago in Japan. Décor is elegant, the Japanese influences a visual pleasure. There are several dining areas: a sushi bar with a fish tank, a tempura counter, a teppanyaki area and a few tables in the centre of the room; there are five separate private rooms, too. The restaurant is renowned for its tempura and teppanyaki. An attractive list of sake is also available.

稻菊來頭殊不簡單，早在百多年前已於日本開業。這裡的裝潢設計典雅高尚，源自日本人對美學的要求，為食客帶來視覺上的享受。餐廳共有幾個用餐區，包括設有魚缸的壽司吧、天婦羅檯、鐵板燒區，以及餐廳中心的幾張餐桌。此外，稻菊還設有五間私人餐室。這裡的天婦羅及鐵板燒享負盛名，而員工亦可為你推介更多菜式。提供一系列清酒名單任君選擇，相當吸引。

■ ADDRESS/地址

TEL. 2733 2933

1F, The Royal Garden Hotel,
69 Mody Road, East Tsim Sha Tsui,
Kowloon
九龍尖東麼地道69號帝苑酒店1樓
www.rghk.com.hk

■ OPENING HOURS, LAST ORDER
營業時間，最後點菜時間
Lunch/午膳 12:00-14:30 (L.O.)
Dinner/晚膳 18:00-22:30 (L.O.)

■ PRICE/價錢

Lunch/午膳	set/套餐	$160-480
	à la carte/點菜	$350-1,100
Dinner/晚膳	set/套餐	$270-1,200
	à la carte/點菜	$350-1,100

IR 1968 (Causeway Bay)   NEW
印尼餐廳1968 (銅鑼灣)

One of Hong Kong's longest standing and best known Indonesian restaurants is now being run by the sons of the couple who opened it back in 1968. The head chef has also been working here for 25 years so continuity is assured. Satay is cooked over charcoal and Nasi Goreng, beef rendang and sweet Semur sauce ox tongue are among the highlights. The dim lighting, antique wood carvings and rattan chairs create an intimate, relaxed atmosphere.

餐廳在1968年開業，是香港其中一家歷史最悠久而最著名的印尼餐廳，現正由創辦人夫婦的兒子經營。主廚已經在這裡工作25年，食物質素絕對有保證。著名菜式包括以炭火燒烤的沙爹串、印尼炒飯、巴東牛肉和炆牛舌。昏暗的燈光、古董木雕與藤椅，營造親切、輕鬆的氣氛。

■ ADDRESS/地址

TEL. 2577 9981
28 Leighton Road, Causeway Bay
銅鑼灣禮頓道28號
www.ir1968.com

■ OPENING HOURS, LAST ORDER
營業時間，最後點菜時間
12:00-23:00 (L.O.)

■ PRICE/價錢
à la carte/點菜 $ 150-300

Island Tang
港島廳

✿

🍴🍴🍴

🚪40 ☎🍴

This elegant art deco inspired room, with its chandeliers, rich wood panelling and mirrors, is reminiscent of forties Hong Kong; and it should come as no surprise to learn that Sir David Tang is behind it. The menu offers a range of sophisticated and delicious Cantonese dishes, from king prawns with lobster sauce and baked crab meat to terrific Peking duck and many other classics. As befits the surroundings, service is slick and professional.

靈感來自裝飾藝術的高雅房間配有吊燈、厚木鑲板及鏡子，重現四十年代香港的光景；此情此景，發現幕後主腦原是鄧永鏘爵士，面對如斯景致，你應毫不意外毫不意外。菜單上提供一系列獨特美味的廣東菜，從龍蝦醬皇帝蝦、焗蟹肉到出色的北京填鴨及其他不同經典菜色。悉心專業的服務與出色的環境相得益彰。

■ ADDRESS/地址
TEL. 2526 8798
Shop 222, The Galleria,
9 Queen's Road, Central
中環皇后大道中9號嘉軒廣場222號舖
www.islandtang.com

■ OPENING HOURS, LAST ORDER
營業時間，最後點菜時間
Lunch/午膳 12:00-14:30 (L.O.)
Dinner/晚膳 18:00-22:30 (L.O.)

■ PRICE/價錢
Lunch/午膳　set/套餐　　$298-398
　　　　　à la carte/點菜 $300-1,200
Dinner/晚膳　à la carte/點菜 $300-1,200

Jade Garden (Lockhart Road)
翠園 (駱克道)

🛆12 ☎🍽

Jade Garden is located in a very busy street, and the restaurant is just as lively. It reopened in May 2010 following an extensive refurbishment and is now more contemporary in style and rather elegant. The dim sum trolleys at lunch still draw the crowds. In the evening, take your time to enjoy some of the chef's specials from the keenly priced Cantonese menu. Service is very attentive and friendly.

翠園位處繁忙街道上，與餐廳同樣充滿生氣。經過大規模裝修後，餐廳於2010年5月重新開張，變得更富時代感，也不失優雅。午市的點心車一如既往吸引著無數顧客。傍晚時分，你可把握時間品嚐廚師精選。服務殷勤貼心。

■ ADDRESS/地址

TEL. 2573 9339

3F, Causeway Bay Plaza II,
463-483 Lockhart Road, Causeway Bay
銅鑼灣駱克道463-483號
銅鑼灣廣場第2期3樓
www.maxims.com.hk

■ OPENING HOURS, LAST ORDER
營業時間，最後點菜時間
07:00-23:00 (L.O.)

■ PRICE/價錢

Lunch/午膳	set/套餐	$ 120-490
	à la carte/點菜	$ 110-420
Dinner/晚膳	set/套餐	$ 220-490
	à la carte/點菜	$ 230-420

Joi Hing　NEW
再興

The Chow family have had many barbecue shops but this one has been a feature here in Stewart Road since 1975 and is run very capably by the affable Mrs Chow. Her special recipe for the marinade is an integral part of the appeal. Pork, duck and goose are the primary meats, with pork being highly recommended. There's no menu – just cards stuck on the walls. If barbecue is not your thing then their curry sauce is pretty legendary too.

周氏家族曾擁有多間燒臘店，這家自1975年於史劍域道開業，由和藹可親的周太太主理的燒臘店一直是備受矚目。她的秘製滷汁是此店吸引人的主因。這裡主要供應豬、鴨、鵝，尤以豬肉為佳。這裡沒有菜單——只有貼在牆上的牌。如果燒臘非你所好，這裡的咖哩也相當值得嘗試。

■ ADDRESS/地址
TEL. 2519 6639
1C Stewart Road, Wan Chai
灣仔史劍域道1號C

■ ANNUAL AND WEEKLY CLOSING
　　休息日期
Closed 2 weeks Lunar New Year,
Sunday and Public Holidays
農曆新年兩星期、週日及公眾假期休息

■ OPENING HOURS, LAST ORDER
　　營業時間，最後點菜時間
09:30-22:30

■ PRICE/價錢
à la carte/點菜　　　　　$ 25-45

Kau Kee
九記

You'll probably have to line up in the street first to eat here: Kau Kee has been trading since the 1930s and has consequently built up a huge following which includes some well known faces from show business and politics. It's all very basic and you'll have to share your table but the food is delicious. Beef noodles are the speciality; different cuts of meat with a variety of noodles in a tasty broth or spicy sauce. Try the iced milk tea too.

要在九記用膳，你可能要在街上排隊等候：九記自一九三零年代起開始經營，聚集了大量支持者，包括部分政商名人。九記陳設回歸基本，進餐時要和其他人士共用餐桌，但食物極具水準。九記的特色在於其牛肉麵；不同部位的肉塊與美味清湯或辣醬麵的搭配。奶茶亦值得一試。

■ ADDRESS/地址
TEL. N/A
21 Gough Street, Central
中環歌賦街21號

■ ANNUAL AND WEEKLY CLOSING
　休息日期
Closed 10 days Lunar New Year, Sunday and Public Holidays
農曆新年10天、週日及公眾假期休息

■ OPENING HOURS, LAST ORDER
　營業時間，最後點菜時間
12:30-22:30

■ PRICE/價錢
à la carte/點菜　　　$ 27-68

Kimberley Chinese Restaurant NEW
君怡閣

⌷ 200

Its sober atmosphere and traditional looks may be in sharp contrast to more contemporary establishments nearby, but there is no doubting the quality of the cooking here at the Kimberley hotel's Chinese restaurant, which opened over twenty years ago. Cantonese and Mandarin traditions dominate but consider pre-ordering the roast suckling pig stuffed with rice. Other specialities include braised ribs of beef with lemongrass gravy and sea prawns with white pepper.

這裡沈實的氣氛和傳統的外觀可能與附近較時尚的環境形成鮮明對比，但作為已經營20多年的君怡酒店中餐廳，這裡的食物質素絕對無可置疑。君怡閣以粵菜和京菜為主，招牌菜金陵全豬烤香苗必須預訂。其他精選菜式包括香茅汁扣牛脇骨煲與白胡椒乾焗海中蝦。

■ ADDRESS/地址

TEL. 2723 3888

MF, Kimberley Hotel, 28 Kimberley Road, Tsim Sha Tsui, Kowloon
九龍尖沙咀金巴利道28號君怡酒店閣樓
www.kimberleyhotel.com.hk

■ OPENING HOURS, LAST ORDER
營業時間，最後點菜時間
Lunch/午膳 11:00-15:00 (L.O.)
Dinner/晚膳 18:00-23:00 (L.O.)

■ PRICE/價錢
à la carte/點菜 $ 180-900

Kin's Kitchen
留家廚房

❀ ✗

📞🍴

A vivacious atmosphere and enthusiastic service greet you here at this single room restaurant. However, the focus of the operation is firmly on the cooking. The kitchen successfully blends traditional dishes, such as braised pork ribs in a curry sauce, with more innovative ones like stewed fish lips in a duck sauce. The good value menu also offers a selection of Pearl River Delta specialities; for example, braised goose feet with pomelo skin.

這家餐廳只有一個廳房，誠意待你光臨的是充滿活力的氣氛和熱心的服務。然則，最大的賣點還是在於其美食。留家廚房成功將傳統菜式，如留家五味骨與較有創意的菜式，如鴨汁魚唇融合為一。價錢相宜的餐單提供一系列珠江三角洲美食，如古法柚皮鵝掌。

■ ADDRESS/地址
TEL. 2571 0913
9 Tsing Fung Street, Tin Hau
天后清風街9號
www.yellowdoorkitchen.com.hk

■ ANNUAL AND WEEKLY CLOSING
　休息日期
Closed 3 days Lunar New Year
農曆新年休息3天

■ OPENING HOURS, LAST ORDER
　營業時間，最後點菜時間
Lunch/午膳 11:00-15:00 L.O. 14:30
Dinner/晚膳 18:00-23:00 L.O. 22:30

■ PRICE/價錢
Lunch/午膳　à la carte/點菜 $ 150-360
Dinner/晚膳　set/套餐　　 $ 348-580
　　　　　　à la carte/點菜 $ 150-360

Kwan Cheuk Heen NEW
君綽軒

Dark wood panelling, smart table settings and a welcoming atmosphere give this restaurant on the fifth floor of the Harbour Grand hotel a feeling of permanence and professionalism. A number of set menus with marked differences in price are available. Along with a comprehensive list of teas, the à la carte menu features specialities such as deep-fried pork ribs in hawthorn sauce and pan-fried crab claw coated with shrimp paste.

深色木質鑲板、精心設計的餐桌擺設和令人賓至如歸的氣氛，令這家位於港島海逸君綽酒店五樓的中菜廳予人專業和恆久的感覺。這裏提供多款不同價錢的套餐，更搜羅了一系列的中國茶供客人選擇。散餐牌的菜式亦具特色，如山楂脆香骨及百花炸釀蟹鉗。

■ ADDRESS/地址
TEL. 2121 2688
5F, Harbour Grand North Point Hotel,
23 Oil Street, North Point
北角油街23號港島海逸君綽酒店5樓
www.harbourgrand.com/hongkong

■ OPENING HOURS, LAST ORDER
營業時間，最後點菜時間
Lunch/午膳 12:00-14:30
Dinner/晚膳 18:00-24:00

■ PRICE/價錢
set/套餐　　　　　$550-1,388
à la carte/點菜　　$220-1,050

L'Atelier de Joël Robuchon

The counter is the place to sit, as you're at the centre of the operation, but if perching on a high chair is not for you, or you require a little more formality, then the more discreet Le Jardin would be a better choice. The red and black colours marry perfectly and the contemporary French cuisine, which uses prime, seasonal ingredients, produces dishes of exquisite depth, balance and flavour. The superb wine list offers an impressive range.

建議坐在吧檯旁邊,以便觀賞開放式廚房的運作,但若高腳椅並非你的選擇,或者希望能更正式一點,那麼Le Jardin也許更佳。紅色與黑色的配搭與這裡的新派法國菜配合得天衣無縫－－選用上等時令食材,烹調出即有深度又恰當的各種美味的佳餚。出色的酒牌選擇繁多,令人目不暇給。

■ ADDRESS/地址

TEL. 2166 9000
Shop 401, 4F, The Landmark,
15 Queen's Road, Central
中環皇后大道中15號
置地廣場4樓401號舖
www.robuchon.hk

■ OPENING HOURS, LAST ORDER
　營業時間,最後點菜時間
Lunch/午膳 12:00-14:30 (L.O.)
Dinner/晚膳 18:30-22:30 (L.O.)

■ PRICE/價錢

Lunch/午膳	set/套餐	$390-1,850
	à la carte/點菜	$500-1,500
Dinner/晚膳	set/套餐	$560-1,850
	à la carte/點菜	$500-1,500

Lau Sum Kee (Fuk Wing Street)
劉森記麵家 (福榮街)

This is one noodle shop that is not afraid of the competition. In a street overflowing with noodle shops, Lau Sum Kee (and its sister shop around the corner) are packed with customers buzzing in and out. It is run by the third generation of the family, the noodles are pressed by bamboo and the wontons are freshly made at the shop. Recommendations include wonton noodles, dry prawn roe mix with noodles and pork knuckles mixed with noodles.

這家麵店可謂經得起競爭。在滿佈各家麵店的街上，劉森記麵家（及其轉角位的姐妹店）擠滿來往的食客。此麵店由家族第三代經營，在店內新鮮製造竹昇麵及雲吞。推薦菜式包括雲吞麵、蝦子麵及豬手麵。

■ ADDRESS/地址

TEL. 2386 3583
82 Fuk Wing Street, Sham Shui Po, Kowloon
九龍深水埗福榮街82號

■ ANNUAL AND WEEKLY CLOSING
　休息日期
Closed 3 days Lunar New Year
農曆新年休息3天

■ OPENING HOURS, LAST ORDER
　營業時間，最後點菜時間
12:30-23:30 (L.O.)

■ PRICE/價錢
à la carte/點菜　　　　$ 24-50

Lei Bistro NEW
利小館

Providing healthy, good value cooking for everyone is the aim of this new restaurant concept from the Lei Garden group. Influences are Northern and Southern Chinese but there are also Cantonese dishes along with some new creations. Specialities include steamed pork dumpling in Shanghai style; double-boiled Chinese Francolin in smoked coconut, and chilled mango with grapefruit and sago. Despite a capacity of 150, it is still advisable to book.

為所有客人提供健康，物有所值的小菜，正是利苑集團開設這間新餐廳的概念。菜式來自大江南北，亦有提供新派廣東菜。特式菜包括上海小籠包、椰皇燉鷓鴣和始創楊枝金露。雖然餐廳可容納150名客人，但亦建議預先訂座。

■ ADDRESS/地址
TEL. 2602 8283
Shop B217-218, Basement 2,
Times Square, 1 Matheson Street,
Causeway Bay
銅鑼灣勿地臣街1號
時代廣場地庫2樓B217-B218號舖
www.leibistro.com

■ OPENING HOURS, LAST ORDER
　營業時間，最後點菜時間
11:00-23:00 L.O.22:30

■ PRICE/價錢
à la carte/點菜 $ 80-400

Lei Garden (Elements)
利苑酒家 (圓方)

✕✕

♿ ⟨□⟩40

The restaurant is located in the blue-tinted 'water' area of this large shopping mall and its décor is more contemporary than some of the other Lei Garden branches. It is composed of a huge dining room, which can be a little noisy when full, and other more intimate rooms. The cooking throughout is reliable Cantonese, with a broad range of interesting seafood preparations as well as some highly unusual double-boiled tonic soups.

這家裝潢華麗優雅的餐館位於巨大的購物商場中的藍色「水」區，比其他利苑分店更有時代感。這裡設有一個巨形的主廳，滿席的時候可能有點吵鬧，亦可選擇其他更能提供私人空間的飯廳。菜色是清一色的廣東菜，但以各種方法烹調的海鮮和與別不同的燉湯，都令這裡顯得分外出色。

■ ADDRESS/地址

TEL. 2196 8133

Shop 2068-70, 2F, Elements,
1 Austin Road West, Kowloon

九龍柯士甸道西1號圓方2樓2068-70號鋪

www.leigarden.com.hk

■ OPENING HOURS, LAST ORDER

營業時間，最後點菜時間

Lunch/午膳 11:30-14:45 (L.O.)
Dinner/晚膳 18:00-22:45 (L.O.)

■ PRICE/價錢

à la carte/點菜 　　　$ 180-1,000

Lei Garden (IFC)
利苑酒家 (國際金融中心)

✿ 　　　　　　　　　　　　　　　　　　　　　✗✗✗

　　　　　　　　　　　　　　　　　　　　♿ 💺14 ☎️🍴

Forward planning is advisable here – not only when booking but also when selecting certain roast meat dishes which require advance notice. The extensive menu features specialist seafood dishes and the lunchtime favourites include shrimp and flaky pastries filled with shredded turnip. All this is served up by good-natured staff in clean, contemporary surroundings.

到利苑用餐，無論是預訂座位，還是食燒臘，提早預約都十分重要。這裡菜式繁多，其中以海鮮炮製的佳餚最具特色，而午市時段的美食首推的銀蘿千層酥。格局設計富時代感，潔淨雅致，服務令人賓至如歸。

■ ADDRESS/地址
TEL. 2295 0238
Shop 3008-3011, Podium Level 3,
IFC Mall, 1 Harbour View Street, Central
中環港景街1號國際金融中心商場
第2期3樓3008-3011號舖
www.leigarden.com.hk

■ ANNUAL AND WEEKLY CLOSING
　休息日期
Closed 3 days Lunar New Year
農曆新年休息3天

■ OPENING HOURS, LAST ORDER
　營業時間，最後點菜時間
Lunch/午膳 11:30-14:30 (L.O.)
Dinner/晚膳 18:00-22:30 (L.O.)

■ PRICE/價錢
set/套餐　　　　　　$ 150-300
à la carte/點菜　　　$ 150-450

Lei Garden (Kowloon Bay)
利苑酒家 (九龍灣)

🛋 40   📞🍴

Service is one of the strengths of this Lei Garden, located in a shopping mall near the MTR station. Signature dishes include the 10 different varieties of double-boiled tonic soups (to be ordered in advance), sautéed scallops with macadamia nuts and yellow fungus, and braised boneless spare-ribs with sweet and sour sauce. Those who like to eat lunch early or at pace are rewarded with a discount if they vacate their tables before 12.45pm.

這家利苑分店位於地鐵站附近的商場內，服務周到是她的的強項。招牌菜包括10種不同的燉湯（須提前預訂）、米網黃耳夏果炒帶子、宮庭醬烤骨。對於喜歡提早吃午飯或者時間不太足夠可因其下午12:45前離席而獲得折扣優惠。

■ ADDRESS/地址
TEL. 2331 3306
Shop Unit F2, Telford Plaza 1,
33 Wai Yip Street, Kowloon Bay, Kowloon
九龍灣偉業街33號德福廣場F2號鋪
www.leigarden.com.hk

■ ANNUAL AND WEEKLY CLOSING
   休息日期
Closed 3 days Lunar New Year
農曆新年休息3天

■ OPENING HOURS, LAST ORDER
   營業時間，最後點菜時間
Lunch/午膳 11:30-15:00 (L.O.)
Dinner/晚膳 18:00-23:00 (L.O.)

■ PRICE/價錢
à la carte/點菜 $ 160-850

Lei Garden (Kwun Tong)
利苑酒家 (觀塘)

✗✗

&♿; ⌨20

Avoid the escalators and use the shuttle lift to get to the fifth floor in this confusingly arranged shopping mall. Once there, the set up will seem familiar if you've experienced other Lei Garden branches: dishes are standard Cantonese but are reliably cooked using fresh ingredients. The place is as frantic as the others but has been partitioned into different seating areas by smart trellises. Try not to sit near the entrance as it's noisy.

由於這新建商場的設計混亂且複雜，最好不要使用扶手電梯；升降機可直達5樓。假如你曾光顧利苑的其他分店，你絕不會感到陌生：依然是清一色的廣東菜與可靠的美食及新鮮的材料。當然，這裡同樣擠滿了利苑的忠實擁躉，店內設計簡潔的屏風巧妙地將餐廳分隔成不同的用餐區。入口附近太嘈吵，最好不要選擇那裡的座位。

■ ADDRESS/地址

TEL. 2365 3238
Shop L5-8, Level 5, apm, Millennium City 5, 418 Kwun Tong Road, Kwun Tong
觀塘觀塘道418號創紀之城第5期apm5樓L5-8號舖
www.leigarden.com.hk

■ OPENING HOURS, LAST ORDER
營業時間，最後點菜時間
Lunch/午膳 11:30-15:00 (L.O.)
Dinner/晚膳 18:00-23:30 L.O. 23:00

■ PRICE/價錢
à la carte/點菜　　　$ 160-900

Lei Garden (Mong Kok)
利苑酒家 (旺角)

Many flock to this perennially popular restaurant so it's essential to book. This was the original Lei Garden and opened in the 1970s. The contemporary décor is spread over two floors and the upper space has views out onto the busy street. The long and varied Cantonese menu certainly represents good value and includes such excellent seafood recommendations as giant sea whelk and mantis shrimp sautéed with salt, pepper and garlic.

由於這家長青的餐廳實在太受歡迎，要光顧者必須提前訂座。這家利苑總店開業於1970年代。富時代感的餐廳共分為兩層，樓上可看到旺角繁華的街景。以廣東菜為主的菜單花樣多變令人目不暇給，菜色物有所值，特別推薦薄殼大響螺及椒鹽富貴蝦。

■ ADDRESS/地址
TEL.2392 5184
121 Sai Yee Street, Mong Kok, Kowloon
九龍旺角洗衣街121
www.leigarden.com.hk

■ OPENING HOURS, LAST ORDER
營業時間，最後點菜時間
Lunch/午膳 11:30-15:00 (L.O.)
Dinner/晚膳 18:00-23:30 (L.O.)

■ PRICE/價錢
à la carte/點菜 $ 220-1,700

Lei Garden (North Point)
利苑酒家 (北角)

🛏20 📞🍴

Discreetly tucked away on the first floor of an office block but overlooking a pleasant courtyard garden, this branch of the popular chain can get frenetic: the place accommodates up to 300 people. The lengthy Cantonese menu mirrors what's available at other branches, but particular dishes worth noting here are braised prawn with chilli sauce casserole, crispy roasted pork and braised wagyu beef tongue with red wine.

隱藏在商業大廈的一樓，從餐廳望出去可看到一個美麗的後花園—這家受歡迎的連鎖餐廳分店絕對可以滿足瘋狂的食客：寬敞的餐廳足可容納三百人！這裡的菜單與其他利苑分店相差無幾，特別推薦生中蝦煲，冰燒三層肉和紅酒燜和牛脷。

■ ADDRESS/地址
TEL. 2806 0008
1F, Block 9-10, City Garden, North Point
北角城市花園9-10座1樓
www.leigarden.com.hk

■ OPENING HOURS, LAST ORDER
營業時間，最後點菜時間
Lunch/午膳 11:30-14:30 (L.O.)
Dinner/晚膳 18:00-22:30 (L.O.)

■ PRICE/價錢
à la carte/點菜 $ 195-1,050

Lei Garden (Sha Tin)
利苑酒家 (沙田)

This Lei Garden may have been an old name around town for 20 years but refurbishment has kept it feeling fresh. It is located in New Town Plaza Sha Tin, which means that it can get especially busy at weekends when everyone needs refuelling after a day spent shopping. The menu largely follows the theme of others in the group; always ask for the daily special. Pre-ordering the soup and barbecued pork is particularly recommended.

這家利苑酒家已是二十年的老字號，但經過重新裝潢後，一點也不顯老舊。酒家位於沙田新城市廣場，因此週末購物一整天過後前來小歇一番的茶客更是絡繹不絕。菜單與集團的其他餐廳主題相若；謹記留意是日精選。建議預訂老火湯及叉燒。

■ ADDRESS/地址

TEL. 2698 9111

6F, Phase I New Town Plaza,
Sha Tin, Kowloon

九龍沙田新城市廣場第1期6樓

www.leigarden.com.hk

■ OPENING HOURS, LAST ORDER
營業時間，最後點菜時間
Lunch/午膳 11:30-15:00 L.O. 14:45
Dinner/晚膳 18:00-23:30 L.O. 23:00

■ PRICE/價錢
à la carte/點菜 $ 120-420

Lei Garden (Tsim Sha Tsui)
利苑酒家 (尖沙咀)

The entrance takes you past an intricately carved wooden wall and a series of large fish tanks into a big, bustling, traditional dining room that's brightly lit and comfortable. There's pagoda detailing on the ceiling, bare red-brick walls and an army of staff in attendance. The varied Cantonese menu reiterates what's on offer at the other Lei Gardens using fine quality ingredients and cooking them respectfully.

要進入這家餐廳，你要先經過雕刻精緻的木質牆壁和一列大魚缸，最後來到寬敞熱鬧的傳統客廳。餐廳燈光明亮，座位亦十分舒適；天花上畫有精美寶塔圖案，牆壁上也鋪有紅磚，侍應生就如軍隊一般隨時候命。這裡的廣東菜單與其他利苑分店相若，而同出一轍的就是一級的材料和廚師認真的烹調態度。

■ ADDRESS/地址

TEL. 2722 1636
B2F, Houston Centre, 63 Mody Road, East Tsim Sha Tsui, Kowloon
九龍尖東麼地道63號好時中心地庫2樓
www.leigarden.com.hk

■ OPENING HOURS, LAST ORDER
營業時間，最後點菜時間
Lunch/午膳　11:30-14:45 (L.O.)
Dinner/晚膳　18:00-22:45 (L.O.)

■ PRICE/價錢
Lunch/午膳　à la carte/點菜 $200-1,500
Dinner/晚膳　à la carte/點菜 $250-1,500

Lei Garden (Wan Chai)
利苑酒家 (灣仔)

P　🚗18　☎🍴

An inventory of restaurants in Wan Chai wouldn't be complete without a Lei Garden. This branch may at first appear cavernous but the busy and bustling atmosphere does make it feel more intimate. It follows the tried and tested formula evident in its sister restaurants. The extensive menu offers not just luxury ingredients but also less elaborate and classic Cantonese preparations; specialities include deep-fried rock oyster in port wine.

灣仔的餐廳清單若少了利苑，便不算完整。這家分店驟眼看來有點空洞，但店內忙碌的氣氛增添了不少親切感。這裡的菜單沿用了其他利苑分店多次實驗的成功菜式。包羅萬有的菜單不僅有鮑參翅肚，也有較為簡單的經典粵菜；招牌菜有砵酒焗蠔。

■ ADDRESS/地址

TEL. 2892 0333
1F, CNT Tower, 338 Hennessy Road, Wan Chai
灣仔軒尼詩道338號北海中心1樓
www.leigarden.com.hk

■ ANNUAL AND WEEKLY CLOSING
　休息日期
Closed 3 days Lunar New Year
農曆新年休息3天

■ OPENING HOURS, LAST ORDER
　營業時間，最後點菜時間
Lunch/午膳 11:30-14:45 (L.O.)
Dinner/晚膳 18:00-22:45 (L.O.)

■ PRICE/價錢
à la carte/點菜　　　　$ 160-750

Le 188° NEW

Sitting triumphantly on the top floor of the Harbour Grand hotel, with floor-to-ceiling windows on three sides (hence the name) providing spectacular views, is this intimate, 'fine dining' restaurant. The menu focuses primarily on modern European cuisine and seafood from the oyster counter. Typical dishes could include pan-fried sea bass with artichoke, tomato compote and braised abalone or crispy roast chicken with marjoram and bell pepper.

座落於海逸君綽酒店的頂樓，三邊落地玻璃窗（餐廳因此得名）讓客人飽覽出色景觀，是一家為客人提供優雅舒適進餐環境的高級食府。餐牌以現代歐陸菜和生蠔吧的海鮮為主。特色菜包括香煎鱸魚配亞枝竹、燴番茄茸及鮑魚與烤脆雞配馬祖琳香草及燒圓椒。

■ ADDRESS/地址

TEL. 2121 2688
41F, Harbour Grand North Point Hotel,
23 Oil Street, North Point
北角油街23號港島海逸君綽酒店41樓
www.harbourgrand.com/hongkong

■ OPENING HOURS, LAST ORDER
營業時間，最後點菜時間
Lunch/午膳 12:00-14:30 (L.O.)
Dinner/晚膳 18:00-24:00 (L.O.)

■ PRICE/價錢
set/套餐 $ 488-788
à la carte/點菜 $ 450-830

Lin Heung Kui
蓮香居

 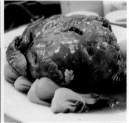

Opened in May 2009, this huge eatery on two floors aims to build on the success of the famous Lin Heung Tea House in Wellington Street. It's modest inside, but hugely popular and the dim sum trolley is a must with customers keen to be the first to choose from its extensive offerings. The main menu offers classic Cantonese dishes with specialities such as Lin Heung special duck house style. The pastry shop below is worth a look on the way out.

佔地甚廣的蓮香居於二零零九年開幕,樓高兩層,秉承威靈頓街蓮香樓的輝煌成績。樸素的內部裝潢擋不住人氣,點心車最讓急不及待從其各式各樣點心中選擇心愛好。菜單上提供傳統廣東菜及特色小菜,如蓮香霸王鴨。離開時路經樓下的中式餅店,亦值得留意。

■ ADDRESS/地址

TEL. 2156 9328
2-3F, 40-50 Des Voeux Road West,
Sheung Wan
上環德輔道西40-50號2-3樓

■ OPENING HOURS, LAST ORDER
營業時間,最後點菜時間
06:00-22:30

■ PRICE/價錢
à la carte/點菜 $ 120-300

Lin Heung Tea House
蓮香樓

A famous name for over 80 years, this restaurant was lightly renovated in 2009. Dim sum is served from 6am to late afternoon, while classic Cantonese dishes are offered at night. Don't underestimate this place: many come early for their dim sum and not only do you need to find a table but the favourites, like steamed egg cake, are gone the second those trolleys roll out. Try a few Lin Heung specials in the evening, like the duck and pork ribs.

八十年來聞名四方的蓮香樓於二零零九年六月稍作裝修。清晨六時至下午供應點心，晚上則供應粵菜。不要低估了這茶樓：很多人清早慕名前來品嘗其點心，你不但要忙著佔桌，更要找尋著名美點，如蒸馬拉糕，點心車甫出現就被掃個片甲不留了。晚上可嚐嚐蓮香精選蓮香霸王鴨及招牌醬燒骨。

■ ADDRESS/地址

TEL. 2544 4556
160-164 Wellington Street, Central
中環威靈頓街160-164號

■ ANNUAL AND WEEKLY CLOSING
　　休息日期
Closed 3 days Lunar New Year
農曆新年休息3天

■ OPENING HOURS, LAST ORDER
　　營業時間，最後點菜時間
06:00-23:00 L.O.22:30

■ PRICE/價錢
à la carte/點菜　　　　　$ 120-300

Liu Yuan Pavilion
留園雅敘

✗✗ ✗✗

🎴16 📞🍽

Thanks to its loyal following, who clearly appreciate the good food and smart appearance, it's advisable to arrive having booked ahead. The light and airy décor is a pleasing environment in which to enjoy some seriously tasty Shanghainese cuisine, especially the dim sum. Perhaps start with some steamed pork dumplings and pan-fried pork buns and try fried green crab with salty eggs from the vast seafood choice.

留園雅敘的一眾忠心擁躉顯然非常欣賞這裡的佳餚與醒目的裝修。建議提早預約。輕巧通爽的裝潢提供舒適環境，可供享受極為出色的上海佳餚，特別是點心。先試試蒸豬肉餃、生煎包，鹹蛋黃炒蟹之外更有一系列海鮮可供選擇。

■ ADDRESS/地址

TEL. 2804 2000
3F, The Broadway, 54-62 Lockhart Road, Wan Chai
灣仔駱克道54-62號博匯大廈3樓

■ OPENING HOURS, LAST ORDER
　營業時間，最後點菜時間
Lunch/午膳 12:00-15:00 L.O.14:30
Dinner/晚膳 18:00-23:00 L.O.22:30

■ PRICE/價錢
Lunch/午膳　à la carte/點菜 $ 200-400
Dinner/晚膳　à la carte/點菜 $ 300-600

Loaf On
六福菜館

36

Hidden one block behind the strip of seafood restaurants in Sai Kung is this neat little restaurant, spread over three floors. Their soup of the day depends on what the owner finds and buys from the local fishermen. You can even bring your own seafood and have staff prepare it for you. Besides seafood, Loaf On also offers simple but flavoursome Cantonese dishes like stir-fry prawns with eggs, Loaf On-style chicken, and salt and pepper calamari.

這家小菜館隱藏在西貢的海鮮餐廳一帶的後街，佔地三層。是日例湯視乎店主當天從當地漁民處買到的新鮮食材。你甚至可自行攜帶海鮮，交由店員烹調。除了海鮮，六福菜館還提供簡單而美味的小菜如滑蛋蝦仁、風沙雞及椒鹽鮮魷。

■ ADDRESS/地址
TEL. 2792 9966
49 See Cheung Street, Sai Kung
西貢市場街49號

■ ANNUAL AND WEEKLY CLOSING
　休息日期
Closed 2 days Lunar New Year
農曆新年休息2天

■ OPENING HOURS, LAST ORDER
　營業時間，最後點菜時間
11:00-23:00 L.O. 22:30

■ PRICE/價錢
Lunch/午膳　à la carte/點菜 $150-500
Dinner/晚膳　à la carte/點菜 $200-500

Lobster Bar and Grill
龍蝦吧

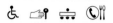

The clubby atmosphere here derives from the colonial style furniture and décor: you can even enjoy an aperitif or single malt whisky in a cosy armchair upholstered in Scottish tartan. Specialities are Maine and Spiny lobsters prepared in a choice of styles, as well as a variety of oysters, fish and meats from the grill. Largely business-orientated at lunchtime but more relaxed, with live music, during the evening.

殖民地傢具和裝潢襯托出夜店般的氣氛：你可以躺在舒適的蘇格蘭格仔扶手椅上享受一杯餐前酒或單一麥芽威士忌。鎮店菜式有各式波士頓（緬因州）龍蝦與刺龍蝦，以及多種經燒烤的蠔、魚及肉。午餐時段較多商務人士，晚上氣氛則較悠閒，有現場樂隊演奏。

■ ADDRESS/地址

TEL. 2820 8560

6F, Island Shangri-La Hotel, Pacific Place, Supreme Court Road, Admiralty

中區法院道太古廣場
港島香格里拉酒店6樓
www.shangri-la.com

■ OPENING HOURS, LAST ORDER
營業時間，最後點菜時間
Lunch/午膳 12:00-14:30 (L.O.)
Dinner/晚膳 18:30-22:30 (L.O.)

■ PRICE/價錢
à la carte/點菜 $ 500-900

Lo Chiu (Jordan)
老趙 (佐敦)

The Chinese owner spent several years in Vietnam before arriving in Hong Kong and opening this Vietnamese restaurant back in 1978. He now has two other shops but this is his flagship. Steamed stuffed rice rolls, noodles in beef soup and cold vermicelli with pork, beef or chicken are some of the highlights, but the hotpot curry is also worth trying. The environment is basic but clean and the staff are helpful.

老闆是曾經在越南住過幾年的華僑，回來香港後，在1978年開始經營這餐廳。他現在已擁有兩家分店，但此店依然是他的旗艦店。越式蒸粉包、牛肉湯河，豬肉、牛肉或雞肉凍檬都是不錯的選擇，椰香咖喱也非常值得嘗試。餐廳只有簡單裝修，但侍應服務周到。

■ ADDRESS/地址

TEL. 2384 2143
25-27 Man Yuen Street, Jordan, Kowloon
九龍佐敦文苑街25-27號

■ ANNUAL AND WEEKLY CLOSING
　休息日期
Closed 4 days Lunar New Year
農曆新年休息4天

■ OPENING HOURS, LAST ORDER
　營業時間，最後點菜時間
12:00-23:00 (L.O.)

■ PRICE/價錢
set/套餐　　　　　　$ 104-116
à la carte/點菜　　　$ 65-110

Lo Chiu (Tsim Sha Tsui)
老趙 (尖沙咀)

The second branch of this Vietnamese group may have opened in 1999 but its vivid orange colours and chandeliers are more evocative of the 1970s. However, what the room may lack in its levels of comfort, it makes up for in its food and sunny service. The large choice includes traditional Vietnamese soup and noodles but it also purports to be the "king prawn specialist"; these can be served simply grilled on charcoal or with tamarind or chilli paste.

這個越南集團的第二分店在1999年開幕，但她鮮豔的橙色和吊燈更較人想起七零年代。雖然，這間餐廳的環境不算非常舒適，但它的食物質素和陽光般溫暖的服務卻令人倍感自在。豐富的選擇包括傳統越南湯河，它也號稱「大頭蝦專門店」，大頭蝦可簡單地碳烤或加上酸子醬或辣椒蓉。

■ ADDRESS/地址

TEL. 2314 7966

10-12 Hillwood Road, Tsim Sha Tsui, Kowloon

九龍尖沙咀山林道10-12號

■ ANNUAL AND WEEKLY CLOSING
　休息日期
Closed 4 days Lunar New Year
農曆新年休息4天

■ OPENING HOURS, LAST ORDER
　營業時間，最後點菜時間
12:00-23:00 L.O. 22:30

■ PRICE/價錢

Lunch/午膳	set/套餐	$48-58
	à la carte/點菜	$80-220
Dinner/晚膳	à la carte/點菜	$80-220

Loong Toh Yuen NEW
隆濤院

🍽️40 📞🍴

Traditional Shanghainese tea houses are the inspiration behind the pleasant decorative style of this Chinese restaurant within Hullett House, a colonial-style building dating from 1881. The menu features Cantonese recipes combined with some Hong Kong classics and even a few contemporary touches. Typical dishes could include deep-fried shrimp rolls, barbecue pork with honey and baked cod with spinach in a walnut sauce.

Hullett House是一棟充滿殖民地風格的建築，歷史可追溯至1881年。而這家位於Hullett House內的中餐館，則從傳統的上海茶館找到美麗裝潢的靈感。餐牌內的廣東佳餚大多揉合了香港的經典和現代色彩。典型菜式包括沙律皮旦蝦筒、蜜汁叉燒與碧湖銀雪。

■ ADDRESS/地址
TEL. 3988 0107
Hullett House, 2A Canton Road,
Tsim Sha Tsui, Kowloon
九龍尖沙咀廣東道2A Hullett House
www.hulletthouse.com

■ OPENING HOURS, LAST ORDER
營業時間，最後點菜時間
Lunch/午膳 11:30-14:30 (L.O.)
Dinner/晚膳 18:00-22:30 (L.O.)
■ PRICE/價錢
Lunch/午膳　set/套餐　　$148
　　　　　à la carte/點菜 $350-820
Dinner/晚膳　set/套餐　$780-1,340
　　　　　à la carte/點菜 $350-820

Luk Yu Tea House
陸羽茶室

🍴

🏮17

Luk Yu Tea House manages the difficult trick of appealing to both local regulars and tourists. Large numbers from both groups come mainly for the traditionally prepared and flavoursome dim sum and the three floors fill up quickly. The animated atmosphere and subtle colonial decoration are appealing but no one really stays too long; the serving team in white jackets have seen it all before and go about their work with alacrity.

陸羽茶室能同時吸引本地常客和外地遊客，可見其過人之處。大量常客和遊客主要是為了以傳統方法製造的美味點心而來，所以佔地三層的茶室經常滿座。生氣盎然的環境和帶點殖民地色彩的裝潢很吸引，但沒有人會長久駐足觀賞——穿著白色外套的侍應們早以見怪不怪，只會敏捷地專注工作。

■ ADDRESS/地址
TEL. 2523 5464
24-26 Stanley Street, Central
中環士丹利街24-26號

■ ANNUAL AND WEEKLY CLOSING
  休息日期
Closed 4 days Lunar New Year
農曆新年休息4天

■ OPENING HOURS, LAST ORDER
  營業時間，最後點菜時間
07:00-22:00 (L.O.)

■ PRICE/價錢
Lunch/午膳   à la carte/點菜 $100-300
Dinner/晚膳   à la carte/點菜 $200-300

Lung King Heen
龍景軒

✿✿✿

🕸 ← ☞ 🅿 ⛶16 ☎🍴 🕸

Translated as 'view of the dragon', it now offers a panorama of Victoria Harbour whilst the interior is smart and uncluttered, with hand-embroidered silk, columns and glass screens. Ingredients here are of the highest quality – particularly the seafood which is impeccably fresh; all dishes are expertly crafted, nicely balanced and enticingly presented. The serving team is highly professional and describe dishes with great care and obvious pride.

龍景軒名副其實,坐擁動人心弦的維港全景;餐廳內部亦時尚整潔,飾以手工刺繡絲綢、圓柱和玻璃屏幕。食材品質上等,特別是海鮮,絕對新鮮。菜式全是悉心烹調,精心雕琢,賣相一流。服務專業,侍應會細心自豪地介紹菜式。

■ ADDRESS/地址

TEL. 3196 8880
4F, Four Seasons Hotel,
8 Finance Street, Central
中環金融街8號四季酒店4樓
www.fourseasons.com/hongkong

■ OPENING HOURS, LAST ORDER
　營業時間,最後點菜時間
Lunch/午膳　12:00-14:30 (L.O.)
Dinner/晚膳　18:00-22:30 (L.O.)

■ PRICE/價錢
Lunch/午膳　set/套餐　　　$430
　　　　　à la carte/點菜 $300-1,300
Dinner/晚膳　set/套餐　　$1,080
　　　　　à la carte/點菜 $300-1,300

Lung Wah Roast Meats　NEW
龍華燒臘

You might have heard of Lung Wah before but were never quite sure why. It is for roasted meats that their reputation was formed: goose, pigeon and pork - but what about their stuffed pig's trotter or skewers of pork and liver? They are so good you'll want to buy some to take home. It all started back in 1963 and this clean and tidy little shop is now being run by the third generation of the family, with most family members involved.

你也許曾聽説過龍華的名字，但卻不知為何。這裡以燒臘聞名：燒鵝、乳鴿與燒肉。但釀豬蹄與金錢雞呢？它們極之美味，你定會忍不住要買回家品嚐。這家整潔的小店自1963年開業，現在由家族第三代幾乎全家總動員一起經營。

■ ADDRESS/地址

TEL. 2576 6549

41-45 Tang Lung Street, Causeway Bay
銅鑼灣登龍街41-45號

■ ANNUAL AND WEEKLY CLOSING
　休息日期
Closed 3 days Lunar New Year
農曆新年休息3天

■ OPENING HOURS, LAST ORDER
　營業時間，最後點菜時間
07:00-22:30 L.O.22:00

■ PRICE/價錢
set/套餐　　　　　　　　$ 43-68
à la carte/點菜　　　　　$ 37-70

Mak An Kee Noodle (Wing Kut Street)
麥奀記(忠記)麵家 (永吉街)

This narrow shop, at Des Voeux Road and Wing Kut Street, tucked away behind the market, quickly fills up at lunch break time. The regular clientele will happily move up to allow you to share their tables. The legendary beef and wonton noodles is the speciality of the house; using the best quality raw ingredients, these exquisite bowls are bursting with flavour. Furthermore, this quality comes at prices that represent very good value for money.

這家窄小的麵店位於德輔道與永吉街交界，隱藏在街市後方，午飯時間座無虛席。店內常客很樂意稍移座位，與你共用餐桌。其傳統牛腩雲吞麵甚具特色，用料上乘，泡製出每一碗都香濃美味。此外，更是價格相宜，物超所值。

■ ADDRESS/地址

TEL. 2541 6388

37 Wing Kut Street, Central
中環永吉街37號

■ ANNUAL AND WEEKLY CLOSING
    休息日期
Closed 3 days Lunar New Year
農曆新年休息3天

■ OPENING HOURS, LAST ORDER
    營業時間, 最後點菜時間
10:30-20:00 (L.O.)

■ PRICE/價錢
à la carte/點菜 $ 23-60

Mak's Noodle
麥奀雲吞麵世家

A small place with a big reputation: Mak Chi Ming's father opened the original Mak's Noodle in 1960, while his grandfather was 'king of the wonton' in the 1930s. The premises may be modest but the operation runs like clockwork. The staff - strict, efficient and overseen by the boss - serve nothing but noodles, with fresh, authentic recipes utilising seasonal vegetables produced to order. Most prized dish is the mouth-watering chutney pork.

地方淺窄的餐廳卻享負盛名：麥志明祖父是30年代的「雲吞麵大王」，父親則於1960年創立了麥奀記老店。店裡地方不大，設備簡單，員工由老闆監督著，既嚴謹又有效率。餐廳供應的只有麵，採用新鮮食材、正宗食譜，以及季節性蔬菜。最特別的菜式是令人垂涎欲滴的炸醬麵。

■ ADDRESS/地址

TEL. 2854 3810
77 Wellington Street, Central
中環威靈頓街77號

■ OPENING HOURS, LAST ORDER
　營業時間，最後點菜時間
11:00-20:00 L.O.19:45

■ PRICE/價錢
à la carte/點菜　　　　　$ 28-60

Malaysia Port Klang Cuisine   NEW
馬拉盞星馬美食

You'll find this small, friendly, family-run Malaysian restaurant on a busy street; its façade covered with the photos of the local celebrities who have visited. Inside is equally modest but this time the photos shown are of the dishes on offer. The Malaysian community appear much taken with the traditional bah kut teh, the seafood laksa, the special prawn noodle with soup and the stir fry vegetables with shrimp paste sauce.

這家細小、親切、友善的家族式馬來西亞餐廳位處繁忙的街道，門口貼滿了曾光顧的本地名人照片，店內同樣貼滿各式菜餚的照片。馬來西亞人似乎相當喜愛這裡的肉骨茶、海鮮叻沙、特色蝦湯麵與馬拉盞通菜。

■ ADDRESS/地址
TEL. 2555 6444
143 Sai Yee Street, Mong Kok, Kowloon
九龍旺角洗衣街143

■ ANNUAL AND WEEKLY CLOSING
　　休息日期
Closed 5 days Lunar New Year and
Monday
農曆新年5天及週一休息

■ OPENING HOURS, LAST ORDER
　　營業時間,最後點菜時間
12:00-23:00

■ PRICE/價錢
à la carte/點菜　　　　　$ 100-160

Mandarin Grill + Bar
文華扒房+酒吧

A luminous dining room - Sir Terence Conran's refurbishment has kept the Oriental references; if you want to be seen, this is the place to eat. Alternatively, if you want to see the oyster chefs at work, sit at the bar and watch them – guaranteed freshness! On the other side, behind a window, the kitchen team prepare appealing and contemporary European cuisine. Soufflé lovers adore this place as they have a large selection from which to choose.

明亮的餐廳經過20世紀著名的室內設計師Sir Terence Conran的裝修後，仍然保留文華東方的味道。如果你的用餐不介意張揚，這家餐廳則十分適合。又或者，如果你想看看師傅如何準備生蠔，坐在吧檯觀看吧，生蠔保證新鮮！餐廳的另一邊，你可透過窗戶看到廚房團隊用心準備令人垂涎三尺的當代歐洲菜。梳乎厘的愛好者鍾情於這個地方，因為這裡的選擇琳瑯滿目。

■ ADDRESS/地址
TEL. 2825 4004
1F, Mandarin Oriental Hotel,
5 Connaught Road, Central
中環干諾道中5號文華東方酒店1樓
www.mandarinoriental.com/hongkong

■ ANNUAL AND WEEKLY CLOSING
　休息日期
Closed lunch Saturday and Sunday
週六、日午膳休息

■ OPENING HOURS, LAST ORDER
　營業時間，最後點菜時間
Lunch/午膳 12:00-14:30 (L.O.)
Dinner/晚膳 18:30-22:30 (L.O.)

■ PRICE/價錢
Lunch/午膳　set/套餐　　　$588
　　　　　à la carte/點菜 $650-1,000
Dinner/晚膳　set/套餐　　　$888
　　　　　à la carte/點菜 $650-1,000

Man Ho
萬豪殿

XX

♿ 👉🔑 🍽48

A 2009 renovation updated the décor of these two large and elegant dining rooms, located just below the lobby of the JW Marriott Hotel. But regulars weren't too bothered because, more importantly to them, the food remained as it was. That means traditional Cantonese cuisine and the judicious use of fresh, local ingredients in good-value dishes, such as double-boiled fish maws soup with sea whelks and chicken.

於2009年重新裝潢,令這兩個位於萬豪酒店大堂下層、佔地甚廣的高雅飯廳更添精緻。常客則不會理會裝潢;對他們來説,食物品質維持一貫高水平更為重要——萬豪殿提供以新鮮本地食材烹製的傳統粵菜,如原盅花膠響螺燉雞。

■ ADDRESS/地址
TEL. 2841 3853
3F, JW Marriott Hotel, Pacific Place,
88 Queensway, Admiralty
香港金鐘道88號太古廣場萬豪酒店3樓
www.jwmarriotthongkong.com

■ OPENING HOURS, LAST ORDER
　營業時間,最後點菜時間
Lunch/午膳 11:30-14:30 (L.O.)
Dinner/晚膳 18:30-23:00 (L.O.)

■ PRICE/價錢
à la carte/點菜　　　　$ 280-700

Man Wah
文華廳

Man Wah seems to have been untouched by the hotel's modern renovation and exudes a luxuriously intimate and traditional feel. Tables just off the room entrance have the better harbour views, though everyone can appreciate the décor: brass lanterns hang from the wood ceiling and the ornate screen is from the original opening. The Peking duck is a classic, as is the steamed crab claw with winter melon and ginger and the Wagyu beef Cantonese style.

文華似乎沒有被酒店的現代裝修影響，這裡仍然散發著一種豪華的舒適傳統氣息。雖然近門口的餐桌享有較佳的海景，但所有人都可以欣賞這裡的裝潢：木天花板吊著黃銅燈籠，而華麗的屏幕是從開張使用至今。菜單滿是著經典菜式，這裡的北京填鴨是名副其實的美食，薑汁冬瓜蒸蟹拑及粵式和牛亦不遑多讓。

■ ADDRESS/地址

TEL. 2825 4003
25F, Mandarin Oriental Hotel,
5 Connaught Road, Central
中環干諾道中5號文華東方酒店25樓
www.mandarinoriental.com/hongkong

■ OPENING HOURS, LAST ORDER
　營業時間，最後點菜時間
Lunch/午膳　12:00-14:30 (L.O.)
Dinner/晚膳　18:30-22:30 (L.O.)

■ PRICE/價錢
Lunch/午膳　set/套餐　　　　$428-548
　　　　　　à la carte/點菜 $300-750
Dinner/晚膳　set/套餐　　　　$868-968
　　　　　　à la carte/點菜 $300-750

Ming Court
明閣

Highlights of the sophisticated and expertly prepared Cantonese cooking include stir-fried shrimp with egg white; garoupa with mushrooms and dried shrimp roe; and braised prawn with crab meat, spinach and steamed egg white. A fascinating collection of replica Ching Dynasty pottery, as well as some fine Chinese landscape paintings, lend elegance to the stylish interior with its curved walls. Be sure to reserve your table in the main dining room.

菜單包括精心炮製的精美廣東菜式。招牌菜有：脆芝士龍蝦伴醋香鮑魚天使麵。餐廳收藏了一系列清代陶器的仿製品，以及一些筆法細緻的中國山水畫，令本已獨具風格的裝潢更顯高雅。切記預訂在主廳的座位。

■ ADDRESS/地址

TEL. 3552 3300

6F, Langham Place Hotel,
555 Shanghai Street, Mong Kok,
Kowloon
九龍旺角上海街555號朗豪酒店6樓
www.hongkong.langhamplacehotels.com

■ OPENING HOURS, LAST ORDER
營業時間，最後點菜時間
Lunch/午膳　11:00-14:30 (L.O.)
Dinner/晚膳　18:00-22:30 (L.O.)

■ PRICE/價錢
Lunch/午膳　set/套餐　　$398
　　　　　　à la carte/點菜 $200-420

Dinner/晚膳　set/套餐　　$398-868
　　　　　　à la carte/點菜 $260-900

Mist   NEW

The stainless steel and glass façade hint at the equally chic interior, which comes with walls lined with stone and mirrors, and colour courtesy of the red leather dining chairs. The classic ramen noodle is here given a modern makeover, with many of the dishes displaying an element of fusion. Dinner offers the most interesting menu but then lunch represents excellent value. Can't find your chopsticks? Simply pull out the drawer.

由不銹鋼和玻璃組成的外觀可知內裏的裝潢必定同樣時尚新潮——牆身以石材和鏡子砌成線條，配上紅色皮革椅子，色彩強烈。這裡為傳統日本拉麵換上現代新裝，很多菜式都具備fusion（融合異國特色）的元素。晚餐選擇較吸引，但午餐則絕對物超所值。找不到筷子？拉開抽屜吧！

■ ADDRESS/地址

TEL. 2881 5006
4 Sun Wui Road, Causeway Bay
銅鑼灣新會道4號
www.mist.com.hk

■ OPENING HOURS, LAST ORDER
   營業時間，最後點菜時間
Lunch/午膳 12:00-15:00 (L.O.)
Dinner/晚膳 18:00-23:00 (L.O.)

■ PRICE/價錢
Lunch/午膳   à la carte/點菜 $ 120-170
Dinner/晚膳   set/套餐 $ 380
              à la carte/點菜 $ 140-270

Nanhai No.1 NEW
南海一號

It's highly appropriate that this maritime-themed restaurant – which opened in 2010 and takes as its inspiration a culinary voyage around China and the South Seas – commands such terrific harbour views, thanks to its floor-to-ceiling windows. But the cuisine is not just limited to seafood; the contemporary dishes also have a strong Cantonese element. The Eyebar is an equally good-looking spot that makes the most of the top-floor vistas.

這家以海為主題的餐廳於2010年開張，靈感來自中國及南海一帶的美食航程。落地玻璃讓海港美景一覽無遺。她的美食當然不限於海鮮，創新菜式帶有強烈廣東菜元素。頂樓的Eyebar酒吧景觀同樣出色，讓你飽覽落地玻璃下的廣闊景色。

■ ADDRESS/地址
TEL. 2487 3688
30F, iSquare, 63 Nathan Road,
Tsim Sha Tsui, Kowloon
九龍尖沙咀彌敦道63號iSquare30樓
www.elite-concepts.com

■ OPENING HOURS, LAST ORDER
　營業時間，最後點菜時間
Lunch/午膳 11:30-15:00 L.O.14:30
Dinner/晚膳 18:00-23:30 L.O.22:30

■ PRICE/價錢
à la carte/點菜　　　　$ 200-700

Naozen
なお膳

⌷20   ⊙

There are two distinct rooms to this Japanese restaurant: the first is dominated by a sushi counter, while the back room offers a more discreet environment. Upstairs are three tatami rooms for private dining (remove your shoes when you come up here). The menu features all types of Japanese cuisine: sushi, sashimi, tempura, soba as well as seasonal specialities. Well-priced set lunches are also offered and are the popular choice.

這家日本餐廳設有兩個不同的分區：一個以壽司吧為主角，另一個則為顧客提供更私人的空間。樓上有三間榻榻米房間供私人用餐，进房敬請脫鞋。菜式選擇包括各種日本料理：壽司、刺身、天婦羅、蕎麥麵及時令特選菜式。價格實惠的午市套餐極受歡迎。

■ ADDRESS/地址

TEL. 2877 6668
21-25 Wellington Street, Central
中環威靈頓街21-25號
www.naozen.com

■ ANNUAL AND WEEKLY CLOSING
    休息日期
Closed Lunar New Year and Sunday lunch
年初一及週日午膳休息

■ OPENING HOURS, LAST ORDER
    營業時間，最後點菜時間
Lunch/午膳 11:30-14:30 (L.O.)
Dinner/晚膳 18:00-22:30 (L.O.)

■ PRICE/價錢
Lunch/午膳   set/套餐 $120-190
               à la carte/點菜 $200-700
Dinner/晚膳 set/套餐 $320-780
               à la carte/點菜 $200-700

Nha Trang (Central) NEW
芽莊 (中環)

If you're not here bang on midday then you'll probably find yourself queuing as this fun, fast and frantic Vietnamese restaurant really pulls in the crowds. It has a bright, fresh feel, a mix of individual and communal tables and a young service team who are well organised and efficient. The healthy menu ranges from Vietnamese street snacks and salad rolls through to 'broken rice platters' and lemongrass grilled fish, all at affordable prices.

午市時，你若不早前來，便需要在這家有趣、快速、如臨大敵的餐廳前排隊了。店內感覺明亮而清新，設有小餐桌和可能與人共用的大餐桌，年輕的侍應們工作有條理而有效率。健康菜單從越南街頭小吃與粉卷，到越南碎米飯和香茅燒魚都有，價錢也相當合理。

■ ADDRESS/地址

TEL. 2581 9992
88-90 Wellington Street, Central
中環威靈頓街88-90號
www.nhatrang.com.hk

■ OPENING HOURS, LAST ORDER
營業時間，最後點菜時間
12:00-22:30 (L.O.)

■ PRICE/價錢
à la carte/點菜　　　　　$ 140-230

Nice Congee Shop　NEW
和味生滾粥店

The regulars have been coming to this simple shop for years because they know good congee. The menu is on the wall and the most popular dish is the congee with fish, whether that's the fish lips, tail or slices of fillet. It can come enriched with beef, pork belly, heart and even frogs' legs too. Other small dishes are also available, such as fish balls, deep-fried fish skin and rice dumplings.

熟客多年來經常來訪這家簡樸小店的原因，是他們都懂得欣賞好粥。餐單貼在牆上，最著名的菜式是魚粥，不管是魚嘴、魚尾或魚片粥都同樣出色。要令粥品更豐富，則可選擇牛肉、豬肚、豬心、還有田雞腿。此外亦提供其他小食，如鯪魚球、炸魚皮和咸肉粽。

■ ADDRESS/地址
TEL. 2783 0935
75 Woosung Street, Jordan, Kowloon
九龍佐敦吳松街75號

■ OPENING HOURS, LAST ORDER
營業時間，最後點菜時間
07:30-03:00

■ PRICE/價錢
à la carte/點菜　　　$ 25-50

Nicholini's
意寧谷

XXXX

This stylish circular room has large windows that offer a peek between the adjoining tower blocks, allowing views over the bay. At the back is a large Venetian scene and some intriguing glass sculptures which add a little opulence to proceedings. The cooking mixes traditional Northern Italian recipes and contemporary influences; don't miss the excellent pasta. Recommended dishes include three-way scallops and the wild mushroom lasagne.

這家時尚的圓形餐廳擁有寬大的窗戶，於鄰近摩天大樓中鶴立雞群，坐擁維港美景。餐廳後方的巨型威尼斯佈景和迷人的玻璃塑像，散發著豪華莊重的氣息。烹調方式融合北義大利傳統煮法及現代元素；切勿錯過其出色義大利麵！推薦菜式包括三式帶子及焗野菌千層麵。

■ ADDRESS/地址
TEL. 2521 3838
8F, Conrad Hotel, Pacific Place, 88 Queensway, Admiralty
香港金鐘道88號太古廣場港麗酒店8樓
www.conradhotels.com

■ ANNUAL AND WEEKLY CLOSING
　休息日期
Closed Saturday lunch
週六午膳休息

■ OPENING HOURS, LAST ORDER
　營業時間，最後點菜時間
Lunch/午膳　12:00-15:00 (L.O.)
Dinner/晚膳　18:30-23:00 (L.O.)

■ PRICE/價錢
Lunch/午膳　set/套餐　　　$418
　　　　　　à la carte/點菜 $500-1,000
Dinner/晚膳 set/套餐　　　$618-828
　　　　　　à la carte/點菜 $500-1,000

Nobu

This branch of the über-fashionable, international Nobu brand boasts an impressive ceiling fashioned from sea urchin spines and there are images of cherry blossom behind the bar. At lunch, bento boxes are the popular choice. At dinner, Mr. Matsuhisa's beguiling blend of Japanese and South American tastes continues to work its fashionable magic by featuring sushi and sashimi, good quality seafood and fine salsas.

這家享譽國際的Nobu餐廳分店有著以海膽刺裝飾的天花，讓人印象深刻，背景更配有櫻花美景裝飾。午餐時間最受歡迎的是便當。而晚餐方面，主廚松久信幸融合日本和南美風味，炮製的嶄新口味更是迷人。菜式包括壽司、刺身、優質的海鮮及辛香番茄醬。

■ ADDRESS/地址

TEL. 2313 2340

2F, Intercontinental Hotel,
18 Salisbury Road, Tsim Sha Tsui,
Kowloon
九龍尖沙咀梳士巴利道18號
洲際酒店2樓

■ OPENING HOURS, LAST ORDER
　營業時間，最後點菜時間
Lunch/午膳 12:00-14:30 (L.O.)
Dinner/晚膳 18:00-23:00 (L.O.)

■ PRICE/價錢

Lunch/午膳	set/套餐	$ 298-588
	à la carte/點菜	$ 300-900
Dinner/晚膳	set/套餐	$ 888-1,188
	à la carte/點菜	$ 350-1,200

Olala (St. Francis Street)
一碗麵 (聖佛蘭士街)

Olala has this corner of chic Wan Chai covered, with its charcuterie shop and traiteur. But it is the immaculately kept noodle shop on the corner that is the best of the bunch. Its creator, Mr Chow, has a passion for fine ingredients and imports many of them from Europe. The bones from the Iberico hams form the basis of the big bowls of noodles which are becoming legendary, along with the braised beef variety.

"一碗麵"坐落在灣仔充滿時尚風格的一角，鄰近有肉店與小餐館。但最為出色的就是這家在角落的麵店。伊比利亞火腿的骨頭，正正就是這裡馳名大碗麵條湯底的主要材料，除此以外，亦有紅燒牛肉等不同變化。別忘了嚐嚐這裡的小吃，例如蒜泥白肉。

■ ADDRESS/地址

TEL. 2294 0426
33 St. Francis Street, Wan Chai
灣仔聖佛蘭士街33號

■ OPENING HOURS, LAST ORDER
　營業時間，最後點菜時間
11:30-22:30 (L.O.)

■ PRICE/價錢
Lunch/午膳　à la carte/點菜 $80-150
Dinner/晚膳　à la carte/點菜 $100-250

One Dim Sum NEW
一點心

The owner may be young but he's been involved in the dim sum business for quite a few years and has clearly learnt something because there is often a queue here, despite the shop being able to accommodate up to 40 people. The décor is simple and the two chefs, who have around 30 years of experience, prepare mostly traditional dishes such as steamed prawn dumpling, barbecued pork buns and steamed rice noodles with deep-fried flour roll.

店東雖然相當年輕，但他從事點心專門店已多年，亦顯然對自己的生意有一定的了解，因為儘管店內能容納約40人，卻仍然大排長龍。店內裝潢簡潔，而兩名有30多年經驗的主廚，則努力為客人準備經典點心如薄皮鮮蝦餃、蜜汁叉燒包與炸兩腸粉等。

■ ADDRESS/地址
TEL. 2789 2280
15 Playing Field Road,
Mong Kok, Kowloon
九龍旺角運動場道15號

■ ANNUAL AND WEEKLY CLOSING
　　休息日期
Closed 5 days Lunar New Year
農曆新年休息5天

■ OPENING HOURS, LAST ORDER
　　營業時間，最後點菜時間
11:00-01:00 (L.O.)

■ PRICE/價錢
à la carte/點菜　　　　$ 30-50

One Harbour Road
港灣壹號

One Harbour Road may be set in a hotel, but its beautifully refined ambience will make you think you're on the terrace of an elegant 1930s Taipan mansion. The bright and airy feel comes courtesy of split-level dining offering views of the harbour. A profusion of plants, a lotus pond and the sound of running water soften the bold statement of the huge pillars. Renowned Cantonese menus offer a wide variety of well-prepared meat and fish dishes.

雖然港灣壹號位於酒店內，但這裡的優雅氣氛，令你恍如置身於30年代的優雅大班府第。分層用餐讓你同時飽覽海景，享受明亮又通風的環境。茂盛的植物、大型蓮花池，以及潺潺的流水聲，軟化了龐大柱子給人的感覺。這裡的著名粵菜包括準備妥當、種類繁多的肉類和魚類菜式。

■ ADDRESS/地址
TEL. 2584 7722
8F, Grand Hyatt Hotel,
1 Harbour Road, Wan Chai
灣仔港灣道一號君悅酒店8樓
www.hongkong.grand.hyatt.com

■ OPENING HOURS, LAST ORDER
　營業時間，最後點菜時間
Lunch/午膳　12:00-14:30 (L.O.)
Dinner/晚膳　18:30-22:30 (L.O.)

■ PRICE/價錢
Lunch/午膳　set/套餐　　　　$400-550
　　　　　à la carte/點菜 $450-990
Dinner/晚膳　set/套餐　　　　$790
　　　　　à la carte/點菜 $450-990

On Lee NEW
安利

There can't be many locals who don't know this place. It began in 1966 and has moved around, but never far from its current position. Virtually opposite the temple, it has evolved a little from 'milk tea and toast with butter', although these are still on the menu. Now it's fish balls and beef flanks with handmade noodles and their own chilli sauce. The food arrives quickly so you've hardly time to spot your favourite celebrity signature on the wall.

若你住在這一區，肯定聽過這家茶餐廳。自1966年開業以來，安利在附近搬遷多次，但都離現在的地點不遠。這家在寺廟對面的小店，供應的食物從「奶茶配奶油多」已改良了不少，不過這些經典套餐仍然存在於餐單上。現在餐廳的招牌菜已是魚蛋、牛腩配上手打麵，以及他們自製的辣椒醬。上菜快得讓你無暇在牆上找出你最愛明星的簽名。

■ ADDRESS/地址
TEL. 2513 8398
22 Main Street East, Shau Kei Wan
筲箕灣東大街22號

■ OPENING HOURS, LAST ORDER
營業時間，最後點菜時間
07:00-19:00 (L.O.)

■ PRICE/價錢
à la carte/點菜 $ 19-50

On Lot 10

It's not quite as small as it looks as there's more space upstairs, but this is still a very intimate French restaurant. What it lacks in size, it makes up for in quality. The keen chef tours the markets daily to compile his good value menu of traditional Gallic home cooking; specialities include whole fish with crushed potatoes and roasted chicken with black truffle and sweet peas. Choice is limited at lunch so dinner is the best time to visit.

這家法國餐廳看似地方細小，但其實樓上別有洞天--另有更多座位設於其中，氣氛親切。其優質出品更讓它絲毫不顯遜色。充滿熱情的主廚每天穿梭市場，準備其獨具傳統法國家常菜風格的實惠菜單；店內特色法國菜包括原條魚焗薯蓉、黑松露菌蜜糖豆烤雞。中午時段選擇有限，建議於晚餐時段光顧。

■ ADDRESS/地址

TEL. 2155 9210

34 Gough Street, Central
中環歌賦街34號

■ ANNUAL AND WEEKLY CLOSING
    休息日期
Closed Saturday lunch
週六午膳休息

■ OPENING HOURS, LAST ORDER
    營業時間，最後點菜時間
Lunch/午膳 12:15-14:45 (L.O.)
Dinner/晚膳 18:00-22:30 (L.O.)

■ PRICE/價錢
Lunch/午膳   set/套餐 $116-126
Dinner/晚膳 à la carte/點菜 $280-370

Peking Garden (Admiralty)
北京樓 (金鍾)

🍴 10

Belonging to the Maxim Empire and sitting pretty in Pacific Place, this restaurant offers a stylish, metropolitan atmosphere; the library room is a particularly attractive space for private parties. The menu offers classic Pekingese cuisine: barbequed Peking duck being the best seller, along with deep-fried yellow croaker fish with sweet and sour sauce and, of course, dim sum served here at both lunch and dinner.

這家隸屬美心王國的酒樓位處太古廣場，氣氛具都會時尚特色。一組組的小房間特別適合私人團體使用。提供傳統北京菜：北京填鴨和糖醋黃花魚固然最受歡迎，午市和晚市亦提供點心可供選擇。

■ ADDRESS/地址

TEL. 2845 8452
Shop 005, LG, Pacific Place, 88 Queensway, Admiralty
香港金鐘道88號太古廣場地庫1樓5號舖
www.maxims.com.hk

■ OPENING HOURS, LAST ORDER
營業時間，最後點菜時間
Lunch/午膳 11:30-15:00 (L.O.)
Dinner/晚膳 17:30-23:00 (L.O.)

■ PRICE/價錢
à la carte/點菜　　　$ 220-700

Peking Garden (Central)
北京樓 (中環)

🍴🍴🍴

🛋16 📞🍴

Divided into two large and warmly lit rooms; one more traditionally decorated, the other better suited for bigger family groups. Be sure to time your visit for the noodle-making demonstration, performed by a chef each evening in the restaurant at 8.30pm. The signature dish is, of course, the Peking duck which is prepared with great care and precision. Service is conscientious and the pleasant staff are well organised.

餐廳劃分為兩個溫暖明亮的大廳;一邊裝潢風格較為傳統,另一邊則較為適合大家族。緊記要算準時間,欣賞每晚8時30分的師傅即席拉麵表演。這裡的招牌菜當然是經過精心炮製的北京填鴨。侍應服務周到,辦事俐落。

■ ADDRESS/地址
TEL. 2526 6456
BF, Alexandra House,
18 Chater Road, Central
中環遮打道18號歷山大廈地庫
www.maxims.com.hk

■ OPENING HOURS, LAST ORDER
營業時間,最後點菜時間
Lunch/午膳 11:30-15:00 (L.O.)
Dinner/晚膳 18:00-23:30 (L.O.)

■ PRICE/價錢
à la carte/點菜 $ 260-600

Peking Garden (Kowloon)
北京樓 (九龍)

✗✗

⌂24

A huge, boisterous Peking restaurant with eight rooms and 500 seats, where the staff are either supervising with calm deliberation, or pushing trolleys and serving. The special dishes are the barbecued Peking duck with pancake, and the poached fish with bamboo shoots and salted cabbage - but look out also for the sliced fish with rice wine sauce and fried hand-made noodles with shredded pork.

這家熱鬧大型的北京樓分為8個部分，可容納500個座位。員工分工合作，有的沉著地監督；有的推著餐車；有的在奉菜。招牌菜有北京填鴨，雪筍湯爆魚絲等。值得一試的還有北京糟溜魚片和炒手拉麵。

■ ADDRESS/地址

TEL. 2735 8211
3F, Star House, 3 Salisbury Road,
Tsim Sha Tsui, Kowloon
九龍尖沙咀梳士巴利道3號星光行3樓
www.maxims.com.hk

■ OPENING HOURS, LAST ORDER
　營業時間，最後點菜時間
Lunch/午膳　11:30-15:00 L.O. 14:45
Dinner/晚膳　17:30-23:30 L.O. 23:00

■ PRICE/價錢
Lunch/午膳　set/套餐　　$105
　　　　　à la carte/點菜 $180-450
Dinner/晚膳　à la carte/點菜 $180-450

Peking Garden (Tai Koo Shing)
北京樓 (太古城)

🍴🍴🍴

♿ 🍽12 🚫🍷

Head for the City Plaza's indoor ice rink to find this ultra-smart restaurant. The interior hits the gold standard, its glitter an ornately ubiquitous statement - just what's required to draw in all those shoppers. The accomplished cuisine is mostly Peking, and the hallmark dish is Peking duck, but spice is nice here too: tuck into fried prawns with chilli sauce. Sichuan and Shanghai elements are also on the menu, though dim sum is low key.

向太古城溜冰場的方向走，便會找到這家超時尚的餐廳。餐廳的內部實在金碧輝煌：發出閃閃生輝、無所不在的光芒，如此華麗的氣派正正吸引了購物者到此用餐。餐廳的菜式大部分是北京菜，招牌菜是北京填鴨，而這裡的香料亦頗美味：不仿試試京爆明蝦球。有些菜式含四川和上海元素，但點心則較少。

■ ADDRESS/地址
TEL. 2884 4131
2F, Cityplaza II, Tai Koo Shing
太古城太古城中心第2期2樓
www.maxims.com.hk

■ OPENING HOURS, LAST ORDER
　營業時間，最後點菜時間
Lunch/午膳 11:30-15:00 L.O. 14:30
Dinner/晚膳 18:00-23:30 L.O. 23:00

■ PRICE/價錢
à la carte/點菜　　　　$ 135-290

Petrus
珀翠

Perched on the 56th floor with dramatic views, this is firmly in the classical European style with moulded ceilings, chandeliers, elegantly draped curtains and refined table settings. The professional service blends in perfectly and demonstrates great attention to detail. All this is matched by very proficient French cooking that relies on a roll-call of top quality ingredients. Exceptional wine list; live music at night.

餐廳座落於酒店56樓，可飽覽海港美景，設計別出心裁：雕有線條的天花、高雅的窗簾、吊燈及排列優雅的餐桌，盡顯經典歐洲格調。服務十分專業，細心周到。餐廳的法國菜廚藝一流，與絕對新鮮食材，相得益彰。出色的美酒清單，晚上更有現場演奏。

■ ADDRESS/地址

TEL. 2820 8590

56F, Island Shangri-La Hotel, Pacific Place, Supreme Court Road, Admiralty
中區法院道太古廣場
港島香格里拉酒店56樓
www.shangri-la.com

■ OPENING HOURS, LAST ORDER
營業時間，最後點菜時間
Lunch/午膳 12:00-14:30 (L.O.)
Dinner/晚膳 18:30-22:30 (L.O.)

■ PRICE/價錢
Lunch/午膳　set/套餐　　$428
　　　　　à la carte/點菜 $850-1,500
Dinner/晚膳　set/套餐　　$1,380
　　　　　à la carte/點菜 $850-1,500

Pierre

❀ ❀   XXXX

             ♿ ← 🖐 ⎚16 ☎🍴 🐾

The top floor of the Mandarin Oriental provides suitably chic surroundings for celebrated French chef Pierre Gagnaire's culinary pyrotechnics. The intricate and innovative dishes and their component parts arrive in a number of vessels, all carefully explained by the charming staff. The views are terrific and the room itself is stylish, moodily lit and very comfortable. The focus here is on enjoyment, with an atmosphere free from pomposity.

文華東方酒店頂樓的環境，與法國名廚Pierre Gagnaire讓人驚歎的美味菜式非常合襯。精緻而創新的菜式與配菜以不同容器盛載而上，全部由殷勤的侍應細心介紹。餐廳景觀迷人，而餐廳本身的裝潢也甚具現代感，配合富情調的照明，非常舒適。在這裡，你大可盡情融入美景，專心享受美食。

■ ADDRESS/地址

TEL. 2825 4001

25F, Mandarin Oriental Hotel,
5 Connaught Road, Central
中環干諾道中5號文華東方酒店25樓
www.mandarinoriental.com/hongkong

■ ANNUAL AND WEEKLY CLOSING
　休息日期
Closed Saturday lunch, Sunday
and Public Holidays
週六午膳、週日及公眾假期休息

■ OPENING HOURS, LAST ORDER
　營業時間, 最後點菜時間
Lunch/午膳 12:00-14:30 (L.O.)
Dinner/晚膳 19:00-22:30 (L.O.)

■ PRICE/價錢

Lunch/午膳	set/套餐	$440-1,488
	à la carte/點菜	$950-1,500
Dinner/晚膳	set/套餐	$1,488
	à la carte/點菜	$950-1,500

Queen's Palace
帝后殿

It's not just locals who appreciate Queen's Palace, as it draws plenty of customers from further afield. The chef can often be found engaging with his customers and will happily make recommendations. The cooking is a blend of Peking, Shanghai and Sichuan influences. Among the specialities are sautéed prawn balls with salted eggs and glazed Yunnan ham with honey sauce. It's worth trying to get one of the window tables.

懂得欣賞帝后殿的不只本地人，就連許多外國觀光客也慕名前來。主廚經常與顧客閒談，並非常樂意為顧客推薦菜式。這裡的菜式揉合了京、滬、川菜的特色，招牌菜則有黃金明蝦球與蜜汁烤雙方。極力推薦選擇靠窗的座位。

■ ADDRESS/地址

TEL. 2591 6338

27F, QRE Plaza, 202 Queen's Road East, Wan Chai

灣仔皇后大道東202號QRE Plaza 27樓

www.queenspalace.com.hk

■ OPENING HOURS, LAST ORDER
營業時間，最後點菜時間
10:00-23:00 L.O.22:30

■ PRICE/價錢
Lunch/午膳 à la carte/點菜 $ 110-250
Dinner/晚膳 à la carte/點菜 $ 160-300

Red Seasons (Lam Tei)   NEW
季季紅 (藍地)

P   🛋36   ☎🍴

Red Seasons restaurant is renowned for its roast suckling pig – it comes stuffed with rice and dried prawns, must be ordered in advance and is perfect for a large party. It's just one of a number of specialities, along with pork patties with lotus root and pork ribs with plum sauce. Such is their reputation that reservations need to be made well in advance. The restaurant even has its own small temple at the back.

季季紅最著名的菜式是蝦禾米乳香豬－－乳豬內釀了飯和蝦，須提前預訂，十分適合大型派對。其他鎮店名菜包括有香煎蓮藕餅與冰淋醬烤骨。由於酒樓名氣甚廣，請提早訂座。酒樓後方更設有小祠堂。

■ ADDRESS/地址

TEL. 2462 7038
1 Lam Tei Main Street, Tuen Mun, New Territories
新界屯門藍地大街1號
www.redseasons.com.hk

■ OPENING HOURS, LAST ORDER
營業時間，最後點菜時間
05:00-23:00 (L.O.)

■ PRICE/價錢

Lunch/午膳	set/套餐	$127-155
	à la carte/點菜	$50-250
Dinner/晚膳	à la carte/點菜	$120-250

Regal Palace
富豪金殿

This grand dining room on the third floor of the Regal Hotel, with its vast windows and twinkling glass crystals, provides suitably elegant surroundings to match the classic, expertly prepared Cantonese cooking. Chef Ip's longstanding tenure of the top job ensures that the regulars are rewarded with consistency and reliability. It's worth heading for the 'award' or 'signature' dishes on the menu. Service is formal and well organised.

這家位於富豪酒店3樓的豪華酒家有著巨大的玻璃窗與閃爍的水晶玻璃裝飾，優雅的環境配合著這裡由高手炮製的經典粵菜。正因由名廚葉師傅擔任主廚，這裡的食物水準一直都能保持高水平，從不讓顧客失望。推薦選擇菜單上的「得獎」與「招牌」菜式。服務非常周到，安排妥當。

■ ADDRESS/地址
TEL. 2837 1773
3F, Regal Hotel, 88 Yee Wo Street, Causeway Bay
銅鑼灣怡和街88號富豪酒店3樓
www.regalhotel.com

■ OPENING HOURS, LAST ORDER
　營業時間，最後點菜時間
Lunch/午膳 12:00-15:00 (L.O.)
Dinner/晚膳 18:00-23:00 (L.O.)

■ PRICE/價錢
à la carte/點菜　　　　$ 300-500

Roka

The Hong Kong outpost for this small but expanding group of restaurants offering contemporary Japanese Robatayaki cuisine has an appealing minimalist interior featuring wood, earth, iron and rice paper. The charcoal robata grill is used to great effect to cook fresh seafood, which arrives daily from Japan, and meat, mostly from Australia. Sashimi and tempura are also offered. If you want to watch the action, sit at the counter.

正在擴張的Roka飲食集團在香港開設的分店提供現代日式爐端燒美食，內部裝潢簡潔吸引，以木、泥、鐵及米紙為主。炭燒爐端燒是炮製每天從日本運到的新鮮海鮮、或是澳洲運抵的鮮肉的上佳方法。店內亦提供刺身及天婦羅。如有興趣觀賞烹製過程，請坐在櫃檯位置。

■ ADDRESS/地址

TEL. 3960 5988

Shop 002, LG1, Pacific Place, 88 Queensway, Admiralty
香港金鐘道88號太古廣場地庫1樓2號舖
www.rokarestaurant.com

■ OPENING HOURS, LAST ORDER
營業時間，最後點菜時間
11:30-22:30 (L.O.)

■ PRICE/價錢

Lunch/午膳	set/套餐	$288-488
	à la carte/點菜	$220-780
Dinner/晚膳	à la carte/點菜	$220-780

Sabah　NEW
莎巴

It may have an unremarkable façade, but it's easy to find thanks to the huge horizontal neon sign. It's equally modest inside which alerts you to the fact that diners don't come for the interior design but for the authentic Malay specialties. Satay, pork rib soup, king prawns with butter and deep-fried egg yolk are some of the highlights. They are known for the Ipoh bean sprout chicken and it's worth trying the chef's recipe for banana fritters.

這家餐廳的外觀也許很不起眼，但是靠著巨大的霓虹燈招牌，我們可輕易找到它。內部的裝潢與外部一樣平凡，但直得注意的是吸引眾多食客的並不是餐廳的室內設計，而是正宗的馬拉菜。精選菜式包括沙嗲、肉骨茶與金絲奶油大蝦。這裡最著名的招牌菜是怡保銀芽雞，主廚秘方炮製的炸香蕉也十分惹味。

■ ADDRESS/地址

TEL. 2143 6626
98-102 Jaffe Road, Wan Chai
灣仔謝菲道98-102號

■ ANNUAL AND WEEKLY CLOSING
　休息日期
Closed 3 days Lunar New Year
農曆新年休息3天

■ OPENING HOURS, LAST ORDER
　營業時間，最後點菜時間
11:00-23:30 (L.O.)

■ PRICE/價錢
Lunch/午膳　set/套餐　　　$60
　　　　　à la carte/點菜 $70-150
Dinner/晚膳　à la carte/點菜 $70-150

Sabatini

The original Sabatini is in Rome, so this version enjoys a fine pedigree and ticks all the right boxes. A comfy lounge bar sets you up nicely before your meal. The main dining room is large, with a trattoria décor of a wooden beamed ceiling, a shiny tiled floor, rustic furniture and yellow walls embellished with Italian style frescoes. The menu runs the gamut from antipasti to soup, pasta, fish, meat and dessert trolley. Live music from 7pm.

首家Sabatini始創於羅馬,可見帝苑酒店的Sabatini來頭不小,美食正宗,佳釀一流。舒適的雅座酒吧是享用正餐的完美前奏。主餐室地方寬敞,天花由木橫樑組成,光滑的地板以磚鋪成,黃色牆壁掛著意式壁畫,加上質樸的傢俱,彰顯餐廳的意大利風格。餐廳的菜單非常全面,涵蓋各種意式前菜、湯類、意大利麵食、魚類、肉類,以至甜品車。現場演奏由每晚七時開始。

■ ADDRESS/地址

TEL. 2733 2000

3F, The Royal Garden Hotel,
69 Mody Road, East Tsim Sha Tsui,
Kowloon
九龍尖東麼地道69號帝苑酒店3樓
www.sabatini.rghk.com.hk

■ OPENING HOURS, LAST ORDER
　營業時間, 最後點菜時間
Lunch/午膳 12:00-14:30 (L.O.)
Dinner/晚膳 18:00-23:00 (L.O.)

■ PRICE/價錢
Lunch/午膳 set/套餐 $338-368
　　　　　 à la carte/點菜 $650-1,000
Dinner/晚膳 à la carte/點菜 $650-1,000

Sang Kee
生記

🍴🍴

🌙🍴

They thrived for over 30 years in Wan Chai, but it was inevitable that larger premises would have to be found for this family business. None of the philosophies were forgotten in the move, like their regular trips to the market for the best ingredients, particularly seafood. Steamed crab with preserved plums and garlic sauce, and fried fresh squid in salt are of note. It's all overseen by Vicky and Dicken Wong and their dedicated team.

生記在灣仔已立足三十多年，這檔家族生意無可避免地必須擴充其面積，但其宗旨始終如一。如堅持定期前往街市尋找最佳材料，海鮮尤甚。梅子雙蒜蒸蟹和椒鹽鮮魷值得一提。餐廳由黃氏家族及其盡忠職守的工作團隊主理。

■ ADDRESS/地址

TEL. 2575 2236
1-2F, Hip Sang Building,
107-115 Hennessy Road, Wan Chai
灣仔軒尼詩道107-115號恊生大廈1-2樓
www.sangkee.com.hk

■ ANNUAL AND WEEKLY CLOSING
   休息日期
Closed Sunday lunch and first Monday
of the month except Public Holidays
週日午膳及每月第一個週一(公眾假期除
外)休息

■ OPENING HOURS, LAST ORDER
   營業時間，最後點菜時間
Lunch/午膳 11:30-14:15 (L.O.)
Dinner/晚膳 18:00-22:15 (L.O.)

■ PRICE/價錢
à la carte/點菜 $ 150-400

Sang Kee Congee & Noodles (Sheung Wan) NEW
生記清湯牛腩麵家 (上環)

The same menu is available here as in the original premises which still operate just a few steps away in Burd Street and opened over forty years ago. However, as this ten-year old sibling is somewhat larger, it's a little easier to get a table here without waiting too long. Piping hot bowls of congee and tender beef brisket noodles draw the crowds, while the ladies who run it do so with alacrity and efficiency.

在這裡，菜單與相隔數步，早於四十年前已開幕的畢街總店相同。不過，由於這位年僅十歲的「弟弟」面積較大，在這裡不用久等就能取得座位。店裡不斷送上的一碗碗熱騰騰的粥和牛腩麵吸引大量食客，勤快的女店員動作敏捷、效率高。

■ ADDRESS/地址
TEL. 2541 8199
20 Hillier Street, Sheung Wan
上環禧利街20號

■ ANNUAL AND WEEKLY CLOSING
　　休息日期
Closed 1 week Lunar New Year,
Sunday and Public Holidays
農曆新年7天、週日及公眾假期休息

■ OPENING HOURS, LAST ORDER
　　營業時間，最後點菜時間
07:00-21:00

■ PRICE/價錢
à la carte/點菜　　　　　　　$19-35

Ser Wong Fun
蛇王芬

This restaurant was established 70 years ago and is now under the stewardship of the fourth generation, so it is little wonder that there has been a book celebrating the family history and their cherished recipes. Regulars flock here for the snake soup and snake banquets in winter. No less than 15 varieties of double-boiled soups and a vast array of seasonal pot dishes are also offered; add to that barbecue dishes and assorted seafood.

七十年前開店的蛇王芬如今由第四代傳人主理，更有出版書籍介紹家族歷史及其著名菜式。熟客經常來此品嚐蛇羹，冬天甚至品嚐蛇宴。超過十五種老火燉湯任君選擇，亦提供一系列煲仔飯；此外更提供燒烤雜錦海鮮。

■ ADDRESS/地址
TEL. 2543 1032
30 Cochrane Street, Central
中環閣麟街30號

■ ANNUAL AND WEEKLY CLOSING
  休息日期
Closed 4 days Lunar New Year
農曆新年休息4天

■ OPENING HOURS, LAST ORDER
  營業時間，最後點菜時間
11:00-22:30 (L.O.)

■ PRICE/價錢
Lunch/午膳   à la carte/點菜 $70-100
Dinner/晚膳 à la carte/點菜 $150-180

Shanghai Garden
紫玉蘭

🍽120 ☎🍴

It is known for its range of classic dishes from the provinces of Shanghai, Sichuan and Beijing and is hugely popular with local office staff at lunchtimes. The décor in the two large dining rooms may not be particularly noteworthy but it is the cuisine that's the attraction here. Specialities include deep-fried yellow croaker fish with sweet and sour sauce and sautéed freshwater shrimp; Beggar's chicken is worth ordering in advance.

紫玉蘭午市的經典上海、四川、北京菜在本地白領間早已聞名；相較兩個大型中菜廳，這裡的菜餚似乎更吸引。著名美食包括北京大紅袍松鼠黃魚及上海清炒河蝦仁。富貴雞應提早預訂——絕不會令你失望。

■ ADDRESS/地址
TEL. 2524 8181
1F, Hutchison House,
10 Harcourt Road, Central
中環夏慤道10號和記大廈1樓
www.maxims.com.hk

■ OPENING HOURS, LAST ORDER
營業時間，最後點菜時間
Lunch/午膳 11:30-14:30 (L.O.)
Dinner/晚膳 17:30-23:00 (L.O.)

■ PRICE/價錢
à la carte/點菜　　　　$ 180-438

Shanghai Xiao Nan Guo (Kowloon Bay)
上海小南國 (九龍灣)

✂✂

♿ 🛋20

What started off as a small family business in Shanghai has now grown into an international chain, with branches all over China and Hong Kong and even in Tokyo. This Kowloon outpost provides a stylish and contemporary environment in which to enjoy the flavoursome dishes. Along with drunken chicken in Shaoxing wine, look out for grandma's braised pork belly and pan-fried crispy pork soup bun. Dim sum is available at both lunch and dinner.

從上海一家小規模經營的家族生意開始,餐廳如今已成為國際知名的連鎖店,在中國、香港甚至東京都有分店。位於九龍的新店裝潢時尚現代,另你更投入享受佳肴。除了紹興花雕醉雞,更應嚐嚐外婆紅燒肉及灌湯生煎包。午餐及晚餐時段均供應點心。

■ ADDRESS/地址

TEL. 2545 0880

Unit 2, Level 6, Megabox,
38 Wang Chiu Road, Kowloon Bay
九龍灣宏照道38號Megabox6樓2號舖

■ OPENING HOURS, LAST ORDER
營業時間,最後點菜時間
Lunch/午膳 11:30-15:00 L.O. 14:30
Dinner/晚膳 18:00-23:00 L.O. 22:30

■ PRICE/價錢
à la carte/點菜 $ 200-650

Shang Palace
香宮

Four golden statues by the entrance welcome you to this sumptuous room that vividly evokes the grandeur of the Sung Dynasty. Red lacquered walls, antique paintings and classic lanterns only add to the authentic atmosphere. Highlights of the Cantonese menu include lobster, garoupa and scallop dumpling in supreme soup; pan-fried lamb chop with goose liver paste; braised Wu Xi spare rib casserole, and sautéed rice with crab meat and egg white.

大門的四個金色塑像歡迎你來到這家豪華的餐廳，宋朝的顯赫氣派活靈活現。紅色漆牆、古董國畫，以及傳統燈籠交織出古色古香的氣氛。這裡的粵菜亦同樣精巧，更提供不錯的素食菜式。烹調技巧出色，特色美色包括高湯龍皇果、鵝肝醬煎紐西蘭羊架、無錫焗排骨煲及宮廷兩儀飯。

■ ADDRESS/地址

TEL. 2733 8754

Lower level, Kowloon Shangri-La Hotel, 64 Mody Road, East Tsim Sha Tsui, Kowloon

九龍尖東麼地道64號
九龍香格里拉酒店地庫1樓
www.shangri-la.com

■ OPENING HOURS, LAST ORDER
營業時間，最後點菜時間
Lunch/午膳 12:00-15:00 (L.O.)
Dinner/晚膳 18:00-23:00 (L.O.)

■ PRICE/價錢

Lunch/午膳	set/套餐	$238-788
	à la carte/點菜	$300-1,000
Dinner/晚膳	set/套餐	$680-788
	à la carte/點菜	$300-1,000

She Wong Yee
蛇王二

Their signature snake soup has long been renowned and in winter around 1200 bowls are served each day, up until midnight. Regulars are quick to occupy one of the few tables for this memorable experience and it is no surprise that the recipe has remained unchanged for years. These days, those regulars come also for the famed barbecued meats and speciality sausages with rice; the roast goose and double-boiled soups are good too.

此著名蛇羹集團一向聞名四方，冬天平均每天賣出多達1200碗，營業至深夜零時。熟客急不及待佔駐其中一張桌，享受一貫的美味，不出所料，製法多年來從未改變。如今，熟客對其著名燒味及燒臘配飯亦趨之若鶩，燒鵝還有燉湯更具水準。要先在外面等等才有座位？你的等待將是有意義的。

■ ADDRESS/地址
TEL. 2831 0163
24 Percival Street, Causeway Bay
銅鑼灣波斯富街24號

■ ANNUAL AND WEEKLY CLOSING
   休息日期
Closed 3 days Lunar New Year
農曆新年休息3天

■ OPENING HOURS, LAST ORDER
   營業時間，最後點菜時間
11:30-00:00 (L.O.)

■ PRICE/價錢
à la carte/點菜 $ 50-80

212

Siu Shun Village Cuisine
肇順名匯河鮮專門店

Specialities such as stir-fried freshwater lobster with ginger and shallots; steamed pork spare ribs; fresh prawns in XO sauce, and the fish lips casserole draw plenty of locals to this restaurant specialising in Shun Tak cuisine. Located in a shopping mall, it's always crowded and noise levels can reach the lively end of the scale. Imitation bamboo and birdcage lampshades add to the somewhat eccentric decorative style.

這裡的著名菜式包括薑葱龍蝦球、檀香骨、XO醬炒花枝鮮蝦球、瓦撐煎焗魚咀吸引很多香港人來此品嘗順德菜。餐廳位於商場內，經常坐無虛席，從吵鬧聲可見其熱鬧氣氛。仿竹及雀籠燈罩令這裡的裝潢風格更顯特色。

■ ADDRESS/地址
TEL. 2798 9738
7F, MegaBox, 38 Wang Chiu Road, Kowloon Bay, Kowloon
九龍灣宏照道38號MegaBox7樓

■ OPENING HOURS, LAST ORDER
營業時間，最後點菜時間
Lunch/午膳　09:00-16:30 (L.O.)
Dinner/晚膳　18:00-23:30 (L.O.)

■ PRICE/價錢
Lunch/午膳　à la carte/點菜 $100-550
Dinner/晚膳　à la carte/點菜 $140-550

Snow Garden (Causeway Bay)
雪園 (銅鑼灣)

✕✕

🍴16 ◐🍴

Established in 1992 at this sleek business address and known for its carefully prepared, traditional Shanghainese cuisine, this contemporary styled restaurant operates like clockwork. Staff all share the same enthusiasm which is immediately evident in the warm welcome. The long-standing chef's specialities are steamed herring and deep-fried chicken skin with four spices. Dishes arrive thoughtfully assembled and bursting with flavour.

餐廳於1992年創辦於此商業區熱點，其賣點在於精心烹調的上海菜，人流絡繹不絕。聲聲溫暖的歡迎字句反應所有員工具的熱忱。四寶片皮雞是歷久不衰的廚師精選。菜式上碟經過精心編排，香味四溢。

■ ADDRESS/地址

TEL. 2881 6837
2F, Ming An Plaza, 8 Sunning Road, Causeway Bay
銅鑼灣新寧道8號民安廣場2樓
www.snow-garden.com

■ ANNUAL AND WEEKLY CLOSING
   休息日期
Closed 3 days Lunar New Year
農曆新年休息3天

■ OPENING HOURS, LAST ORDER
   營業時間，最後點菜時間
Lunch/午膳 11:30-14:45 (L.O.)
Dinner/晚膳 18:00-22:45 (L.O.)

■ PRICE/價錢
Lunch/午膳   set/套餐 $120
           à la carte/點菜 $250-650
Dinner/晚膳 set/套餐 $488
           à la carte/點菜 $250-650

Sorabol (Causeway Bay) NEW
新羅寶（銅鑼灣）

♟ ♺70

A Korean restaurant, often busy with larger groups who come to share dishes and do their own barbecuing on the grills on each table. Beef is obviously one of the most popular choices but it is worth considering the specials and the hotpots, including the threateningly named Genghis Khan. With plenty of side dishes included with the main dishes, everyone leaves satisfied and the professional staff are on hand to keep things moving along.

前來韓國餐廳的客人，通常都是一行數人，前來一同分享美食及享受自助韓國燒烤的樂趣。牛肉肯定是最受歡迎的選擇之一，但不要忘了特色精選及火鍋，包括名字很吸引的「成吉思汗」。此外，大量伴菜和主菜令每個人都能飽腹，專業的員工忙得停不下來，以維持餐廳順暢運作。

■ ADDRESS/地址
TEL. 2881 6823
17F, Lee Theatre Plaza, 99 Percival Street, Causeway Bay
銅鑼灣波斯富街99號利舞臺廣場17樓
www.sorabol.com.hk

■ OPENING HOURS, LAST ORDER
營業時間，最後點菜時間
Lunch/午膳 11:30-15:00 L.O. 14:30
Dinner/晚膳 18:00-23:00 L.O. 22:30

■ PRICE/價錢
Lunch/午膳   set/套餐 $68-95
             à la carte/點菜 $150-500
Dinner/晚膳 à la carte/點菜 $250-500

Spoon by Alain Ducasse

Fantastic views, stylish seating, a ceiling lined with spoons and an impressive glass cellar holding around 600 wines – characteristics of this fashionable outpost of the Alain Ducasse empire. The carefully prepared, French cuisine suits this environment well. Signature dishes include steamed duck foie gras with fruit condiment and brioche, and baked suzuki with asparagus, black truffle and Argenteuil sauce.

美妙景觀、時尚雅座、排列著匙羹的天花板，加上擺放了接近600瓶佳釀令人嘆為觀止的玻璃酒櫃，打造成名廚艾倫杜卡斯（Alain Ducasse）美食王國的香港分部，實為潮流時尚之選。精心炮製的當代法國菜與優美環境相得益彰。招牌菜包括蒸法國鴨肝伴乾果醬配牛油包及焗鱸魚伴青露筍跟黑松露菌。

■ ADDRESS/地址
TEL. 2313 2256
GF, Intercontinental Hotel,
18 Salisbury Road, Tsim Sha Tsui,
Kowloon
九龍尖沙咀梳士巴利道18號
洲際酒店地下
www.hongkong-ic.intercontinental.com

■ OPENING HOURS, LAST ORDER
　營業時間，最後點菜時間
Sunday lunch/週日午膳 12:00-14:30
Dinner/晚膳 18:00-23:30 (L.O.)
■ PRICE/價錢
Sunday lunch/週日午膳 set/套餐 $558
　　　　　à la carte/點菜 $ 660-1,420
Dinner/晚膳　set/套餐　　$988
　　　　　à la carte/點菜 $ 660-1,420

Spring Moon
嘉麟樓

An elegant and luxurious Cantonese restaurant, which appears to be very much at home in The Peninsula. Admire the tropical hardwood or the bamboo flower arrangements while sipping tea at the tea bar, or dine in the restaurant or on the more intimate mezzanine floor where refined service oversees authentic dishes with flavour. There are 25 different teas available and you can even call upon the services of a 'tea sommelier'.

嘉麟樓位於半島酒店內，是一家優雅豪華的粵菜餐廳，令人感覺舒適。食客可以邊在"茶檔"茗茶，邊欣賞餐廳內的熱帶硬木或竹花排列。你可以選擇在餐廳內或在較隱蔽的私家房內用餐，完善的服務配合味道濃郁的原味菜餚。這裏有25種茶可供選擇，你甚至可要求「茗茶師」為你調配名茶。

■ ADDRESS/地址
TEL. 2315 3160
1F, The Peninsula Hotel, Salisbury Road, Tsim Sha Tsui, Kowloon
九龍尖沙咀梳士巴利道半島酒店1樓
www.peninsula.com

■ OPENING HOURS, LAST ORDER
營業時間, 最後點菜時間
Lunch/午膳 11:30-14:30 (L.O.)
Dinner/晚膳 18:00-22:30 (L.O.)

■ PRICE/價錢
Lunch/午膳	set/套餐	$368-448
	à la carte/點菜	$300-800
Dinner/晚膳	set/套餐	$928-1,988
	à la carte/點菜	$500-1,500

Steik World Meats   NEW

XX ⚹

⟷26

There may be lobster, mussels, tiger prawns and scallops on the menu but the majority of the customers come here for the beef. The assorted cuts come mostly from the USA, Australia, Scotland and Japan; the dry-ageing is done in-house and in-view above the partially open kitchen. The restaurant is contemporary, but undoubtedly masculine in style; the booths are the most popular spots. Its discreet location also adds to the clubby feel.

餐牌上不乏龍蝦、青口、虎蝦和帶子，但大部份客人都是慕牛肉之名而來。這裡的牛扒主要來自美國、澳洲、蘇格蘭及日本。半開放式廚房設有dry-aged（風乾）櫃，既可自行風乾牛肉，又可吸引客人注目。餐廳設計時尚，風格充滿陽剛味，廂座很受歡迎。獨特的位置也令餐廳更添俱樂部感覺。

■ ADDRESS/地址

TEL. 2530 0011

Level 3, K11, 18 Hanoi Road,
Tsim Sha Tsui, Kowloon
九龍尖沙咀河內道18號K11 3樓
www.epicurean.com.hk

■ OPENING HOURS, LAST ORDER
  營業時間，最後點菜時間
Lunch/午膳 12:00-15:00 (L.O.)
Dinner/晚膳 18:00-23:30 L.O.22:30

■ PRICE/價錢

Lunch/午膳	set/套餐	$ 166-326
	à la carte/點菜	$ 250-1,000
Dinner/晚膳	set/套餐	$ 538-638
	à la carte/點菜	$ 250-1,000

St. George   NEW

The beams, vaulted ceiling, chandeliers and fireplaces add intimacy to a comfortable and discreet first floor dining room, whose atmosphere evokes that of a gentlemen's club. The private dining rooms are equally appealing and also come furnished with antiques. By contrast, the French and European inspired cuisine is far more contemporary, with dishes given such titles as 'scallops cappuccino' or 'white jaffa'.

橫樑、拱形天花、吊燈與壁爐為這位於一樓，既舒適又隱密的餐廳增加不少親切感，餐廳的氣氛讓人聯想起昔日的紳士俱樂部。餐廳的私人宴會廳，以古董做裝飾，同樣格調典雅華麗。與裝潢剛好相反，由法國菜及歐洲菜得到靈感的菜式非常大膽創新，從"帶子卡布奇諾"或"白雅法"等新奇名字即可見一斑。

■ ADDRESS/地址

TEL. 3988 0220
Hullett House, 2A Canton Road, Tsim Sha Tsui, Kowloon
九龍尖沙咀廣東道2A Hullett House
www.hulletthouse.com

■ ANNUAL AND WEEKLY CLOSING
   休息日期
Closed Sunday
週日休息

■ OPENING HOURS, LAST ORDER
   營業時間，最後點菜時間
Lunch/午膳 12:00-14:30 (L.O.)
Dinner/晚膳 19:00-22:30 (L.O.)

■ PRICE/價錢
Lunch/午膳	set/套餐	$320-398
	à la carte/點菜	$650-1,100
Dinner/晚膳	set/套餐	$888-1,188
	à la carte/點菜	$650-1,100

Summer Palace
夏宮

They've created a charming environment here in this 5th floor room, with its crystal chandeliers, traditional Chinese screens and well-placed tables. The Cantonese menu features all the true classics and the kitchen uses carefully chosen ingredients prepared without fussiness or over-elaboration. To drink, there's a varied selection of wines by the glass, Chinese liquors and exquisite teas.

他們在這位於五樓的空間營造了迷人的環境，配上水晶吊燈、傳統中國屏風及精心佈置的餐桌。粵菜菜譜提供所有經典名菜，廚房精心挑選食材，烹調時井井有條，毫不過火。餐酒方面具杯裝西洋餐酒、中國酒和高級茗茶。

■ ADDRESS/地址
TEL. 2820 8553
5F, Island Shangri-La Hotel, Pacific Place,
Supreme Court Road, Admiralty
中區法院道太古廣場
港島香格里拉酒店5樓
www.shangri-la.com

■ OPENING HOURS, LAST ORDER
營業時間，最後點菜時間
Lunch/午膳 11:30-14:30 (L.O.)
Dinner/晚膳 18:30-22:30 (L.O.)

■ PRICE/價錢
Lunch/午膳　set/套餐　　$ 590-1,340
　　　　　　à la carte/點菜 $ 280-1,200
Dinner/晚膳 set/套餐　　$ 400-1,540
　　　　　　à la carte/點菜 $ 280-1,200

Sun Kau Kee Noodle Shop NEW
新九記粥麵

Most residents of Wan Chai will know this shop as it's been here for around twenty years and, although it's now under the stewardship of the former managers and chef, little has really changed in all that time. This is one of the few places to offer congee hotpot so try it and you can be assured of a table; if you want noodles then you'll just have to join the queue. It's also worth sampling the beef flank with tendons.

大部分灣仔居民都認識這已有約二十年歷史的店鋪。這裡雖然掌管的經理和廚師都不同了，但除此之外改變不大。這是少數提供火鍋以粥做湯底的地方，試試看，絕不會讓你失望。如果你想吃麵，就要花時間排隊了。這裡的牛筋腩也非常有名。

■ ADDRESS/地址
TEL. 2865 2827
9 Tai Wong Street East, Wan Chai
灣仔大王東街9號

■ ANNUAL AND WEEKLY CLOSING
　休息日期
Closed 10 days Lunar New Year and Sunday
農曆新年10天及週日休息

■ OPENING HOURS, LAST ORDER
　營業時間，最後點菜時間
11:00-01:00

■ PRICE/價錢
à la carte/點菜　　　　　　$ 20-40

Sun Tung Lok NEW
新同樂

✿ ✿ ✿   ✗✗✗✗

🍽20 ☎🍴

After 40 years in Happy Valley, Sun Tung Lok is now comfortably installed on the fourth floor of the Miramar shopping centre. A contemporary colour palette of grey, brown and beige is used to good effect in this stylish restaurant; ask for one of the three booths for extra privacy. 80% of the menu is Cantonese; examples include rib of beef with house gravy, stuffed crab shell, and roast suckling pig.

在跑馬地經營了40年後，新同樂現在於美麗華商場的4樓重新開張。充滿時代感的灰色、咖啡色與米色在這家摩登酒家裡被巧妙運用。設有3個廂坐，以供需要多點私隱的客人選擇。八成菜式是粵菜，包括燒汁乾逼牛肋骨、鮮蘑菇焗釀蟹蓋及燒乳豬件。

■ ADDRESS/地址
TEL. 2152 1417
4F, Miramar Shopping Centre,
132 Nathan Road, Tsim Sha Tsui,
Kowloon
九龍尖沙咀彌敦道132號美麗華商場4樓

■ OPENING HOURS, LAST ORDER
營業時間，最後點菜時間
Lunch/午膳 11:30-15:00 (L.O.)
Dinner/晚膳 18:00-23:00 (L.O.)

■ PRICE/價錢

Lunch/午膳	set/套餐	$150-7,680
	à la carte/點菜	$220-5,000
Dinner/晚膳	set/套餐	$498-7,680
	à la carte/點菜	$220-5,000

Sun Yuen Hing Kee　NEW
新園興記

This traditionally styled, simple but well maintained barbecue shop has been run by the same family since the mid 1970s. Over the years they've built up quite an appreciative following so the small place fills quickly. The appetising looking suckling pigs hanging next to the kitchen are not the only draw here: roasted pork, duck and pigeon all have their followers, as does the soft-boiled chicken. It's located next to Sheung Wan market.

這家格調傳統，簡單而又保養得宜的燒味店自70年代中一直由同一家族經營。多年來，他們已累積了不少忠實顧客，所以小小的地方很快便坐無虛席。這裡受歡迎的不僅是掛在廚房旁邊，賣相令人垂涎欲滴的乳豬、燒肉、烤鴨、乳鴿，和白切雞都各有忠實擁躉。燒味店位於上環街市旁邊。

■ ADDRESS/地址
TEL. 2541 2207
327-329 Queen's Road Central,
Sheung Wan
上環皇后大道中327-329號

■ ANNUAL AND WEEKLY CLOSING
　休息日期
Closed 5 days Lunar New Year
農曆新年休息5天

■ OPENING HOURS, LAST ORDER
　營業時間，最後點菜時間
08:00-19:45 (L.O.)

■ PRICE/價錢
à la carte/點菜　　　　　$ 80-150

Sushi Kato
加藤壽司

A friendly little eatery that's worth searching out – don't be put off because it's on the first floor of an apartment block. The cosy interior has hand-made wood panelling, and Mr Kato himself is at the sushi bar. Straightforward menus are served at simple tables: sashimi, salads, soups, bento boxes, noodles, and a selection of grilled, fried or steamed favourites. It's good value; all the dishes are fresh, carefully prepared and authentic.

這家親切的小壽司店,位於一幢公寓大樓的一樓,但不要因此而卻步,這店實在值得專程尋找。店裡很舒適,採用了手工製作的木質鑲板,而加藤先生就在壽司吧親自下廚。簡單的餐桌配合簡單的菜單,菜式包括魚生、沙律、湯類、便當、麵食,以及一系列的精選烤物、炸物或蒸物。菜式純正,採用新鮮食材,準備細心,是超值之選。

■ ADDRESS/地址

TEL. 2807 3613
Shop 7-9, 1F, 20-36 Wharf Road, North Point
北角和富道20-36號1樓7-9號舖

■ ANNUAL AND WEEKLY CLOSING
　休息日期
Closed Tuesday
週二休息

■ OPENING HOURS, LAST ORDER
　營業時間,最後點菜時間
Lunch/午膳　12:00-14:00 (L.O.)
Dinner/晚膳　18:00-22:00 (L.O.)

■ PRICE/價錢
Lunch/午膳　set/套餐　　　　$100-200
　　　　　　à la carte/點菜　$150-300
Dinner/晚膳　à la carte/點菜　$350-680

Sushi Kuu
壽司喰

Casual and relaxed, Sushi Kuu is unlike the more formal style Japanese restaurant you might be used to. The bar features an impressive sake list, while the sushi counter is always popular with late-night revellers. You can also eat at tables by the bar, or in window booths overlooking busy Wyndham Street. There's a good choice of Japanese specialities, including traditional sushi and sashimi arriving every day from Japan; tempura and noodles.

壽司喰洋溢著輕鬆隨意的氣氛，不像那些風格較為正式的日本餐廳。吧檯提供令人驚喜的清酒選擇，而壽司吧則永遠都受夜遊客歡迎。食客亦可以選擇在吧檯附近的餐桌用餐，或是靠窗的雅座，邊吃邊俯瞰繁忙的雲咸街。這裡有不錯的日本菜選擇，包括傳統壽司、魚生，每天由日本新鮮運到，更有天婦羅及麵食可供選擇。

■ ADDRESS/地址

TEL. 2971 0180
1F, Wellington Place, 2-8 Wellington Street, Central
中環威靈頓街2-8號威靈頓廣場1樓

■ ANNUAL AND WEEKLY CLOSING
　休息日期
Closed Lunar New Year
年初一休息

■ OPENING HOURS, LAST ORDER
　營業時間，最後點菜時間
Lunch/午膳　12:00-15:00 (L.O.)
Dinner/晚膳　18:00-23:00 (L.O.)

■ PRICE/價錢
Lunch/午膳　set/套餐　　　　$130-280
　　　　　　à la carte/點菜　$250-600
Dinner/晚膳　à la carte/點菜　$250-600

Sushi Shota
壽司翔太

Here you're guaranteed respite from the bustle of Lockhart Road; so just take a seat at the counter and watch the master at work. Sushi, sashimi, maki and tempura are the specialities but fish is also steamed with impressive precision. Need some help on what to order? The chef and his equally friendly assistants are only too willing to advise. A concise but well chosen sake list completes the picture.

在此，你肯定可獲得一絲寧靜，遠離駱克道的煩囂；坐在壽司吧前看看師傅的手藝吧。壽司、魚生、手卷、天婦羅是精選餐點，蒸魚的時間亦控制得非常準確。不知道該怎麼選擇？大廚與他友善的助手們會熱情地向你提供建議。日本酒的選擇不算多，卻五臟俱全。

■ ADDRESS/地址

TEL. 2834 3031

8F, Kyoto Plaza, 491-499 Lockhart Road, Causeway Bay

銅鑼灣駱克道491-499號京都廣場8樓

■ OPENING HOURS, LAST ORDER
營業時間，最後點菜時間
Lunch/午膳 11:45-14:30 (L.O.)
Dinner/晚膳 18:00-22:30 (L.O.)

■ PRICE/價錢

Lunch/午膳	set/套餐	$ 250-320
	à la carte/點菜	$ 250-680
Dinner/晚膳	set/套餐	$ 500-680
	à la carte/點菜	$ 250-680

226

Tai Wing Wah
大榮華

Anyone travelling all the way to Yuen Long (in the North of New Territories) can seek reward for doing so by visiting this restaurant. Tai Wing Wah is found above its own cake shop, which specialises in moon cakes and Chinese sausages. It serves dim sum throughout the day and 'Walled Village' cuisine, alongside classic Cantonese dishes. Many come for the chicken in five spices, baked fish roe with eggs and, above all, the steamed egg cake.

很多人長途跋涉來到元朗(新界北部),只有一個原因:為了來大榮華。大榮華位於其餅店樓上,餅店專門售賣月餅和臘腸。除了全日提供的點心外,還提供圍村菜及經典粵菜。五味雞、魚春蒸蛋之外,當然少不了奶黃馬拉糕。

■ ADDRESS/地址
TEL. 2476 9888
2F, 2-6 On Ning Road,
Yuen Long, New Territories
新界元朗安寧路2-6號2樓

■ OPENING HOURS, LAST ORDER
營業時間,最後點菜時間
06:30-23:30 (L.O.)

■ PRICE/價錢
à la carte/點菜 $ 80-250

Tai Woo (Causeway Bay)
太湖海鮮城 (銅鑼灣)

⚔⚔

🕧 24

In a dense, busy street, this is easy to spot from the series of aquaria displayed on the outside. Inside, the staircase lined with culinary awards leads to some fairly modest but busy dining rooms where the freshest of seafood is brought – both live and cooked – up to a never-ending stream of regulars. Prawns in salted egg yolk and baked lobster with supreme sauce are perennial favourites. Most tables opt for the signature crispy juicy stewed beef.

即使在人來人往的繁華街道上，太湖海鮮城亦容易被找到，皆因外面展示著一系列的魚缸。餐廳的樓梯羅列著眾多的美食獎項，帶來並不奢華卻擠滿捧場客的進餐區。這裡的海鮮極其新鮮，大量生猛海鮮以供選購，故此捧場客絡繹不絕。西施伴霸王及上湯焗龍蝦等菜式長期大受歡迎。大部分食客都會點上一味馳名三弄回味牛肉。

■ ADDRESS/地址

TEL. 2893 0822

27 Percival Street, Causeway Bay
銅鑼灣波斯富街27號
www.taiwoorestaurant.com

■ OPENING HOURS, LAST ORDER
營業時間，最後點菜時間
10:30-03:00 L.O. 02:15

■ PRICE/價錢

Lunch/午膳   set/套餐 $268
              à la carte/點菜 $200-390

Dinner/晚膳   à la carte/點菜 $200-390

Tak Lung
得龍

Tak Long moved to its current San Po Kong location in 1963, and this successful operation is now being run by the second-generation owner. It comes divided into two dining rooms; try to get a table in the brighter main room. Business remains brisk thanks to the sensible prices and the popularity of signature dishes such as baked oyster in port wine, sweet and sour pork and 'grandpa chicken' which involves a 100 year old recipe from Guangzhou.

得龍大飯店於1963年搬遷至新蒲崗現址，這家成功的飯店現在由第二代繼承人經營。飯店由兩個舖位組成，盡可能選擇在較明亮的一邊。由於價錢相宜，招牌菜又廣受歡迎，這裡客似雲來。招牌菜包括砵酒焗桶蠔、山楂咕嚕肉，以及按有100歷史的廣州食譜炮製的古法太爺雞。

■ ADDRESS/地址
TEL. 2320 7020
25-29 Hong Keung Street,
San Po Kong, Kowloon
九龍新蒲崗康強街25號
www.taklung.com.hk

■ OPENING HOURS, LAST ORDER
營業時間，最後點菜時間
06:00-23:30 L.O.23:00

■ PRICE/價錢

Lunch/午膳	set/套餐	$118-288
	à la carte/點菜	$80-250
Dinner/晚膳	à la carte/點菜	$80-250

Tak Yue   NEW
得如茶樓

Tak Yue would never win any design awards. Indeed, its two large dining rooms could be considered somewhat ugly and are not helped by the presence of spittoons. It opened in the 1920s and some of the waiters give the impression they started working here not long after. What sets it apart, however, is the quality of its dim sum, served from 5.30am, as well as the Cantonese dishes such as sweet corn soup, prawns and the pork cooked with cashew nuts.

得如茶樓肯定不會贏得任何設計獎項。的確,兩個大型飯廳外貌可能並不吸引,即使有痰盂也不能彌補甚麼。茶樓於1920年代開張,有些侍應似乎在開店後不久就已經在這裡工作。不過,說到點心的品質,這裡絕對是首選。早上5:30已開始供應點心,更有廣東菜如粟米羹、醬爆腰果豬肉蝦粒。

■ ADDRESS/地址
TEL. 2388 3884
378 Shanghai Street,
Yau Ma tei, Kowloon
九龍油麻地上海街378號

■ OPENING HOURS, LAST ORDER
營業時間,最後點菜時間
Lunch/午膳 05:00-14:30 (L.O.)
Dinner/晚膳 18:00-21:30 (L.O.)

■ PRICE/價錢
Lunch/午膳　à la carte/點菜 $ 60-180
Dinner/晚膳　à la carte/點菜 $ 100-180

Tam's Yunnan Noodles (Jordan Road)
譚仔雲南米線 (佐敦道)

One thing you won't be able to do is miss the bright yellow and green sign. This is one of a chain of eateries popular for its Sichuan-style spicy rice noodles. You simply pick one of three soup bases (clear soup, sour & spicy and super spicy); decide on the level of heat and then choose your own toppings to go with it. There are also three types of delicious chicken wings to add as a side dish. Just be prepared to do some queuing.

你絕不可能錯過這明亮的黃綠色招牌！這四川風味麻辣米線店極受歡迎，可從三種湯底（清湯、酸辣、麻辣）挑選，再選擇辣度和你喜歡的配料。另外，更有三款美味鷄翼可作為小菜。做好排隊的心理準備吧。

■ ADDRESS/地址

TEL. 2302 0982
36 Jordan Road, Jordan, Kowloon
九龍佐敦佐敦道36號

■ ANNUAL AND WEEKLY CLOSING
　休息日期
Closed 5 days Lunar New Year
農曆新年休息5天

■ OPENING HOURS, LAST ORDER
　營業時間，最後點菜時間
11:15-23:15 (L.O.)

■ PRICE/價錢

set/套餐	$ 40
à la carte/點菜	$ 21-50

Tam's Yunnan Noodles (Sham Shui Po)
譚仔雲南米線 (深水埗)

It's easy to see why there are now more than ten branches of this family-owned noodle business. For a start, the concept works well: you choose your own spice level and the ingredient you would like added to your clear soup – the choice ranges from beef slices and tofu to cabbage or meatballs. Then you simply find a space and share a table with others. If it's too busy you can always just cross the street to find another of their shops.

不難發現這家家庭式經營的麵店迅速擴張至十家分店的原因。一開始，概念就對了：你可以選擇適合自己的辣度和喜歡加到清湯裡的材料。選擇繁多，從牛肉片到豆腐到椰菜或肉丸都有。然後，你只需找個空位，與其他食客「搭桌」。餐廳經常都很忙碌，但在對面街就可輕易找到其另一家分店。

■ ADDRESS/地址
TEL. 2708 7055
107 Fuk Wing Street,
Sham Shui Po, Kowloon
深水埗福榮街107號

■ OPENING HOURS, LAST ORDER
    營業時間，最後點菜時間
10:30-24:00 (L.O.)

■ PRICE/價錢
à la carte/點菜 $ 25-50

T'ang Court
唐閣

Rich silks and contemporary art line the walls of the lavishly furnished main dining room, on the first floor above the hotel's grand lobby. There's also a dramatic staircase leading up to a second floor of tables and exclusive private dining rooms named after famous Tang Dynasty poets. The cooking displays considerable skill, with particular emphasis on seafood. The service is also well structured and polished.

豐厚的絲緞配合富當代氣息的牆身，裝潢豪華的主菜廳位於酒店大堂樓上。一道極盡奢華的樓梯連上二樓各餐桌，更設有以唐代著名詩人命名的貴賓廳。菜餚極具功夫，海鮮更是當中首推菜式。服務經過精心編排。

■ ADDRESS/地址
TEL. 2375 1133
1F, The Langham Hotel, 8 Peking Road, Tsim Sha Tsui, Kowloon
九龍尖沙咀北京道8號朗廷酒店1樓
www.hongkong.langhamhotels.com

■ OPENING HOURS, LAST ORDER
營業時間，最後點菜時間
Lunch/午膳 12:00-15:00 L.O. 14:30
Dinner/晚膳 18:00-23:00 L.O. 22:30

■ PRICE/價錢
Lunch/午膳   set/套餐 $248-650
           à la carte/點菜 $160-2,000
Dinner/晚膳   set/套餐 $650
           à la carte/點菜 $300-2,000

Tasty (Happy Valley)
正斗粥麵專家 (跑馬地)

Worth searching out because this is more than your average noodle dining experience. There's a sophisticated air, with polished wood enhancing a feeling of exclusivity. Waitresses wear colourful uniforms, and many customers call them over for the legendary wonton noodles. The range of congee toppings is comprehensive, while chef's special dim sum includes roast pork bun with saucy filling and pomelo skin with shrimp roe.

這裡值得你花時間走一趟，因為此店有非一般的水準。這裡氣氛濃厚，拋光的木飾更添一種獨享感覺。服務員制服色彩繽紛，許多客人被口碑載道的雲吞麵深深吸引。粥的配菜種類很全面，同樣是廚師的點心特別推介包括流汁叉燒飽及蝦子柚子皮。

■ ADDRESS/地址
TEL. 2838 3922
21 King Kwong Street, Happy Valley
跑馬地景光街21號

■ OPENING HOURS, LAST ORDER
　營業時間，最後點菜時間
11:30-24:00 (L.O.)

■ PRICE/價錢
Lunch/午膳　à la carte/點菜 $35-65
Dinner/晚膳　à la carte/點菜 $60-120

Tasty (Hung Hom)
正斗粥麵專家 (紅磡)

It's quite modest and simple inside, with dark wood walls and Chinese decorations but it's all enlivened by friendly and efficient waitresses. You can't reserve here and it's often so busy you're forced to queue. It's worth it, though, for the quality of the noodles, soup, congee and dim sum. Try dishes like salted lean pork and preserved egg congee or stir-fried rice noodle with beef. You won't be disappointed and you won't pay much either.

餐廳裝潢樸實簡單，深木色的牆身和中國傳統擺設。友善而高效率的女侍應更增加餐廳活力。這裡食客眾多，但沒有訂座服務，因此經常需要排隊輪候。不過，這裡的麵、湯、粥和點心都是優質美食，實在值得排隊等候。推介菜式包括皮蛋瘦肉粥或乾炒牛河。此外，這裡的菜式價錢相宜，絕對不會令你失望！

■ ADDRESS/地址

TEL. 3152 2328
Shop 111, 1F, Whampoa Plaza,
Site 8, Hung Hom, Kowloon
九龍紅磡黃埔花園第8期1樓111號舖

■ OPENING HOURS, LAST ORDER
營業時間，最後點菜時間
11:30-23:30 (L.O.)

■ PRICE/價錢
à la carte/點菜 $ 75-150

Tasty (IFC)
正斗粥麵專家（國際金融中心）

Sleek mall surroundings enhance Tasty's strikingly elaborate facade of ornate wood and coloured glass. Inside it's just as vivid: walls covered with 30,000 chopsticks, handmade chairs with intricate floral patterns, and eye-catching metal pots. You'll probably be asked to share a table before tucking into the hallmark shrimp wonton or the much-loved beef and rice noodle stir fry. Also recommended from the vast choice is congee with prawns.

豪華的商場環境突顯了正斗的木飾和彩色玻璃外觀。餐廳裡同樣有生氣：牆壁佈滿一萬五千雙筷子，手工椅子上有複雜精細的花卉圖案，還有引人注目的金屬壺。你可能需與人搭枱，不過能享用美食便值回票價。熱門菜包括招牌鮮蝦雲吞麵，或備受喜愛的干炒牛河。此外，在芸芸選擇中，我們特別推介生猛大蝦粥。

■ ADDRESS/地址
TEL. 2295 0101
Shop 3016, Podium Level 3, IFC Mall,
1 Harbour View Street, Central
中環港景街1號國際金融中心商場
3樓3016號舖

■ OPENING HOURS, LAST ORDER
營業時間，最後點菜時間
11:30-22:45 (L.O.)

■ PRICE/價錢
à la carte/點菜 $ 75-150

Tasty (Kowloon Bay)   NEW
正斗粥麵專家 (九龍灣)

Old black and white photos of local streets are here to remind diners that this growing chain began life as a street food business back in the 1950s. This branch, located within the Telford Plaza shopping mall, is delightfully decorated with Chinese inspired furniture and the kitchen is on view behind the window. The menu offers a large selection of traditional congee, noodles in soup, fried noodles and dim sum served all day.

香港街道的黑白照，提醒著顧客這家正不斷發展的連鎖麵店，其實早在50年代巳由街頭小店開始經營。這家位於德福廣場的分店，採用中式傢俬，顧客可透過店內的大玻璃窗清楚看到廚房的情況。餐牌羅列了許多全日供應的傳統粥品、湯麵、炒麵與點心。

■ ADDRESS/地址
TEL. 2795 2828
Shop F1, Level 1, Telford Plaza 1, Kowloon Bay
九號灣德福廣場第1期1樓F1號舖

■ OPENING HOURS, LAST ORDER
營業時間，最後點菜時間
11:30-23:00 L.O.22:45

■ PRICE/價錢
à la carte/點菜 $ 70-170

Thai Basil

Shoppers in Pacific Place mall can seek sustenance here, from a wide ranging menu of straightforward dishes which include the likes of soft shell crab tempura and king prawns in yellow curry. Don't miss the sticky banana pudding with honey ice cream to boost those energy levels. The simple wooden furniture and friendly young team of servers help create a relaxed atmosphere in this large dining room, which is open all day.

於太古廣場購物的人士可在此一解飢腸，餐單提供林林總總的選擇，從較簡單的菜式一如軟殼蟹米紙卷，或是大虎蝦黃咖喱，任君選擇。別錯過讓你精神百倍的雪糕香蕉布甸。簡約的木製家具和友善年輕的服務生在此偌大的餐廳營造悠閒氣氛，全日開放。

■ ADDRESS/地址

TEL. 2537 4682
Shop 001, LG, Pacific Place,
88 Queensway, Admiralty
香港金鐘道88號太古廣場地庫1樓1號舖

■ OPENING HOURS, LAST ORDER
營業時間，最後點菜時間
11:30-22:30 (L.O.)

■ PRICE/價錢
à la carte/點菜　　　　$ 220-320

Thai Chiu　NEW
泰潮

Hainannese chicken; tom yum kung with seafood; fried egg with herbs and the various different styles of curry are just some of the highlights from an extensive menu prepared by native Thai chefs at this simple little restaurant. It's made up of two modest dining rooms, both decorated in bright green and yellow, with plastic tables and small stools. But the food is good and the prices are competitive.

海南雞、海鮮冬蔭功、香草炒蛋及一系列咖哩只是選擇繁多的菜單的其中一部分，一律由這家簡樸小餐廳的泰藉廚師主理。餐廳由兩個飯廳組成，都以亮綠及黃色裝潢，加上膠桌和小板凳。食物美味，價錢相宜。

■ ADDRESS/地址
TEL. 2314 3333
101-103 Fuk Wing Street,
Sham Shui Po, Kowloon
九龍深水涉福榮街101-103號

■ ANNUAL AND WEEKLY CLOSING
　　休息日期
Closed 3 days Lunar New Year
農曆新年休息3天

■ OPENING HOURS, LAST ORDER
　　營業時間，最後點菜時間
12:00-23:30 L.O.23:00

■ PRICE/價錢

Lunch/午膳	set/套餐	$36
	à la carte/點菜	$60-150
Dinner/晚膳	set/套餐	$40
	à la carte/點菜	$60-150

The Chairman   NEW
大班樓

🍴🍴

🛋20   📞🍴

The Chairman looks to small suppliers and local fishermen for its ingredients and much of the produce used is also organic. Showing respect for the provenance of ingredients, and using them in such flavoursome dishes as steamed crab with aged ShaoXing or braised beef brisket in a herbed broth, has clearly attracted a loyal following. The restaurant is divided into four different sections and service is pleasant and reassuringly experienced.

大班樓的食材來自小型供應商和本地漁民，大部分都是有機材料。如此重視採購，更將精挑細選的材料用於美味菜式，如雞油花雕蒸大花蟹、紅麴糯米酒醬油炆金錢蹍，吸引不少忠實擁躉。餐廳分成四個不同用餐區，服務令人賓至如歸。

■ ADDRESS/地址
TEL. 2555 2202
18 Kau U Fong, Central
中環九如坊18號
www.thechairmangroup.com

■ OPENING HOURS, LAST ORDER
營業時間，最後點菜時間
Lunch/午膳 12:00-14:30
Dinner/晚膳 18:00-22:30

■ PRICE/價錢
Lunch/午膳   set/套餐 $148
           à la carte/點菜 $380-470
Dinner/晚膳   set/套餐 $428-528
           à la carte/點菜 $380-470

The Chinese Restaurant
凱悅軒

As the name more than suggests, this restaurant, located on the 3rd floor of the Hyatt Regency, offers Chinese cuisine. Dishes such as double boiled crab meat soup; fried prawns with premium soy sauce; roast barbecued pork and crispy chicken Loong Kong are among the specialities. At lunch, the all-you-can-eat dim sum is a bestseller. The décor adds Chinese influences to a contemporary palette. There's also a large terrace.

餐廳一如其名，坐落凱悅酒店三樓，供應中菜。四寶燉萬壽果、頭遍生抽焗花竹蝦、蜜汁叉燒及脆皮龍崗雞均屬名菜之列。中午時分的任食點心最受歡迎。餐廳裝潢在現代色彩中加上一抹中國特色。餐廳亦有大型露台。

■ ADDRESS/地址
TEL. 2311 1234
3F, Hyatt Regency, 18 Hanoi Road,
Tsim Sha Tsui, Kowloon
九龍尖沙咀河內道18號凱悅酒店3樓
www.hongkong.tsimshatsui.hyatt.com

■ OPENING HOURS, LAST ORDER
    營業時間，最後點菜時間
Lunch/午膳 11:30-14:30 (L.O.)
Dinner/晚膳 18:30-22:30 (L.O.)

■ PRICE/價錢
Lunch/午膳   set/套餐 $198
                  à la carte/點菜 $240-560
Dinner/晚膳 à la carte/點菜 $240-560

The Drawing Room

The Drawing Room is a warm and stylish restaurant on the first floor of the chic JIA boutique hotel. The striking and original metal art pieces from local creators are quite a feature and the bar sets the mood – this is a place to be seen. Choose from the two daily-changing Italian set menus created with the best available ingredients. This is accompanied by a comprehensive wine list covering most regions of Italy.

位於時尚酒店JIA的一樓，溫暖而具流行風格。本地藝術家創作了讓人一見難忘的原創金屬藝術品，甚具特色，酒吧更洋溢情調，這裡的一切都是賞心悅目的視覺饗宴。可從兩款每日更替的菜單中選擇，全由當日最佳新鮮食材炮製。這裡的意大利菜單配合齊全的酒牌，網羅來自意大利各地的美酒。

■ ADDRESS/地址
TEL. 2915 6628
1F, 1-5 Irving Street, Causeway Bay
銅鑼灣伊榮街1-5號1樓
www.thedrawingroom.com.hk

■ ANNUAL AND WEEKLY CLOSING
　休息日期
Closed Sunday
週日休息

■ OPENING HOURS, LAST ORDER
　營業時間，最後點菜時間
Dinner/晚膳 18:00-23:00 (L.O.)

■ PRICE/價錢
Dinner/晚膳　set/套餐　　　$620-780
　　　　　　à la carte/點菜 $610-700

The Lounge

Nestling in the lobby corner of the Four Seasons hotel is this all-day dining restaurant. Its contemporary décor, great harbour views and live music (piano or jazz trio) create a perfect blend of informal elegance. The cuisine blends East and West: Scottish salmon with smoked caviar served with yuzu cream, Niçoise salad, squid ink linguine pasta and roasted pigeon on Savoy cabbage are just some examples. Afternoon tea is also popular.

位於四季酒店大堂一隅，餐廳全日提供服務。當代裝潢，醉人海景及現場音樂演奏（鋼琴或爵士三重奏）締造輕鬆而不失優雅的氣氛。餐單方面包括東西方精選：蘇格蘭三文魚伴煙魚子醬及柚子忌廉、尼斯沙律、墨魚汁幼麵烤乳鴿配皺葉捲心菜。下午茶亦甚受歡迎。

■ ADDRESS/地址
TEL. 3196 8820
1F, Four Seasons Hotel,
8 Finance Street, Central
中環金融街8號四季酒店1樓
www.fourseasons.com/hongkong

■ OPENING HOURS, LAST ORDER
營業時間，最後點菜時間
Lunch/午膳 11:00-15:00 (L.O.)
Dinner/晚膳 17:30-23:30 (L.O.)

■ PRICE/價錢
à la carte/點菜 $ 350-750

The Mistral   NEW
海風餐廳

✗✗

♿ ☞ 🍴20

They've neatly captured that faux-rustic atmosphere typical of so many Italian restaurants, thanks to the beams, terracotta tiled flooring, yellow and blue tablecloths and open kitchen. Much of the produce comes directly from Italy and the menu features dishes from all regions. For lunch, a buffet and set menu are offered alongside the à la carte. The restaurant may be in the basement of a hotel but the kitchen is clearly proud and capable.

這裡利用橫樑、赤陶地磚、黃色與藍色的枱布及開放式廚房，巧妙地營造了許多意大利餐廳的典型「人造鄉村」氣氛。餐廳所用的食材大部分直接從意大利進口，餐牌內可找到意大利不同地方的菜式。午餐除了餐牌內的菜式外，還供應自助餐和套餐。儘管餐廳位於隱蔽的酒店地庫，卻無損食物一流水準。

■ ADDRESS/地址
TEL. 2731 2870
B2, Intercontinental Grand Stanford Hotel, 70 Mody Road, East Tsim Sha Tsui, Kowloon
九龍尖東麼地道70號海景嘉福酒店B2樓
www.hongkong.intercontinental.com

■ OPENING HOURS, LAST ORDER
營業時間，最後點菜時間
Lunch/午膳 12:00-14:30 (L.O.)
Dinner/晚膳 19:00-22:30 (L.O.)

■ PRICE/價錢
Lunch/午膳   set/套餐 $248-688
          à la carte/點菜 $ 420-1,200
Dinner/晚膳 set/套餐 $688-788
          à la carte/點菜 $ 420-1,200

The Press Room

A local newspaper once occupied these premises but it's now home to a typically French brasserie that offers a pleasant, relaxed atmosphere. The panelling and high ceiling is enlivened by some interesting contemporary Chinese art. There's still plenty to read, from a large menu of classics that covers everything from soups and salads to grills and seafood. The extensive range of cheeses and wines by the glass are certainly newsworthy.

這物業範圍曾是某本地報社的所在位置,但如今已變身為法式小菜館,氣氛舒適宜人。隔板及高天花以有趣的現代中國藝術裝飾。餐牌提供眾多選擇,從餐湯、沙律、烤肉、海鮮,應有盡有。餐廳提供的芝士和餐酒,更是絕不能錯過。

■ ADDRESS/地址
TEL. 2525 3444
108 Hollywood Road, Central
中環荷里活道108號
www.thepressroom.com.hk

■ OPENING HOURS, LAST ORDER
營業時間,最後點菜時間
12:00-23:00 (L.O.)
Weekends/週末 10:00-23:00

■ PRICE/價錢

Lunch/午膳	set/套餐		$132
	à la carte/點菜	$300-600
Dinner/晚膳	set/套餐		$260
	à la carte/點菜	$300-600

The Square
翠玉軒

One always feels a sense of anticipation as one climbs the small staircase up to The Square and expectations will now be heightened thanks to a comprehensive makeover that has given it a handsome new look. Meanwhile, the menu offers a very diligently prepared selection of Cantonese dishes, including such specialities as braised conpoy with bean curd, signature crispy fried chicken and vegetable purée broth, and golden crispy prawns with tangerine sauce.

緩步通往翠玉軒的梯級之際，內心不期然泛起盼望，既是對其精緻美味佳餚的懷念嚮往，更多的是對其全新裝潢後的熱切期待。餐廳的粵菜菜式烹調甚見巧思，美食包括瑤柱豆腐菜茸羹，招牌脆皮雞及柑橘脆蝦球。

■ ADDRESS/地址
TEL. 2525 1163
4F, Two Exchange Square,
8 Connaught Place, Central
中環康樂廣場8號交易廣場第2期4樓
www.maxims.com.hk

■ OPENING HOURS, LAST ORDER
營業時間，最後點菜時間
Lunch/午膳 11:00-15:00 (L.O.)
Dinner/晚膳 18:00-22:45 (L.O.)

■ PRICE/價錢
Lunch/午膳　set/套餐　　$218-868
　　　　　　à la carte/點菜 $170-600
Dinner/晚膳　set/套餐　　$298-868
　　　　　　à la carte/點菜 $170-600

The Steak House

One of the most sophisticated grill rooms in town, with its own dramatic wine bar and a spectacular wine list, 70% of which is from the USA, including an impressive number of top Californian wines. The ingredients used here are unimpeachable: beef sourced from Australia, the U.S. and Japan is supplemented by great seafood. You even get to choose your knife from 10 different models. Service is both professional and friendly.

城中功力最到家的扒房之一--The Steak House，擁有一流的酒吧，讓人目不暇給的齊全酒牌－－當中70%產自美國，更包括了許多頂級加州葡萄酒。這裡採用的全是一流食材：來自澳洲、美國與日本的牛肉，配合鮮美的海鮮。你甚至可以從10種餐刀中挑選最適合自己的款式！服務既專業又友善。

■ ADDRESS/地址

TEL. 2313 2405

LF, Intercontinental Hotel,
18 Salisbury Road, Tsim Sha Tsui,
Kowloon
九龍尖沙咀梳士巴利道18號
洲際酒店地庫1樓

■ OPENING HOURS, LAST ORDER
　營業時間，最後點菜時間
Sunday lunch/週日午膳　12:00-14:30
Dinner/晚膳　18:00-23:00 (L.O.)

■ PRICE/價錢
Sunday lunch/週日午膳
　　　　　　set/套餐　　$598-1,018
Dinner/晚膳　à la carte/點菜　$750-2,100

Tim Ho Wan (Mong Kok)
添好運 (旺角)

It would not be an exaggeration to say that this little dim sum shop has brought life into this quiet street in Mong Kok. In 2009, two chefs joined forces and opened here; it has been a success ever since, hence the queue outside. There's no doubt about their ingredients; special mention can be given to the steamed dumpling 'chiu chow style', the steamed egg cake and, most definitely, the baked bun with barbecued pork. The wait will be worth it.

説這家小小的點心店為旺角較為靜寂的街角增添了生氣，這個説法並不為過。2009年，兩位師傅聯手創辦此店。值得留意的有潮洲蒸粉果、香滑馬拉糕，酥皮焗叉燒包更是絕對不能錯過。你會發現，這裡的點心絕對不負期待。

■ ADDRESS/地址
TEL. 2332 2896
8 Kwong Wa Street, Mong Kok, Kowloon
九龍旺角廣華街8號

■ OPENING HOURS, LAST ORDER
營業時間，最後點菜時間
10:00-21:15 (L.O.)

■ PRICE/價錢
à la carte/點菜　　　　$ 30-50

Tim Ho Wan (Sham Shui Po)   NEW
添好運 (深水埗)

Mid 2010 saw the opening of this second branch of Tim Ho Wan, this time in a more residential area. Although able to accommodate more customers than the original, it won't be long before queues start appearing here too. The 25 different dim sum choices are reasonably priced and carefully prepared. Highlights include steamed shrimp dumpling, baked bun with bbq pork and steamed beef balls. There are four small private rooms on the first floor.

這家坐落於住宅區的首家添好運分店於2010年中開張。儘管這家分店比總店能容納更多客人，相信不用多久便會出現人龍。25款價錢實惠的點心由廚師精心炮製。出名的點心包括蝦餃、酥皮焗叉燒包和陳皮牛肉球。一樓還設有4個小型貴賓房。

■ ADDRESS/地址
TEL. 2788 1226
9-11 Fuk Wing Street, Sham Shui Po, Kowloon
九龍深水埗福榮街9-11號

■ OPENING HOURS, LAST ORDER
營業時間, 最後點菜時間
08:00-22:00

■ PRICE/價錢
à la carte/點菜 $ 30-50

Tim's Kitchen
桃花源小廚

✿✿   ✗✗✗

🛋20   ☎️🍴

Success has lead to these new premises for Tim's Kitchen – in the same area but, with two floors and a capacity of 100, much larger. Chef-owner Tim's son designed the colourful, modern room; and his daughter marshals the professional service. Greater menu choice is also now on offer, along with the popular specialities such as Crystal prawn, pomelo skin and pork stomach, all of which showcase the kitchen's respect for the ingredients.

桃花源小廚的成功令其開辦新店——新店位於同區，佔地2層，可容納100人，比舊店大得多。店主兼廚師黎先生的兒子設計了色彩豐富、現代化的房間，他的女兒則提供專業服務。現時，此店更提供更多菜式可供選擇，當然也少不了鎮店菜式如玻璃蝦球、柚皮及豬肚，每種都能證明廚房對優質材料的高度重視。

■ ADDRESS/地址

TEL. 2543 5919

84-90 Bonham Strand, Sheung Wan
上環文咸東街84-90號
www.timskitchen.com.hk

■ ANNUAL AND WEEKLY CLOSING
   休息日期
Closed Sunday
週日休息

■ OPENING HOURS, LAST ORDER
   營業時間，最後點菜時間
Lunch/午膳 11:30-14:30 (L.O.)
Dinner/晚膳 18:00-22:30 (L.O.)

■ PRICE/價錢
Lunch/午膳 à la carte/點菜 $ 150-300
Dinner/晚膳 à la carte/點菜 $ 300-1,000

Tokoro

Based around the robatayaki concept of the Japanese barbecue, with many raw ingredients on display here for you to select. Once that's done, you take your seat either at a counter or in one of three bird cages which swivel if you want to face the kitchen. Interaction between guests and chefs makes for an animated atmosphere and there's plenty of sake on hand to lubricate things further. There is also a small but lively and contemporary sushi bar.

這家以爐端燒為主題的餐廳特色是展示多種原材料供食客挑選。選料後可隨意選擇座位，既可以坐在櫃檯用餐，亦可選擇三個可旋轉至面向廚房的鳥籠的其中一個。客人和廚師之間的互動令這裡充滿生氣。餐廳提供多種米酒，並設有一個時尚的小型壽司吧。

■ ADDRESS/地址

TEL. 3552 3330

3F, Langham Place Hotel,
555 Shanghai Street, Mong Kok,
Kowloon
九龍旺角上海街555號朗豪酒店3樓
www.tokoro.com.hk

■ OPENING HOURS, LAST ORDER
　營業時間，最後點菜時間
Lunch/午膳　12:00-14:30 (L.O.)
Dinner/晚膳　18:30-22:30 (L.O.)

■ PRICE/價錢
Lunch/午膳　set/套餐　　　　$167-217
　　　　　　à la carte/點菜　$200-450
Dinner/晚膳　set/套餐　　　　$450-950
　　　　　　à la carte/點菜　$200-450

Trusty Congee King   NEW
靠得住

The owner, Mr Lam, opened his first shop after his friends were so impressed by his ability to throw together a quick congee meal that they suggested he should start selling it. His was purported to be the first congee shop in Hong Kong to use a fish soup base for congee and indeed fish remains a speciality here. The shop is brightly lit, clean and tidy. With a name that includes the words 'trusty' and 'king', how can you go wrong?

店鋪主人林先生的友人驚嘆於他的巧手，能迅速炮製一餐粥品美食，便提議他開店售賣，於是他開了第一間店。靠得住據說是全港首家採用魚湯煮粥底的粥店，而魚粥直到現在還是這家店的招牌。店內燈火通明、整齊清潔。名字已説明一切——「靠得住」。這店怎麼會令你失望？

■ ADDRESS/地址
TEL. 2882 3268
7 Heard Street, Wan Chai
灣仔克街7號

■ ANNUAL AND WEEKLY CLOSING
　休息日期
Closed 4 days Lunar New Year
農曆新年休息4天

■ OPENING HOURS, LAST ORDER
　營業時間，最後點菜時間
11:00-23:00

■ PRICE/價錢
à la carte/點菜 $ 26-68

Tsim Chai Kee (Queen's Road)
沾仔記 (皇后大道中)

Formerly of Connaught Road, Tsim Chai Kee moved here in 2008. The simple, but neat and clean basement room is hidden away somewhat, with steps leading down from its narrow entrance. However, it's the good value, straightforward cooking that people come for. The concise menu lists dishes such as king prawn wonton noodle, fresh minced fish ball or fresh sliced beef noodle; choose between yellow or flat white noodles or vermicelli.

以往位於干諾道的沾仔記於2008年遷至此處。簡約清潔的地下室有樓梯連至其窄小入口。人們前來只為一嘗其物有所值、直接了當的菜式。餐牌雖然選擇不多，但五臟俱全，列出招牌雲吞麵、鮮鯪魚球、鮮牛肉麵；從麵、河、米粉中選出一種吧。

■ ADDRESS/地址
TEL. 2581 3369
153 Queen's Road Central, Central
中環皇后大道中153號

■ OPENING HOURS, LAST ORDER
營業時間，最後點菜時間
09:00-22:00 (L.O.)

■ PRICE/價錢
à la carte/點菜 $ 17-25

Tsim Chai Kee (Wellington Street)
沾仔記 (威靈頓街)

This highly regarded, simple noodle shop may have been here since 1998 but it's still looking good. The staff are as bright as their aprons; the popular side booths are quickly snapped up and the regulars know to eat outside peak times when the pace is less frenetic. The attraction is the handmade fish balls, the generously filled wontons and the fresh beef served with the noodles. It's easy to spot – just look for the lunchtime queues.

享負盛名的沾仔記於一九九八年開業，裝修簡單，但依然整潔舒適。侍應制服明亮潔淨。卡位非常受歡迎，經常滿座；熟客會在非繁忙時間光顧，氣氛則較為輕鬆。著名菜式包括自製的鮮鯪魚球、餡料豐富的招牌雲吞，以及鮮牛肉麵。餐廳容易尋找，午市時段外面大排長龍的那家就是了！

■ ADDRESS/地址

TEL. 2850 6471

98 Wellington Street, Central
中環威靈頓街98號

■ ANNUAL AND WEEKLY CLOSING
　休息日期
Closed 4 days Lunar New Year
農曆新年休息4天

■ OPENING HOURS, LAST ORDER
　營業時間，最後點菜時間
09:00-22:00 (L.O.)

■ PRICE/價錢
à la carte/點菜　　　　　$ 17-25

Tuscany by H

🍴16 📞🍴 🎱

The name doesn't give the whole picture as this soberly dressed, modern restaurant looks to all parts of Italy for its influences, not just Tuscany. Expect a wide range of classics, all exuding a certain rustic style of cooking that is all about the flavours. The 36 month aged Parma ham, the beef cheek ravioli and the veal chop are some of the dishes to pair with a choice of over 200 bottles from the wine list.

餐廳名字不足以表達其全貌；這家經過精心裝潢、富現代感的餐廳受到義大利不同地區的影響，不只是塔斯卡尼。餐廳提供一系列經典，全都表現出濃厚意式鄉土風味，注重調味。三十六個月的風乾巴拿馬火腿，牛頰肉意式雲吞和小牛排是其中一些精選擇，配上酒牌上超過二百種餐酒可供選擇。

■ ADDRESS/地址

TEL. 2522 9798
58-62 D'Aguilar Street,
Lan Kwai Fong, Central
中環蘭桂芳德己立街58-62號
www.tuscany-by-h.com

■ ANNUAL AND WEEKLY CLOSING
　　休息日期
Closed lunch Sunday and Public Holidays
週日午膳及公眾假期午膳休息

■ OPENING HOURS, LAST ORDER
　　營業時間，最後點菜時間
Lunch/午膳 12:00-14:30 (L.O.)
Dinner/晚膳 18:30-23:00 (L.O.)

■ PRICE/價錢
Lunch/午膳　set/套餐　　　$218
　　　　　　à la carte/點菜 $300-800
Dinner/晚膳　set/套餐　　$488-880
　　　　　　à la carte/點菜 $300-800

Unkai
雲海

Lots of small rooms emanating from a central bamboo provide a characteristic Japanese minimalist setting for Unkai. There's a tatami room for a taste of real Japan, private rooms for intimacy, or rooms where the chefs will prepare teppanyaki in front of your eyes – not forgetting the ubiquitous sushi bar. Cuisine from the Osaka region is a speciality here, while sake lovers will raise a smile over the fact there are 62 varieties of it on offer.

由中央的竹，延伸至用來間隔小房閭的到頂的木條，構成了雲海的日本極潔抽象風格。餐廳包括一個榻榻米房間、較有私隱的私人餐室，以及廚師即席在人前烹調鐵板燒的房間。此外，壽司吧亦無處不在。這裡的特色美食包括大阪菜式，而這裡有62種清酒之多，愛好清酒者真是口福不淺！

■ ADDRESS/地址
TEL. 2369 1111
3F, Sheraton Hotel, 20 Nathan Road, Tsim Sha Tsui, Kowloon
九龍尖沙咀彌敦道20號喜來登酒店3樓
www.sheraton.com/hongkong

■ OPENING HOURS, LAST ORDER
營業時間，最後點菜時間
Lunch/午膳　12:00-14:30 L.O.14:15
Dinner/晚膳　18:30-22:30 L.O.22:15

■ PRICE/價錢

Lunch/午膳	set/套餐	$180-950
	à la carte/點菜	$400-900
Dinner/晚膳	set/套餐	$350-1,200
	à la carte/點菜	$400-900

Uno Más

Sit back with friends and absorb the atmosphere, while the open kitchen prepares classic tapas like boquerones (anchovies) or croqueta de jamon (ham croquettes) alongside grilled dishes like octopus Gallega. Fine imported charcuterie is good, as are the olives. And no meal is complete without the addictive churros dipped in chocolate. Sitting at one of the first floor terrace tables, one can easily think this is Barcelona, not Lockhart Road.

和三五知己一同安坐於這裡，享受 Uno Mas 的氣氛吧。開房式廚房裡烹調著西班牙醋醃鯷魚或西班牙火腿炸件（croqueta de jamon），以及燒烤菜式，如烤西班牙八爪魚（Gallega）。精緻的入口雜錦前菜（charcuterie）和橄欖同樣出色。當然，缺乏了令人上癮的炸西班牙油條（churros）沾巧克力醬，就不算一頓完整的美食。坐在一樓的露天雅座，你可輕易想像自己是身處巴塞隆納，而非駱克道。

■ ADDRESS/地址

TEL. 2527 9111

1F, 54-62 Lockhart Road, Wan Chai
灣仔駱克道54-62號1樓
www.uno-mas.com

■ OPENING HOURS, LAST ORDER
　營業時間，最後點菜時間
Lunch/午膳　12:00-15:00 L.O.14:30
Dinner/晚膳　18:00-24:00 L.O.22:45

■ PRICE/價錢
Lunch/午膳　set/套餐　　　　$110
　　　　　à la carte/點菜 $150-450
Dinner/晚膳　à la carte/點菜 $150-450

Wagyu Kaiseki Den

Don't let the name confuse you - Wagyu beef is not the only ingredient. In fact, its just one of numerous imported items that appears on the daily-changing, no choice Kaiseki menu, where some modern touches sit alongside more traditional elements. Seasonality and freshness are fundamental to the passionate Japanese chef here; watch him and his team perform by reserving at the counter. The charming, detailed decoration enhances the experience.

別讓店名模糊了視線——和牛並非唯一食材。其實，和牛只是無數每天新鮮入口的不同食材的其中一種，由廚師決定的懷石菜單，傳統中帶有現代修飾。對充滿熱情的日籍廚師來說，時令及新鮮程度是基本要素。預訂櫃檯位置，看看他和團隊如何施展渾身解數吧。迷人精緻的裝潢，令用餐體驗更臻完美。

■ ADDRESS/地址

TEL. 2851 2820

263 Hollywood Road, Sheung Wan
上環荷李活道263號

■ ANNUAL AND WEEKLY CLOSING
　休息日期
Closed 3 days Lunar New Year
and Sunday
農曆新年3天及週日休息

■ OPENING HOURS, LAST ORDER
　營業時間，最後點菜時間
Dinner/晚膳 18:30-23:00 (L.O.)

■ PRICE/價錢
Dinner/晚膳　set/套餐　　$1,780

Wang Fu   NEW
王府

It's all about charming Madame Wang (that's not her real name but that's what everybody calls her): she helps make the dumplings, cooks them and oversees the eating of them. Hers was one of the first shops on Wellington Street and her Pekingese dumplings are renowned. Pork and chive or even tomato and egg are part of an extensive range and this is the only place you'll find winter melon dumplings. Check the kitchen window for the day's special.

一切都靠著王女士（不是她的真名，不過大家都這樣叫）：她幫忙包粽子、煮粽子，看著大家吃粽子。王府是威靈頓街最早期的店鋪之一，北京水餃更是遠近馳名。韭菜豬肉或番茄蛋都屬眾多選擇之一，而且，這是你唯一可以找到冬瓜水餃的店鋪。看看廚房的窗子，就可見到每日精選。

■ ADDRESS/地址

TEL. 2121 8006
65 Wellington Street, Central
中環威靈頓街65號

■ OPENING HOURS, LAST ORDER
　營業時間，最後點菜時間
11:00–22:30 (L.O.)

■ PRICE/價錢
à la carte/點菜 $ 26–120

Wasabisabi
山葵

This über-chic environment manages to blend together Japanese simplicity with something far more futuristic. As you step onto a subtly lit catwalk passage, you'll find the brash red of the Lipstick Lounge on one side and the cooler tones of the main dining room on the other. Culinary styles too are thrown up in the air and incorporate everything from mustard beef tenderloin bento boxes to Japanese tiramisu.

餐廳裝潢融合了日本簡約風格和未來主義,走在時尚尖端。踏上燈光黯淡的catwalk大道,可見一邊是豔紅色的Lipstick Lounge,而另一邊的主餐室則以較深沉的色調為主。芥辣籽汁燒牛柳便當、綠茶芝士餅等菜式都實在各有風格。

■ ADDRESS/地址

TEL. 2506 0009

Shop 1301, 13F, Food Forum,
Times Square, 1 Matheson Street,
Causeway Bay

銅鑼灣勿地臣街1號時代廣場
食通天13樓1301號舖

www.aqua.com.hk

■ OPENING HOURS, LAST ORDER
營業時間,最後點菜時間
Lunch/午膳 12:00-14:45 (L.O.)
Dinner/晚膳 18:00-22:45 (L.O.)

■ PRICE/價錢
Lunch/午膳   set/套餐 $118-278
            à la carte/點菜 $370-580
Dinner/晚膳   set/套餐 $588
            à la carte/點菜 $370-580

Watermark

⚒ ⚒

    ♿ ⬅ 🍽24 ☎🍴

The views of Kowloon and the harbour from this large, glass-sided, contemporary restaurant on Pier 7 are superb but are certainly not its only asset. Beef from the USA, Ireland and Australia, as well as supremely fresh seafood feature on a menu that delivers contemporary touches to classic dishes. Non-carnivores should try crispy fillet of red emperor with pinto beans. A great place to while away a Sunday brunch.

這家位於七號碼頭的餐廳其中一邊為落地玻璃，盡覽九龍方向及海港景色，但顯然這並非唯一賣點。來自美國、愛爾蘭與澳洲的牛肉，極其新鮮的海鮮，為傳統的餐牌帶來一絲現代氣息。不好肉類的食客可嚐嚐脆炸紅皇帝石斛伴斑豆。此處亦是星期天早午合餐的絕佳地點。

■ ADDRESS/地址

TEL. 2167 7251

Level P, Central Pier 7, Star Ferry, Central

中環7號碼頭P樓

www.igors.com

■ OPENING HOURS, LAST ORDER

營業時間，最後點菜時間

Lunch/午膳 11:30-14:30 (L.O.)

Dinner/晚膳 18:00-22:30 (L.O.)

■ PRICE/價錢

Lunch/午膳　set/套餐　　$176-216

Dinner/晚膳　à la carte/點菜　$340-430

Whisk   NEW

The appropriately named Whisk brings together contemporary French cooking techniques with modern twists and Asian influences to create dishes with an appealing blend of flavours, such as baked miso-marinated cod in ginger and lime or roasted suckling pub with truffle and red wine sauce. The location for this informal but elegant environment is equally apposite as it is found on the 5th floor of the urbane and vibrant Mira Hotel.

恰如其名的Whisk，以當代法國菜烹調技巧，揉合現代元素和亞洲菜特色，造出多款創新菜式，為味覺帶來新享受，例如味噌鱈魚伴青檸薑汁和燒乳豬班黑松露紅酒醬。這家位於The Mira酒店五樓的餐廳，營造了一個優雅中帶點無拘無束的用餐環境，與酒店的活力和時代感形象互相呼應。

■ ADDRESS/地址
TEL. 2315 5999
5F, The Mira Hotel, 118 Nathan Road,
Tsim Sha Tsui, Kowloon
九龍尖沙咀彌敦道118號The Mira 5樓
www.themirahotel.com

■ OPENING HOURS, LAST ORDER
營業時間，最後點菜時間
Lunch/午膳 12:00-14:30 (L.O.)
Dinner/晚膳 18:00-22:30 (L.O.)

■ PRICE/價錢
Lunch/午膳   set/套餐 $258
     à la carte/點菜 $550-1,750
Dinner/晚膳   à la carte/點菜 $550-1,750

Wing Hap Lung　NEW
永合隆

Take care with the slippery floor and slide gently towards one of the 8 small tables of this tiny shop, which was established more than 40 years ago. Moreish suckling pig and succulent roasted pig are the best sellers but they also serve bbq pork, Peking duck, goose legs and wings; most come simply presented on steamed white rice. It boasts a pleasant neighbourhood atmosphere and there is often a queue outside for takeaway orders.

小心地滑！進入這家有40多年歷史只有八張小桌的細小燒臘店時要步步為營。乳豬和多汁的燒肉最受歡迎，亦有叉燒、燒鴨、鵝掌翼等選擇，大部分都配白飯。這裡有著親切的街坊氣氛，也經常可見排隊外賣的人龍。

■ ADDRESS/地址
TEL. 2380 8511
392 Portland Street, Mong Kok, Kowloon
九龍旺角砵蘭街392號

■ ANNUAL AND WEEKLY CLOSING
　休息日期
Closed Lunar New Year
年初一休息

■ OPENING HOURS, LAST ORDER
　營業時間，最後點菜時間
11:00-22:00

■ PRICE/價錢
à la carte/點菜　　　$ 40-140

Wing Wah
永華雲吞麵家

This simple operation has been maintaining high standards for well over 50 years now, the secret being that they do everything from scratch upstairs, making their noodles by hand using bamboo. So proud are they of their skills that there's a photographic display on the walls showing what they do. Finest offerings include shrimp wonton and barbecued pork noodle as well as a dessert of coconut milk with honeydew melon and sago.

這家簡單的餐廳營運至今逾50年，依然保持一貫的高水準，成功秘訣在於一手包辦所有工作，在樓上用竹昇手打麵條便可見一斑。他們以自家技術深感自豪，牆上貼著製作過程的照片。招牌美食包括鮮蝦雲吞麵及炸醬麵，甜品方面首推蜜瓜椰汁西米露。

■ ADDRESS/地址
TEL. 2527 7476
89 Hennessy Road, Wan Chai
灣仔軒尼詩道89號

■ ANNUAL AND WEEKLY CLOSING
　休息日期
Closed Lunar New Year
年初一休息

■ OPENING HOURS, LAST ORDER
　營業時間，最後點菜時間
12:00-04:00 (L.O.)
Sunday/週日 12:00-01:00 (L.O.)

■ PRICE/價錢
à la carte/點菜　　　　　$ 50

Wooloomooloo Steakhouse (Wan Chai)

Carnivores can choose between wet-aged Black Angus beef from Australia or USDA Prime beef from the USA at this branch of the growing chain. Cuts range from rib-eye and sirloin to porterhouse and New York strip and you also choose the sauce to accompany your meat. Finish with some equally hearty desserts like apple crumble and you'll be sure to leave feeling sated. Staff are helpful, the views are great and the atmosphere fun.

喜愛肉類的你，大可前往這家逐漸擴充的連鎖店，在濕式熟成的澳洲黑安格斯牛肉和美國的USDA頂級牛肉之間選取心頭好。切法從肉眼扒到西冷扒，大丁骨（porterhouse）到紐約特選長牛扒（New York strip steak）應有盡有，還有不同醬汁可供選擇。蘋果脆批等甜品同樣窩心，可為你豐盛的一餐畫上完美的句號，另你「滿載而歸」。員工都很熱心，景觀怡人，氣氛有趣。

■ ADDRESS/地址

TEL. 2893 6960
31F, The Hennessy, 256 Hennessy Road, Wan Chai
灣仔軒尼詩道256號The Hennessy 31樓
www.wooloo-mooloo.com

■ OPENING HOURS, LAST ORDER
營業時間，最後點菜時間
Lunch/午膳 12:00-14:30
Dinner/晚膳 18:00-23:00

■ PRICE/價錢
Lunch/午膳   à la carte/點菜 $270-580
Dinner/晚膳   à la carte/點菜 $400-850

Wu Kong (Causeway Bay)
滬江 (銅鑼灣)

🍽16 🍴

Whether you're a member of the local business community or just in need of a break from shopping, then head down to Wu Kong, established in the heart of Times Square since 1994. Authentic Shanghainese recipes are given due respect here in practiced classics; braised mandarin fish with sweet and sour sauce and the legendary drunken chicken are of note. In contrast, the room has a more modern feel and the young team provide well meaning service.

不管你是本地商界的一員，或是純粹在購物過後小歇一番，都可前往1994年起已座落於時代廣場中心部份的滬江。正宗上海菜完全尊重並按照傳統製法；松子桂花魚和上海醉雞值得一提。相對之下，貴賓房較富當代氣息；年輕團隊提供貼心服務。

■ ADDRESS/地址

TEL. 2506 1018

Shop1303, 13F, Food Forum, Times Square, 1 Matheson Street, Causeway Bay
銅鑼灣勿地臣街1號時代廣場
食通天13樓1303號舖
www.wukong.com.hk

■ ANNUAL AND WEEKLY CLOSING
　　休息日期
Closed 2 days Lunar New Year
農曆新年休息2天

■ OPENING HOURS, LAST ORDER
　　營業時間，最後點菜時間
Lunch/午膳 11:45-14:45 (L.O.)
Dinner/晚膳 17:45-22:45 (L.O.)

■ PRICE/價錢
Lunch/午膳　set/套餐　　　$85
　　　　　　à la carte/點菜 $100-200
Dinner/晚膳 à la carte/點菜 $150-300

Xin Dan Ji
新斗記

 12

Formerly located in Woosung Street, this restaurant, in the heart of Jordan, is known for its seafood and roasted suckling pig, items for which its customers will travel some distance. But the main appeal is clearly the seafood which is bought from the fish market every day and placed in the tank on the ground floor just by the entrance. Look out for the pictures of Old Kowloon in the large first floor dining room.

餐館本來位於吳松街,現時坐落佐敦的中心位置。最著名的是海鮮和燒乳豬,不少顧客為此遠道前來。不過,最吸引的顯然是海鮮,每天從魚市場新鮮購買,然後放進地下入口旁的大魚缸裡。餐館的一樓掛著多幅九龍舊貌的照片,讓人懷舊一番。

■ ADDRESS/地址
TEL. 2388 6020
18 Cheong Lok Street, Jordan, Kowloon
九龍佐敦長樂街18號

■ ANNUAL AND WEEKLY CLOSING
　休息日期
Closed Lunar New Year
年初一休息

■ OPENING HOURS, LAST ORDER
　營業時間,最後點菜時間
Dinner/晚膳 18:00-03:00 L.O. 02:30

■ PRICE/價錢
à la carte/點菜　　　　$ 150-1,000

Xi Yan Sweets
囍宴 甜・藝

The well-thumbed menu is an indication of how popular this vibrant place has become. Created by interior designer/celebrity chef Jacky Yu, it makes quite a statement in its vivid red. The Zhenjiang spare ribs are usually taken by every table, along with the Sichuan spicy chicken and fried soft shell crab in plum sauce. Desserts are renowned, with the lychee ice cream in osmanthus wine one highlight. Service is suitably snappy.

令人食指大動的餐牌顯示這家餐廳的受歡迎程度。由著名室內設計師兼星級廚師余健志打造的美食空間以鮮紅作宣言。幾乎每一桌都會點上一道秘製鎮江骨，金牌口水雞及梅子軒殼蟹。這裡的甜品亦非常著名，包括桂花酒釀荔枝雪糕。敏捷的服務來得恰到好處。

■ ADDRESS/地址
TEL. 2833 6299
8 Wing Fung Street, Wan Chai
灣仔永豐街 8 號
www.xiyan.com.hk

■ OPENING HOURS, LAST ORDER
  營業時間，最後點菜時間
11:30-22:30 (L.O.)

■ PRICE/價錢
Lunch/午膳	set/套餐	$60-88
	à la carte/點菜	$140-250
Dinner/晚膳	à la carte/點菜	$140-250

Cantonese/粵菜 MAP/地圖　14/C-3

Yan Toh Heen
欣圖軒

The authentic Cantonese specialties include golden scallops with minced shrimp and pear; double boiled Black chicken with mushrooms and abalone, and wok-fried lobster with crab roe and milk. Also included in the extensive choice is the 'ihealth menu' - a collaboration between the Intercontinental hotel and the Hong Kong Adventist hospital. It's all served in an elegant room with lovely views and attractive table settings.

這家水準一流的中菜廳精心炮製的粵式佳餚包括龍帶玉梨香、鮮松茸鮑魚燉竹絲雞、龍皇炒鮮奶。此外，由洲際酒店與港安醫院合作的健康餐單 「ihealth餐單」更有大量不同選擇。客人用膳的大廳裝潢優雅，景致宜人，餐桌擺設吸引。

■ ADDRESS/地址

TEL. 2313 2243

GF, Intercontinental Hotel,
18 Salisbury Road, Tsim Sha Tsui,
Kowloon
九龍尖沙咀梳士巴利道18號
洲際酒店地下

■ OPENING HOURS, LAST ORDER
　營業時間，最後點菜時間
Lunch/午膳 12:00-14:30 (L.O.)
Dinner/晚膳 18:00-23:00 (L.O.)

■ PRICE/價錢

Lunch/午膳	set/套餐	$318-498
	à la carte/點菜	$300-1,800
Dinner/晚膳	set/套餐	$988-1,968
	à la carte/點菜	$320-1,800

Yat Lok　　NEW
一樂食館

A family business since the 1950s, the chef-owner still cooks his father's specialities that first made their reputation. There are 25 steps in the preparation of the roast goose, so it is no surprise that this is the top seller. The barbecue pork with its secret sauce is another favourite. Some order noodles but the rice is best if you want to taste those meat juices. His wife runs the service and creates a pleasant family atmosphere.

這家家庭式經營的食館自1950年代開業，老闆兼主廚現在依然炮製當年其父所創、讓食館聞名的招牌菜式。鎮店燒鵝的準備工夫多達25個步驟，不難理解何以最為暢銷。配以秘製醬汁的叉燒亦很受歡迎。部分配以粉麵，但若想品嘗肉汁，白飯則是最佳選擇。老闆娘負責招呼客人，為店裡帶來親切的家庭氣氛。

■ ADDRESS/地址

TEL. 2524 3882
28 Stanley Street, Central
中環士丹利街28號

■ ANNUAL AND WEEKLY CLOSING
　休息日期
Closed 3 days Lunar New Year and last Sunday of the month
農曆新年3天及每月最後之星期日休息

■ OPENING HOURS, LAST ORDER
　營業時間，最後點菜時間
07:00-19:00
Sunday/週日 09:00-16:00

■ PRICE/價錢
à la carte/點菜　　　　　$ 20-40

Yat Tung Heen (Jordan)
逸東軒 (佐敦)

Despite its basement setting, this spacious restaurant is warm and atmospheric, thanks to the soft colours and subtle lighting. A highly personable manager heads up a friendly and efficient team. The menu is strictly Cantonese and the best of the signature dishes include pan-fried chicken with dried mandarin peel; roasted crispy goose; fried rice with assorted meat and conpoy wrapped in lotus leaves and fried prawns balls and diced onion with preserved beancurd paste.

雖然位於酒店地庫，但柔和的色調和精心設計的燈光，令佔地甚廣的逸東軒洋溢著溫暖舒服的氣氛。親切有禮的經理，帶領一班態度友善，工作效率高的員工。餐廳提供純粹粵菜，著名菜式包括陳皮煎軟雞、脆皮燒鵝、荷葉飯、干燒明蝦球等。

■ ADDRESS/地址

TEL.2710 1093
B2F, Eaton Hotel, 380 Nathan Road, Jordan, Kowloon
九龍佐敦彌敦道380號
逸東酒店地庫2樓
www.hongkong.eatonhotels.com

■ OPENING HOURS, LAST ORDER
營業時間，最後點菜時間
Lunch/午膳 11:00-15:30 (L.O.)
Dinner/晚膳 18:00-22:30 (L.O.)

■ PRICE/價錢
Lunch/午膳　set/套餐　　　　$ 98
　　　　　　à la carte/點菜 $ 250-600
Dinner/晚膳　à la carte/點菜 $ 250-600

Yat Tung Heen (Wan Chai)
逸東軒 (灣仔)

✿

🍴🍴

🚃 20   ☎🍴

The business community who occupy the Great Eagle Centre can count themselves lucky to be sharing their building with this restaurant. The menu is firmly Cantonese and along with the classics such as abalone, there are some real gems on it, such as smoked duck breast with citron honey and purple clay casserole dishes; there's also a great sponge cake which is well worth making an investment in. Lunch dim sum is good too.

租用了鷹君中心的商務客可暗自慶幸能與此餐廳共用同一大廈。餐單上的菜式貫徹粵菜風格，除了必備的鮑魚和魚翅外，還有午餐時分出色的點心，菜牌上有些菜式不容錯過：蜂蜜柚子煙鴨胸、紫砂鍋及美味的千層馬拉糕絕對值得投資。

■ ADDRESS/地址
TEL. 2878 1212
2F, Great Eagle Centre, 23 Harbour Road, Wan Chai
灣仔港灣道23號鷹君中心2樓

■ OPENING HOURS, LAST ORDER
營業時間，最後點菜時間
Lunch/午膳 11:00-16:00 (L.O.)
Dinner/晚膳 18:00-24:00 (L.O.)

■ PRICE/價錢
Lunch/午膳	set/套餐	$ 100-850
	à la carte/點菜	$ 195-1,350
Dinner/晚膳	set/套餐	$ 290-850
	à la carte/點菜	$ 195-1,350

Yellow Door Kitchen
黃色門廚房

Take the lift to this inconspicuous restaurant where the closely set tables will have you practically sharing your neighbour's food! You'll feel instantly at home with the friendly service, and even more relaxed when you try the tasty Sichuan and Shanghainese cooking, prepared by the all-female team. Don't be afraid to tackle the evening tasting menu of eight starters, six main courses, dim sum and dessert, all in small, delicious portions.

程搭升降機來到這家不甚起眼的餐廳，裡面的餐枱緊緊排列在一起，使你幾乎可以分享鄰座的晚餐！親切的服務令你賓至如歸；嚐到美味四川和上海菜由全女班團隊炮製。放膽試試包含八道前菜、六道主菜、點心和甜品的推薦套餐，全部都是份量小而美味的菜式。

■ ADDRESS/地址
TEL. 2858 6555
6F, 37 Cochrane Street, Central
中環閣麟街37號6樓
www.yellowdoorkitchen.com.hk

■ ANNUAL AND WEEKLY CLOSING
　休息日期
Closed 3 days Lunar New Year, Sunday and Public Holidays
農曆新年3天、週日及公眾假期休息

■ OPENING HOURS, LAST ORDER
　營業時間，最後點菜時間
Lunch/午膳 12:00-14:30 (L.O.)
Dinner/晚膳 18:30-22:30 (L.O.)

■ PRICE/價錢
Lunch/午膳　à la carte/點菜 $120-250
Dinner/晚膳　set/套餐　　　$298

Yè Shanghai (Admiralty)
夜上海 (金鍾)

🍴 14 ☎

Surrounded by watch and jewellery shops, and with a bijou chocolate shop at the entrance, this large dining room, with floor to ceiling windows, is elegantly decorated. Attentive staff will guide you through the intricacies of the menu which specialises not only in the cuisine of Shanghai but also its neighbouring provinces of Jiangsu and Zhejiang. Try the deep-fried sweet and sour yellow fish with pine nuts or the baked stuffed crab shell.

餐廳附近盡是鐘錶和珠寶店,入口處則設有一家小巧的巧克力店。餐廳佔地寬廣,設有落地玻璃,裝修優雅,侍應樂於為你介紹餐單上的繁複菜式;特色美食不但包括上海菜,更有江蘇及浙江菜。建議一試松子黃魚及蟹粉釀蟹蓋。

■ ADDRESS/地址

TEL. 2918 9833
Shop 332, 3F, Pacific Place,
88 Queensway, Admiralty
香港金鐘道88號太古廣場3樓332號舖
www.elite-concepts.com

■ OPENING HOURS, LAST ORDER
營業時間,最後點菜時間
Lunch/午膳 11:30-14:30 (L.O.)
Dinner/晚膳 18:00-22:30 (L.O.)

■ PRICE/價錢
Lunch/午膳   set/套餐 $380
            à la carte/點菜 $200-600
Dinner/晚膳 set/套餐 $380
            à la carte/點菜 $200-600

Yè Shanghai (Kowloon)
夜上海 (九龍)

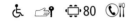

Expertly balanced, subtle cooking is provided here, drawing not only on Shanghai but also the neighbouring provinces of Jiangsu and Zhejiang. Specialities include braised Tianjin cabbage with ham, stir-fried river shrimps with longjin tea and steamed pork belly wrapped in lotus leaves. Contemporary décor recalls 1930s Shanghai in its use of dark woods, subdued lighting and semi-private alcoves. A busy, sophisticated operation.

這裡的烹調水準專業，技術精湛，不但提供上海菜，更涵蓋江蘇及浙江菜。特色美食包括金華火腿津白，龍井蝦仁及稻草扎肉。餐廳以當代風格設計，燈光昏暗，採用深色木材，設有半掩餐室，散發著三十年代上海的味道。餐廳生氣勃勃，營運順暢，服務非常周到。

■ ADDRESS/地址
TEL. 2376 3322
6F, Marco Polo Hotel, Harbour City,
Canton Road, Tsim Sha Tsui, Kowloon
九龍尖沙咀廣東道海運大廈
馬哥孛羅酒店6樓
www.elite-concepts.com

■ OPENING HOURS, LAST ORDER
營業時間，最後點菜時間
Lunch/午膳 11:30-15:30 L.O. 15:00
Dinner/晚膳 18:00-24:00 L.O. 23:00

■ PRICE/價錢
à la carte/點菜　　　　$ 250-550

Yeung's Noodle
楊記麵家

Mr Yeung's done it again, this time in Wan Chai. There's a fresh, modern red and black interior, and the swift and efficient team keep a beady eye on proceedings. The recipes are proven, and the prices very reasonable considering the quality. Fish balls, fresh beef and seasonal vegetables flood out of the small kitchen in steaming bowls of soup or noodles. The shrimp roe lao mian is definitely worth a try.

楊先生再展拳腳,今次選定灣仔,創立楊記麵家。餐廳內部採用了時尚的紅色和黑色設計,感覺煥然一新。高效的侍應有型有格,反應非常敏捷,隨時為食客提供服務。菜式水準有保證,相對下價錢確是十分合宜。侍應不斷從廚房捧出一碗碗的時菜、魚蛋和鮮牛肉湯或麵。這裡的蝦子撈麵絕對值得一試。

■ ADDRESS/地址

TEL. 2511 1336
219 Hennessy Road, Wan Chai
灣仔軒尼詩道219號

■ ANNUAL AND WEEKLY CLOSING
   休息日期
Closed 4 days Lunar New Year
農曆新年休息4天

■ OPENING HOURS, LAST ORDER
   營業時間,最後點菜時間
11:00-22:00 (L.O.)

■ PRICE/價錢
Là la carte/點菜 $ 17-30

Yue Kee
裕記

Over 40,000 geese are needed each year to satisfy demand at this large, second-generation family business, which opened back in 1958. The restaurant has 50 tables, which are divided between eight simply decorated rooms; the geese are sourced from eight different farms in Mainland China. If contentment is indicated by the amount of noise generated, then clearly these roasted geese are much appreciated by the customers.

這裡每年需購入超過40,000隻鵝以確保供應。這家第二代家族經營的大型餐館自1958年開業，共有50桌，分佈於8個佈置簡潔的房間內；這裡的鵝來自中國內地8個不同的農場。若聲浪與滿足程度成正比，這裡的燒鵝肯定非常受客人欣賞。

■ ADDRESS/地址
TEL. 2491 0105
9 Sham Hong Road, Sham Tseng,
New Territories
新界深井深康路9號
www.yuekee.com.hk

■ ANNUAL AND WEEKLY CLOSING
　休息日期
Closed 3 days Lunar New Year
農曆新年休息3天

■ OPENING HOURS, LAST ORDER
　營業時間，最後點菜時間
11:00-23:15 (L.O.)

■ PRICE/價錢
à la carte/點菜 $ 150-300

Yung Kee (Central)
鏞記 (中環)

💺 100

Yung Kee has been a veritable institution for nearly four decades. It can seat over 1,000 people and is spread over four floors, with each one offering a different environment. So you can enjoy the bustle of the simple ground floor, more formality upstairs, or the discreet luxury of the top floor VIP room. It takes an army of waiters to serve the traditional Cantonese dishes, with roast goose being the house speciality.

這裡可容納超過一千人，佔地共四層，每層環境都各有特色。你可以選擇裝潢簡潔、人流絡繹不絕的地下、較正式的樓上、甚至頂樓的至尊貴賓房。一隊井然有序的侍應負責端上傳統廣東菜，招牌菜式是鏞記燒鵝。鏞記屹立四十載，名不虛傳。

■ ADDRESS/地址
TEL. 2522 1624
32-40 Wellington Street, Central
中環威靈頓街32-40號
www.yungkee.com.hk

■ ANNUAL AND WEEKLY CLOSING
　休息日期
Closed 3 days Lunar New Year
農曆新年休息3天

■ OPENING HOURS, LAST ORDER
　營業時間，最後點菜時間
11:00-23:30 (L.O.)

■ PRICE/價錢
à la carte/點菜　　　　　$ 220-600

Yung Kee Siu Choi Wong
容記小菜王

Despite being hidden behind a local market, this restaurant's fame is widely spread - look around and you'll see the shop decked out with photos of the owner and all the famous celebrities who have visited. Must-tries would be their crispy roasted pork and special Yung Kee dish (chives with dried prawns and squid) or the chicken with baked fish intestine. It's always busy, so be prepared to share your table with others.

雖然隱藏在本地街市後，你會發現這家餐廳遠近馳名，不容小覷——看看四周，你會看見店內滿佈店主和來訪著名藝人的合照。不能錯過其脆皮燒肉及小炒王（韭黃蝦乾炒鮮魷），或是鮮雞焗魚腸。餐廳經常滿座，要有和陌生人同檯的心理準備。

■ ADDRESS/地址

TEL. 2387 1051

108 Fuk Wa Street, Sham Shui Po, Kowloon
九龍深水埗福華街108號

■ ANNUAL AND WEEKLY CLOSING
　　休息日期
Closed 4 days Lunar New Year
農曆新年休息4天

■ OPENING HOURS, LAST ORDER
　　營業時間，最後點菜時間
Dinner/晚膳 17:30-02:00 L.O.01:45

■ PRICE/價錢
à la carte/點菜 $ 120-200

Zuma

Currently caught in the zeitgeist of fashion and celebrity, Zuma is spread across 2 floors with a cool sake bar and lounge hovering above the main dining room and linked by a dramatic spiral staircase. Dishes are prepared in three distinct areas: the open kitchen, the sushi bar and the robata grill, allowing a mix of calm precision and dramatic flourish. Over 1,000 wines and 40 types of sake and shochu are available. A DJ plays at weekends.

餐廳風格緊貼名人和時尚潮流，共分為兩層：主餐室樓上設有型格的燒酒吧及酒廊，以螺旋形樓梯連接，設計獨特。廚房包括三個部分：開放式廚房、壽司吧，以及爐端燒，廚藝精巧，味道一流。餐廳提供超過一千種葡萄酒及四十種不同的日本酒及燒酒，週末更有DJ在場打碟。

■ ADDRESS/地址

TEL. 3657 6388

5-6F, The Landmark, 15 Queen's Road, Central
中環皇后大道中15號置地廣場5-6樓
www.zumarestaurant.com

■ OPENING HOURS, LAST ORDER
營業時間，最後點菜時間
Lunch/午膳 12:00-15:00 (L.O.)
Dinner/晚膳 18:00-23:00 (L.O.)

■ PRICE/價錢

Lunch/午膳	set/套餐	$255-445
	à la carte/點菜	$350-900
Dinner/晚膳	set/套餐	$870-1,086
	à la carte/點菜	$350-900

HOTELS
酒店

HOTELS BY ORDER OF COMFORT
酒店 — 以舒適程度分類

The Upper House 奕居	NEW	366
Hullett House	NEW	310
Le Meridien Cyberport 數碼港艾美		334
Lanson Place		332
East 東隅	NEW	294
The Mira	NEW	358

Hyatt Regency Tsim Sha Tsui 尖沙咀凱悦		314
Hyatt Regency Sha Tin 沙田凱悦		312
Harbour Plaza North Point 北角海逸		308
W		368
Royal Plaza 帝京		348
Crowne Plaza 皇冠假日	NEW	292
The Royal Garden 帝苑		364
LKF 蘭桂坊		336
Metropark (Causeway Bay) 銅鑼灣維景		342

The Luxe Manor 帝樂文娜公館	356

JIA		322
Eaton 逸東		296
Cosmopolitan 麗都		290
Panorama 麗景		346
Novotel Century 諾富特世紀		344
Harbour Plaza 8 Degrees 8度海逸	NEW	306

Cosmo 麗悦	288
Lan Kwai Fong 蘭桂坊	330

Conrad
港麗

With its enviable location above the Pacific Place shopping and entertainment complex, this hotel adeptly mixes the traditional with the modern. The vast oval lobby superbly showcases Chinese vases and bronze sculptures. Bedrooms are located between the 40th and 61st floors, ensuring sweeping views; the suites are particularly spacious and have elegantly marbled bathrooms. An outdoor swimming pool offers an equally dramatic panorama of the city.

RESTAURANTS/ 餐廳

Recommended/推薦			Also/其他
Golden Leaf/ 金葉庭	✿	✗✗✗	Brasserie on the Eight/
Nicholini's/ 意寧谷		✗✗✗	懷歐敍
			Garden Café/ 咖啡園
			Lobby Lounge/ 樂敍廊

酒店位處集購物娛樂於一身的太古廣場之上，巧妙地混合了傳統和現代元素。龐大的橢圓形大堂展示著中式花瓶及銅像，優雅而壯麗。寢室全在40至61樓之間，坐擁遼闊美景，而套房則特別寬敞，設有雲石浴室。室外游泳池同樣讓你飽覽香港全景。

■ ADDRESS/地址
TEL. 2521 3838
FAX. 2521 3888
Pacific Place, 88 Queensway,
Admiralty
香港金鐘道88號太古廣場
www.conradhotels.com

■ ROOMS AND SUITES/客房及套房
Rooms/客房 ＝467
Suites/套房 ＝46

■ PRICE/價錢

♦	＄5,000-6,000
♦♦	＄5,000-6,000
Suites/套房	＄6,800-41,000
⊐	＄280

Cosmo
麗悅

♿ ♻

Conveniently located close to Times Square, this fashionable sister hotel to the Cosmopolitan offers travellers well-equipped, good value accommodation. Bedrooms are compact but are brightly colour-coded in 'chic' orange, 'expectation' green and 'comfort' yellow and styled in a modern way. Unusually, room numbers are displayed on floors, not doors. A chic bar, The Nooch, is one of the more fashionable places in which to drink in Wan Chai.

RESTAURANTS/ 餐廳

Recommended/推薦	Also/其他

鄰近時代廣場的麗悅酒店選址便利,是麗都的時尚姐妹酒店,為旅行人士提供設備齊全,物有所值的住宿。睡房小巧精緻,以鮮豔的橙「時尚」、綠「祈望」、黃「舒適」為主色,富有現代風格。房間號碼罕有地顯示在地板上,而非門牌。風格時尚的酒吧The Nooch更是灣仔區最入流的酒吧之一。

■ ADDRESS/地址

TEL. 3552 8388
FAX. 3552 8399
375-377 Queen's Road East, Wan Chai
灣仔皇后大道東375-377號
www.cosmohotel.com.hk

■ ROOMS AND SUITES/客房及套房
Rooms/客房 =139
Suites/套房 =3

■ PRICE/價錢

🧍	$ 1,700-2,400
🧍🧍	$ 1,700-2,400
Suites/套房	$ 3,800-5,000
☕	$ 90

Cosmopolitan
麗都

    ♿ ⚤ 🏃 🚴

This large operation occupies the former premises of the Xin Hua News Agency Building; in effect, the old Chinese embassy before Hong Kong's handover. Today, it is the perfect choice for anyone wanting to attend the Happy Valley Racecourse: some rooms even offer a full view of the proceedings. Bedrooms are smart and unpretentious although some may be a little compact. A complimentary shuttle bus links the hotel to a number of local amenities.

RESTAURANTS/ 餐廳

Recommended/推薦	Also/其他
	La Maison de l'Orient/ 大宅門餐廳

這間大型酒店前身為新華社香港分社的所在地，實際上是香港回歸前的中國大使館。今天，對希望觀看跑馬地賽事的人來說，這間酒店是完美選擇，有些客房甚至讓你看到整場賽事的全貌。寢室設計既時尚又不造作，不過部分房間可能有點小巧。設有免費穿梭巴士，往返酒店及一些著名市區設施。

■ ADDRESS/地址

TEL. 3552 1111
FAX. 3552 1122
387-97 Queen's Road East, Wan Chai
灣仔皇后大道東387-397號
www.cosmopolitanhotel.com.hk

■ ROOMS AND SUITES/客房及套房
Rooms/客房 =435
Suites/套房 =19

■ PRICE/價錢

🧍	$ 1,800-3,200
🧍🧍	$ 1,800-3,200
Suites/套房	$ 4,200-4,500
☕	$ 128

Crowne Plaza
皇冠假日

Upper level bedrooms at this modern, corporate-minded hotel have the best views and these include the Happy Valley racetrack on the south side. All the bedrooms are decently proportioned and come with glass-walled bathrooms; but the Crown Club rooms offer extra luxuries. Club@28 is the chic bar on the top floor for the fashionable crowd; there's even an illuminated floor to help perfect that catwalk strut.

RESTAURANTS/ 餐廳

Recommended/推薦

Also/其他

Kudos

這家為企業客戶精心設計的摩登酒店，高層客房均坐擁香港島最出色的景觀，南邊的高層客房更可飽覽跑馬地馬場全景。所有房間都寬敞舒適，襯以玻璃牆壁的浴室，貴賓樓層客房更提供額外的豪華享受。Club@28是在頂層為一眾時尚人士而設的酒吧，酒吧裏舖設發光地板，讓眾顧客的「Catwalk」更顯完美。

■ ADDRESS/地址

TEL. 3980 3980
FAX. 3980 3900
8 Leighton Road, Causeway Bay
銅鑼灣禮頓道8號
www.cphongkong.com

■ ROOMS AND SUITES/客房及套房
Rooms/客房 ＝253
Suites/套房 ＝10

■ PRICE/價錢

👤	$ 1,550-2,200
👥	$ 1,550-2,200
Suites/套房	$ 4,200-4,850
☕	$ 188

293

East
東隅

NEW

Describes itself as a 'lifestyle business hotel' where even the water feature by the entrance tells you it's a little different. It has it all: an uncluttered lobby, a chic bar, relaxed dining, even a paperless check-in (you sign a screen); plus a stunning rooftop terrace bar named 'Sugar', as this was once a sugar factory. Bedrooms are minimalist and use plenty of glass and wood to create a warm, tasteful feel. Corner rooms have great views.

RESTAURANTS/餐廳

Recommended/推薦	Also/其他
	Feast

標榜為一家悠閒式商務酒店，東隅入口處的水飾已顯出一點兒與別不同。整潔的大堂，時尚的酒吧，氣氛輕鬆的餐廳，甚至電子入住登記（你可在輕觸式螢幕上簽名），加上一個可觀看維港迷人景色的天台露台酒吧 “Sugar” －名字靈感源自酒店前身為糖廠，絕對切合你所需。客房佈置採用簡約風格，利用大量玻璃與木材來塑造溫暖而具品味的感覺。位處轉角的客房景觀尤佳。

■ ADDRESS/地址

TEL. 3968 3968
FAX. 3968 3933
29 Taikoo Shing Road, Island East
港島東太古城道29號
www.east-hongkong.com

■ ROOMS AND SUITES/客房及套房

Rooms/客房 =345

■ PRICE/價錢

🚹	$1,200-2,000
🚹🚹	$1,200-2,000
Suites/套房	$3,500-6,000
☕	$140

Eaton
逸東

This is located near both the Jade Market and the Tin Hau temple; in its 4th floor lobby you'll find a small terrace with fishponds. Bedrooms are compact but neatly kept; a sizeable number have recently been renovated and labelled as Deluxe. The small swimming pool is located on the hotel's roof. This friendly establishment is a firm favourite with marrying couples: it hosts over 700 wedding receptions each year!

RESTAURANTS/ 餐廳

Recommended/推薦	Also/其他
Yat Tung Heen (Jordan)/ 逸東軒 (佐敦) ✗✗	Metro Buffet & Grill
	Yagura

酒店鄰近玉器市場和天后廟，四樓大堂更設有景致宜人的花園和魚池。客房面積不大，但整潔舒適，不少房間最近更翻新為高級客房，酒店天台設有小型游泳池。這家設備完善的酒店廣受新婚人士歡迎，每年舉行超過七百次婚宴。

■ ADDRESS/地址
TEL. 2782 1818
FAX. 2385 8132
380 Nathan Road, Kowloon
九龍彌敦道380號
www.hongkong.eatonhotels.com

■ ROOMS AND SUITES/客房及套房
Rooms/客房 ＝445
Suites/套房 ＝20
■ PRICE/價錢

🛉	$ 800-5,000
🛉🛉	$ 800-5,000
Suites/套房	$ 1,600-5,500
🖵	$ 138

Four Seasons
四季

Standing majestically over the harbour, Four Seasons offers some of the most spacious accommodation in Hong Kong. Bedrooms come either with contemporary detailing or a more Asian feel; bathrooms are large and luxurious. The Blue Bar is the stylish setting for cocktails and live music; the spa is impressive and leads out to the two swimming pools, each kept at a different temperature. Comfort levels are matched by the high standards of service.

RESTAURANTS/ 餐廳

Recommended/推薦			Also/其他
Caprice	✿✿✿	🗙🗙🗙🗙🗙	
Lung King Heen/ 龍景軒	✿✿✿	🗙🗙🗙🗙	
The Lounge		🗙🗙	

四季酒店坐擁壯麗維港景色，提供一些香港最寬敞的時尚客房。部份客房以現代風格佈置，有些則融合東方情懷，更設有大型豪華浴室。Blue Bar專為享受雞尾酒和現場音樂而設。水療設施令人印象難忘，更設有兩個溫度不同的泳池。舒適的環境與高質素服務互相輝映。

■ ADDRESS/地址

TEL. 3196 8888
FAX. 3196 8899
8 Finance Street, Central
中環金融街8號
www.fourseasons.com/hongkong

■ ROOMS AND SUITES/客房及套房
Rooms/客房 =399
Suites/套房 =54

■ PRICE/價錢

👤	$ 4,200-5,300
👥	$ 4,200-5,300
Suites/套房	$ 8,800-55,000
☕	$ 220

Grand Hyatt
君悅

There's a classic 1930s feel to the lobby of this grand hotel, which has been a fixture in the Wan Chai area for over 20 years. Bedrooms, by contrast, are contemporary, being sleek and minimalist in their decoration, with deluxe rooms offering more space and views. Plenty of marble and granite have been used to create particularly opulent bathrooms. There are 14 Plateau rooms with a Japanese feel and direct access to the spa.

RESTAURANTS/ 餐廳

Recommended/推薦		Also/其他
Grissini	🍴	Kaetsu/ 鹿悅
One Harbour Road/ 港灣壹號	🍴	Tiffin/ 茶園

酒店紮根於灣仔區二十年以上而大堂極具三十年代的經典風格。相比之下，客房設計更具現代特色，裝潢流暢簡潔，豪華房間提供更大空間，更寬廣觀景。奢華浴室用大量雲石及花崗岩打造而成。酒店設有十四間靜水沁園日式房間，直接通往水療設施。

■ ADDRESS/地址
TEL. 2588 1234
FAX. 2802 0677
1 Harbour Road, Wan Chai
灣仔港灣道1號
www.hongkong.grand.hyatt.com

■ ROOMS AND SUITES/客房及套房
Rooms/客房 ＝536
Suites/套房 ＝13

■ PRICE/價錢

👤	$5,000-8,500
👥	$5,200-8,700
Suites/套房	$8,500-55,000
☕	$260

Harbour Grand Kowloon
九龍海逸君綽

First impressions do not disappoint here. This shimmering glass structure is right on the waterfront, offering superb views across Victoria Harbour, and there's a spectacular lobby with an impressive white marble staircase. The bedrooms are bright, comfortable and well-equipped, if sober by comparison to other areas. Make the most of the dramatic rooftop pool with its glass-sided walls, as well as the top floor fitness centre and steam bath.

RESTAURANTS/ 餐廳

Recommended/推薦

- Harbour Grill
- Hoi Yat Heen/ 海逸軒

Also/其他

- Robatayaki/ 炉端燒
- The Promenade
- Waterfront Bar & Terrace/ 水雲間

這裡的第一印象絕對不會令你失望。這座閃閃發亮的玻璃建築毗鄰維港，金碧輝煌的大堂設有白色雲石階梯。房間開揚舒適，設備齊全，相比酒店其他設施或較樸實。住客可盡情享受天台設有玻璃幕牆的游泳池、頂樓健身中心和蒸氣浴。

■ ADDRESS/地址

TEL. 2621 3188
FAX. 2621 3311
20 Tak Fung Street, Whampoa Garden, Hung Hom, Kowloon
九龍紅磡黃埔花園德豐街20號
www.harbour-grand.com/kowloon

■ ROOMS AND SUITES/客房及套房

Rooms/客房 =468
Suites/套房 =38

■ PRICE/價錢

	$1,260-3,600
	$1,260-3,900
Suites/套房	$2,700-32,000
	$185

Harbour Grand Hong Kong NEW
港島海逸君綽

This L-shaped hotel at the heart of Hong Kong Island offers unique views of the harbour, while its striking lobby, dominated by a vast Swarovski crystal chandelier, underlines its grandeur. All rooms are contemporary in style; some even come with private patios and Jacuzzis. Dining facilities are numerous and include what is claimed as the longest buffet in Hong Kong. An easy 5-minute walk from the Fortress Hill MTR station.

RESTAURANTS/ 餐廳

Recommended/推薦		Also/其他
Kwan Cheuk Heen/ 君綽軒	✕✕✕	Harbour Grand Café
Le 188°	✕✕✕	Lobby Lounge/ 大堂酒吧
		Nagomi/ 和

這棟位處港島中心地帶的L型酒店讓我們欣賞到獨一無二的維港景致。引人注目的酒店大堂以巨型施華洛世奇水晶吊燈作裝飾,富麗堂皇,氣派不凡。所有房間都走現代風格,部分客房甚至擁有私人露台,附設暖水按摩浴池。這裡有各式各樣的餐廳,提供世界各地美食,包括號稱全港最大型的自助餐。酒店位置方便,從港鐵炮台山站只需步行5分鐘。

■ ADDRESS/地址
TEL. 2121 2688
FAX. 2121 2699
23 Oil Street, North Point
北角油街23號
www.harbour-grand.com/hongkong

■ ROOMS AND SUITES/客房及套房
Rooms/客房 ＝742
Suites/套房 ＝86

■ PRICE/價錢

👤	$ 1,180-5,000
👥	$ 1,180-5,000
Suites/套房	$ 3,000-24,000
☕	$ 195

Harbour Plaza 8 Degrees
8度海逸

An eight degree incline is this tall and contemporary hotel's unique selling point, from the lobby ceiling and walls to the glasses in the restaurant. Bedrooms may be quite compact but they are thoughtfully laid out and come in warm colours; the higher the floor, the brighter the room. The swimming pool is pleasant, even if it's surrounded by walls. The hotel should benefit from the huge development project that's upgrading the local area.

RESTAURANTS/ 餐廳

Recommended/推薦	Also/其他
	8 Degrees Café/ 8度餐廳

傾斜 8 度是這家高聳而現代的酒店的獨特賣點，從大堂天花到牆身以至餐廳玻璃，都是傾斜的。睡房可能比較小巧，但經過精心佈置，以暖色裝潢。樓層越高，房間越開揚。泳池雖然四面被牆圍繞，但環境依然宜人。酒店應可從該區的大型提升環境發展計劃得益。

■ ADDRESS/地址

TEL. 2126 1988
FAX. 2126 1900
199 Kowloon City Road, To Kwa Wan, Kowloon
九龍土瓜灣九龍城道 199 號
www.harbour-plaza.com

■ ROOMS AND SUITES/客房及套房
Rooms/客房 ＝678
Suites/套房 ＝24

■ PRICE/價錢

👤	$ 800-2,800
👥	$ 900-3,000
Suites/套房	$ 2,000-4,300
☕	$ 130

307

Harbour Plaza North Point
北角海逸

For the moment, this has the longest outdoor swimming pool on Hong Kong Island (at 25 metres) as well as a smartly equipped fitness centre. Spread over 32 floors, everything is very contemporary, right from the moment you enter the lobby with its unusual water feature. Bedrooms here are a good size and quiet - most only have a shower so if you require a bath ask when booking. There are 200 serviced suites designed for long-stay clients.

RESTAURANTS/ 餐廳

Recommended/推薦	Also/其他
	Green/ 綠怡廳
	Hoi Yat Heen/ 海逸軒

樓高32層的北角海逸酒店擁有目前港島最大型的戶外游泳池（25米），以及設施齊全的健身中心。酒店的裝飾極富時代感，從大堂的水池即可見一斑。客房寬敞而寧靜：大部分房間只有淋浴設備，如需浸浴，緊記在預訂房時事先詢問。酒店另設有200間為長期住客而設的服務式套房。

■ ADDRESS/地址
TEL. 2187 8888
FAX. 2187 8899
665 King's Road, North Point
北角英皇道665號
www.harbour-plaza.com

■ ROOMS AND SUITES/客房及套房
Rooms/客房 ＝469
Suites/套房 ＝200

■ PRICE/價錢
👤	$ 1,950-2,050
👥	$ 2,150-2,650
Suites/套房	$ 3,650-6,450
🛏	$ 135

Hullett House NEW

The jewel in the 1881 Heritage complex, once the headquarters of the Marine Police, is Hullett House. This handsome colonial building was restored in 2009 and blends together history, culture and contemporary comfort. The strength of the operation certainly lies with the bedrooms – each of the ten very large rooms is individually themed, ranging from art deco or pop art to dynasty and red Chinese. There's a choice of five restaurants.

RESTAURANTS/ 餐廳

Recommended/推薦		Also/其他
Loong Toh Yuen/ 隆濤院	✕✕	Mariners' rest
St. George	✕✕✕	Stables Grill
		The Parlour

Hullett House堪稱1881年建造的前水警總部內的寶石。這棟富有殖民地色彩的美麗建築物在2009年翻新,將歷史、文化與現代的舒適自在共冶一爐。這文物級酒店的強項絕對是他們的房間,十個極為寬敞的房間各按不同主題裝飾,由裝飾藝術或普普藝術到古典中式風格,一應俱全。這裡亦設有五家餐廳可供選擇。

■ ADDRESS/地址

TEL. 3988 0000
FAX. 2368 2325
2A Canton Road, Tsim Sha Tsui, Kowloon
九龍尖沙咀廣東道2A
www.hulletthouse.com

■ ROOMS AND SUITES/客房及套房
Rooms/客房 = 10

■ PRICE/價錢

🧍	$ 4,400-6,000
🧍🧍	$ 4,400-6,000

Hyatt Regency Sha Tin
沙田凱悅

Opened in 2009, this hotel is just a two minute walk from University station (adjacent to the Chinese University). It is styled in a contemporary way, making clever use of neutral colours and natural materials like stone and wood to create a soothing ambience. The 26 floor building includes well-equipped bedrooms with either harbour or mountain views. Facilities include a smart spa and fitness centre.

RESTAURANTS/ 餐廳

Recommended/推薦	Also/其他
	Café/ 咖啡廳
	Sha Tin 18/ 沙田18

沙田凱悅於2009年開幕，從港鐵大學站（毗鄰香港中文大學）
前往僅需步行兩分鐘。酒店設計現代，巧妙運用中性色彩及天
然物料如石材及木材製造柔和融洽的感覺。樓高二十六層的酒
店擁有設備齊全的海景或山景客房，酒店更配備完善水療設備
及健身中心。

■ ADDRESS/地址

TEL. 3723 1234
FAX. 3723 1235
18 Chak Cheung Street, University,
Sha Tin, New Territories
新界沙田大學站澤祥街18號
www.hongkong.shatin.hyatt.com

■ ROOMS AND SUITES/客房及套房
Rooms/客房 ＝434
Suites/套房 ＝133

■ PRICE/價錢

🧍	$ 900-3,100
🧍🧍	$ 900-3,100
Suites/套房	$ 2,900-12,700
☕	$ 198

Hyatt Regency Tsim Sha Tsui
尖沙咀凱悅

NEW

Occupying floors 3 to 24 of the impressive K11 skyscraper, and connected to the K11 Art Mall, means that the bedrooms here at the Hyatt Regency benefit from impressive views of the city or the harbour. The rooms are decorated in a crisp, modern style; those choosing the Regency Club level have access to the private lounge. There are dining options galore and an impressive selection of whiskies available in the Chin Chin Bar.

RESTAURANTS/ 餐廳

Recommended/推薦		Also/其他
Hugo's/ 希戈	✕✕✕	Café/ 咖啡廳
The Chinese Restaurant/ 凱悅軒	✕✕✕	

尖沙咀凱悅佔據令人印象深刻的K11摩天大樓的3至24層，並與
K11購物藝術館相連，代表酒店房間都能看到令人響往的城市繁
華景色，又或者是令人迷醉的維港景致。房間風格俐落摩登，選
擇嘉賓軒樓層的住客更可享受專用酒廊的服務。酒店提供多個餐
飲選擇，值得一提的是請請吧內威士忌種類之多令人目不暇給。

■ ADDRESS/地址
TEL. 2311 1234
FAX. 3721 1235
18 Hanoi Road, Tsim Sha Tsui,
Kowloon
九龍尖沙咀河內道18號
www.hongkong.tsimshatsui.hyatt.com

■ ROOMS AND SUITES/客房及套房
Rooms/客房 ＝348
Suites/套房 ＝33

■ PRICE/價錢

👤	$ 1,600-3,250
👥	$ 1,600-3,250
Suites/套房	$ 2,300-10,000
☕	$ 198

Intercontinental
洲際

♿ ⬳ 👆 🚭 💆 🏊 Spa 🚴

Deceptively unremarkable from the outside, but decidedly impressive once you're in the grand lobby with its magnificent harbour views. All bedrooms are spacious, well-appointed in neutral tones and have large marble bathrooms. Relax in either the attractive swimming pool or the spa pool or take a massage in an outside cabana. Options for dining are particularly good (see separate entries) and the service is meticulous.

RESTAURANTS/ 餐廳

Recommended/推薦			Also/其他
Nobu		╳╳	Harbourside
Spoon by Alain Ducasse	✿	╳╳╳	
The Steak House		╳╳╳	
Yan Toh Heen/ 欣圖軒	✿	╳╳╳	

酒店平凡的外表也許會讓人認為不外如是，但踏入富麗堂皇的酒店
大堂，望著一流海景，絕對會令你留下深刻印象。所有客房都非常
寬敞，淺色調的裝潢亦讓人感覺安靜，更設有寬闊的大理石浴室。
你可以在優雅的游泳池或水療池鬆弛身心，或在戶外的池邊小室享
受一下按摩服務。酒店內的餐飲服務非常出色（請參照其他有關的
介紹），而且服務水準一流。

■ ADDRESS/地址
TEL. 2721 1211
FAX. 2739 4546
18 Salisbury Road, Tsim Sha Tsui,
Kowloon
九龍尖沙咀梳士巴利道18號
www.intercontinental.com

■ ROOMS AND SUITES/客房及套房
Rooms/客房 ＝470
Suites/套房 ＝25

■ PRICE/價錢

👤	$ 2,800-8,700
👥	$ 2,800-8,900
Suites/套房	$ 12,000-78,000
☕	$ 280

Intercontinental Grand Stanford
海景嘉福

Although originally built in 1981, this sizeable 18-storey waterfront property has been drastically upgraded over the last few years but still retains its unusual zigzag frontage. The best bedrooms benefit from excellent views over Victoria Harbour and Hong Kong Island and have charming French Empire-style furniture. A fitness centre and outdoor heated swimming pool are both perched on the roof of the building.

RESTAURANTS/ 餐廳

Recommended/推薦			Also/其他
Hoi King Heen/ 海景軒	✿	⚒⚒⚒	Café on M
The Mistral/ 海風餐廳		⚒⚒	

雖然這幢18層的龐大臨海建築物建於1981年，但在過去幾年已大幅升級，並保留了獨特的曲折正門。酒店內最佳的寢室坐擁維港及港島美景，並採用了迷人的法國帝王式傢具。酒店頂層設有健身室及戶外溫水泳池。

■ ADDRESS/地址

TEL. 2721 5161
FAX. 2732 2233
70 Mody Road, East Tsim Sha Tsui,
Kowloon
九龍尖東麼地道70號
www.hongkong.intercontinental.com

■ ROOMS AND SUITES/客房及套房
Rooms/客房 = 556
Suites/套房 = 23

■ PRICE/價錢

👤	$ 1,300-4,100
👥	$ 1,300-4,100
Suites/套房	$ 3,100-12,000
☕	$ 228

Island Shangri-La
港島香格里拉

The intricate beauty of possibly the world's largest Chinese silk painting towers over the glamorous atrium and rises up all of 16 storeys. More sparkle is provided by the dazzling array of chandeliers placed round the hotel. Up above, the accommodation is classic and sumptuously appointed, especially those on the executive floors (52nd to 55th). The Island Shangri-La feels somewhat like a father-figure of the Hong Kong hotel scene.

RESTAURANTS/ 餐廳

Recommended/推薦			Also/其他
Lobster Bar and Grill/ 龍蝦吧		XX	Café TOO
Petrus/ 珀翠	✿	XXXXX	Nadaman/ 灘萬
Summer Palace/ 夏宮	✿	XX	

屹立在迷人的中庭，高高越過酒店的16層：這幅可能是世上最大的中國絲綢畫，散發著複雜精細的美。酒店四處掛著的吊燈燈光，五光十色，令人眼花撩亂。樓上是奢華典雅的客房，尤其是52至55樓商務樓層的房間，十分豪華。港島香格里拉給人的感覺，就像香港酒店業的前輩一樣。

■ ADDRESS/地址

TEL. 2877 3838

FAX. 2521 8742
Pacific Place, Supreme Court Road, Admiralty
中區法院道太古廣場
www.shangri-la.com

■ ROOMS AND SUITES/客房及套房
Rooms/客房 ＝531
Suites/套房 ＝34

■ PRICE/價錢

👤	$ 4,600-5,850
👥	$ 4,600-5,850
Suites/套房	$ 9,600-32,500
☕	$ 268

JIA

 ♿ ⚥

Jia means 'home' but the idea of having a Philippe Starck designed home is not within most people's reach, so staying at this hip hotel is the next best thing. The interior is as modern as you expect, with bold contemporary pieces contrasting with a white palette. It's located in a fairly vibrant area so asking for a bedroom on an upper floor is a good idea. Continental breakfast, afternoon tea and evening wine are all included in the rate.

RESTAURANTS/ 餐廳

Recommended/推薦   Also/其他

Jia代表「家」,但對大多數人來説,擁有由知名創意設計大師Philippe Starck(菲利浦史塔克)設計的家是遙不可及的;在這家潮流精品酒店住宿,大概是最好的次選了。內部裝潢一如所想,極富現代特色,強烈的當代作品與純白的調色板相映成趣。酒店位於繁華地段,因此選擇較高樓層的房間會是個好主意。房間價錢已包括歐陸早餐、下午茶及黃昏美酒。

■ ADDRESS/地址
TEL. 3196 9000
FAX. 3196 9001
1-5 Irving Street, Causeway Bay
銅鑼灣伊榮街1-5 號
www.jiaboutiquehotels.com

■ ROOMS AND SUITES/客房及套房
Rooms/客房 ＝26
Suites/套房 ＝28
■ PRICE/價錢

♦	$2,500
♦♦	$2,500
Suites/套房	$3,500-6,000

JW Marriott
萬豪

   ♿ ← ☞ **P** ⅟ 🏋 🏊 🚵

This business-oriented hotel boasts 602 rooms spread over 35 storeys and, at its pinnacle, a series of executive floors with their own discreet lounge and meeting rooms. A major renovation in 2009 made the bedrooms more contemporary and functional. There's a pleasant outdoor swimming pool and a well-equipped fitness centre, as well as a large choice of dining options, from Cantonese to Californian, seafood to wine bar and a tea room.

RESTAURANTS/ 餐廳

Recommended/推薦		Also/其他

Man Ho/ 萬豪殿 ✕✕

Fish Bar/ 魚吧
JW's California/ JW's 加州
Marriott Café/ 萬豪咖啡室
The Lounge

以商務住客為主的萬豪酒店樓高三十五層，客房數量達602間。位於頂樓的一列行政套房，更附有設計素雅的休息室和會議室供住客專用。2009年的主要更新是將房間改造得更富現代感、更實用。設有環境宜人的戶外游泳池及設備齊全的健身中心，各地餐飲任君選擇，廣東菜到加州菜應有盡有，海鮮、酒吧、茶室悉隨尊便。

■ ADDRESS/地址
TEL. 2810 8366
FAX. 2845 0737
Pacific Place, 88 Queensway,
Admiralty
香港金鐘道88號太古廣場
www.jwmarriotthongkong.com

■ ROOMS AND SUITES/客房及套房
Rooms/客房 ＝577
Suites/套房 ＝25

■ PRICE/價錢
👤	$3,700-5,900
👥	$4,100-6,200
Suites/套房	$8,800-40,000
☕	$250

Kowloon Shangri-La
九龍香格里拉

It is not just the grandeur of the lobby, with its marble, sparkling chandeliers and tiered water fountain, which will impress at this business-orientated hotel – the bedrooms are also a good size when compared to many other similarly priced hotels. But be sure to ask for one of the recently renovated bedrooms which now have a warmer, brighter feel. The hotel is also a popular destination for traditional afternoon tea.

RESTAURANTS/ 餐廳

Recommended/推薦			Also/其他
Angelini		✕✕✕	Café Kool
Shang Palace/ 香宮	❀	✕✕✕	Nadaman/ 灘萬
			Tapas Bar

不僅是氣派宏偉的雲石酒店大堂，甚至是閃爍的吊燈與多層噴泉，都令你對這家以商務為主的酒店留下深刻印象。與許多其他價格相近的酒店相比，這裡的房間更顯寬敞。切記要求一間最近重新裝潢過、感覺較溫暖明亮的房間。這裡也是一個享受傳統下午茶的熱門地點。

■ ADDRESS/地址
TEL. 2721 2111
FAX. 2723 8686
64 Mody Road, East Tsim Sha Tsui, Kowloon
九龍尖東麼地道64號
www.shangri-la.com

■ ROOMS AND SUITES/客房及套房
Rooms/客房 =645
Suites/套房 =43

■ PRICE/價錢

👤	$ 2,200-3,300
👥	$ 2,200-3,900
Suites/套房	$ 4,800-18,880
☕	$ 220

Langham Place
朗豪

Located in a vibrant, animated neighbourhood, this 42-storey glass tower is filled with every gadget a technophile could ever want and also functions as a wonderful showcase for Chinese modern art - over 1,500 paintings, sculptures and installations are spread around the building. Bedrooms are all crisply contemporary in their style and come in a range from 'Vital' through to 'Prime'. The pool is found on the hotel roof.

RESTAURANTS/ 餐廳

Recommended/推薦			Also/其他
Ming Court/ 明閣	✿✿	XX XX	The Place
Tokoro		XX	

酒店座落於充滿活力的社區內，玻璃塔般的大樓樓高42層，不僅有每個科技發燒友夢寐以求的電子產品，亦是個空間廣闊的中國現代美術展覽場。超過1,500 幅畫作、雕塑與裝置藝術品分佈於整棟大樓之內。客房的設計極富現代感，從「基本」到「全盛」系列，應有盡有。酒店頂樓設有泳池。

■ ADDRESS/地址
TEL. 3552 3388
FAX. 3552 3322
555 Shanghai Street, Mong Kok,
Kowloon
九龍旺角上海街555號
www.hongkong.langhamplacehotels.com

■ ROOMS AND SUITES/客房及套房
Rooms/客房 ＝625
Suites/套房 ＝40

■ PRICE/價錢
👤	$ 1,100-3,000
👤👤	$ 1,100-3,000
Suites/套房	$ 3,400-15,000
☕	$ 178

Lan Kwai Fong
蘭桂坊

A stylish mix of Chinese and contemporary furniture, neutral tones and dark wood veneers has been used to create a calming environment. Try to secure one of the corner bedrooms or a suite with a balcony if you need a little more space. The top floor rooms have the harbour views. The discreet Celebrity Cuisine offers accomplished Cantonese cooking. This is a hotel that can offer a genuine sense of neighbourhood.

RESTAURANTS/ 餐廳

Recommended/推薦	Also/其他

Celebrity Cuisine/ 名人坊 ✿✿ ╳╳

融合了中國傳統與現代的家俱，中性色調及深色木間隔，打造舒適環境。如果你需要更寬敞空間，建議預訂轉角位置的房間或附露臺的套房。頂樓房間可飽覽維港景色。服務周到的名人坊提供美味的廣東菜。酒店可充分表現此區真正特色。

■ ADDRESS/地址

TEL. 3650 0000

FAX. 3650 0088
3 Kau U Fong, Central
中環九如坊3號
www.lankwaifonghotel.com.hk

■ ROOMS AND SUITES/客房及套房
Rooms/客房 ＝157
Suites/套房 ＝5

■ PRICE/價錢

♦	$ 1,200-3,400
♦♦	$ 1,200-3,400
Suites/套房	$ 3,800-6,800
☕	$ 140

Lanson Place

♿ ⇙ 🏃 🚴

An elegant European-style façade marks Lanson Place out as a stylish boutique hotel, which dovetails effortlessly with its chic location. Classical and contemporary designs interweave to create a calm exclusivity. There's a serene patio, and the interior artwork creates a feel of warmth and tranquillity. The spacious rooms include a small kitchen for long-stay guests, and many look out to HK Stadium. A cool, calm lounge fits the bill perfectly.

RESTAURANTS/餐廳

Recommended/推薦   Also/其他

Lanson Place擁有歐洲風格的優雅外觀，是時尚的精品酒店，與時尚的地理位置一脈相承。古典和當代設計交織成這裡的專屬氣派。寧靜的露台配合室內的藝術作品，營造溫暖寧靜的感覺。寬敞客房內的小廚房，專為長期逗留的客人而設。另一方面，很多人都會觀望外面的香港大球場。寧靜安逸的酒廊可說是完全值回票價。

■ ADDRESS/地址
TEL. 3477 6888
FAX. 3477 6999
133 Leighton Road, Causeway Bay
銅鑼灣禮頓道133號
www.lansonplace.com

■ ROOMS AND SUITES/客房及套房
Rooms/客房 ＝188
Suites/套房 ＝6
■ PRICE/價錢

♦	$ 2,500-3,100
♦♦	$ 2,900-3,800
Suites/套房	$ 4,800-10,500
☐	$ 110

Le Méridien Cyberport
數碼港艾美

This design-led, corporate hotel with a spectacular sea-front setting is a chic place to stay. Expect up-to-the-minute business facilities and an attractive outside pool. The hip bedrooms with rain shower bathrooms, aromatherapy bowls and internet radios all enhance the wow factor. Choose from three restaurants, with Japanese, Cantonese or international menus, or just chill out on beanbags in the Podium bar.

RESTAURANTS/ 餐廳

Recommended/推薦	Also/其他
	Nam Fong/ 南方
	Prompt
	Umami

這間以設計作焦點的商務酒店坐擁無敵海景，極度時尚。酒店擁
有最先進的商業設施和吸引的室外泳池。客房設計時尚，豪華裝
置包括陣雨式淋浴系統、香薰設備和網絡收音機，全都令人驚嘆
不已。酒店內有三間餐廳選擇，包括是日式、粵式和國際菜式。
或者你可坐在平台酒吧的雪豆坐椅上小酌一番。

■ ADDRESS/地址

TEL. 2980 7788

FAX. 2980 7888
100 Cyberport Road
數碼港道100號
www.lemeridien.com/hongkong

■ ROOMS AND SUITES/客房及套房
Rooms/客房 ＝167
Suites/套房 ＝3

■ PRICE/價錢

👤	$ 2,300-3,200
👥	$ 2,700-3,700
Suites/套房	$ 8,500
🍽	$ 238

LKF
蘭桂坊

Smaller than most hotels in Central, LKF naturally styles itself in the 'boutique' class. Its hub centres round the higher floors: Slash, on the 29th, is a modern and intimate lounge bar; up the staircase on floor 30, Azure is a cool restaurant offering eye-popping city views. Spacious and contemporary bedrooms have espresso machines to give you a high, and pristine beds with sumptuous goose down pillows to bring you back down.

RESTAURANTS/ 餐廳

Recommended/推薦	Also/其他
	Azure

LKF比中環大部分酒店細，自然歸入「精 品」級酒店。其樞紐中心位處較高樓層：29樓的Slash是舒適的現代酒廊；30樓的Azure是一家風格不凡的餐廳，客人可將迷人的景觀盡收眼底。寬敞及時尚的客房設有特濃咖啡機讓你提提神，而純樸的床放置了豪華的鵝絨枕頭，讓你好好休息。

■ ADDRESS/地址
TEL. 3518 9688
FAX. 3518 9699
33 Wyndham Street, Lan Kwai Fong, Central
中環蘭桂坊雲咸街33號
www.hotel-LKF.com.hk

■ ROOMS AND SUITES/客房及套房
Rooms/客房 ＝86
Suites/套房 ＝9

■ PRICE/價錢

👤	$3,500-4,800
👥	$3,500-4,800
Suites/套房	$6,000-7,000
☕	$185

Mandarin Oriental
文華東方

As it approaches its half century, this hotel continues to be successfully updated whilst remaining true to its own celebrated heritage. Bedrooms are divided between Tai Pan style (wood and brown colours) or Veranda style (with brighter décor), but all rooms come with impressive technological gadgetry. The spa is a spiritual haven and the dining and bar options are many and varied, from the chic top-floor M bar to the legendary Captain's Bar.

RESTAURANTS/ 餐廳

Recommended/推薦

Mandarin Grill + Bar/		
文華扒房+酒吧	✿	✕✕✕✕
Man Wah/ 文華廳		✕✕✕
Pierre	✿✿	✕✕✕

Also/其他

Café Causette

Chinnery/ 千日里

Clipper Lounge/ 快船廊

The Krug Room

縱然邁向半世紀，酒店在保留優良傳統的同時，依然成功地走在時代之端。客房分為大班樣式（木色及棕色）或外廊樣式（較明亮及附海景），兩者同樣設有先進技術裝置。水療設施令客人彷如置身心靈的天堂，餐飲選擇繁多，從時尚的頂樓酒吧M bar到享負盛名的Captain's Bar，任君選擇。

■ ADDRESS/地址

TEL. 2522 0111

FAX. 2810 6190

5 Connaught Road, Central

中環干諾道中5號

www.mandarinoriental.com/hongkong

■ ROOMS AND SUITES/客房及套房

Rooms/客房 =436

Suites/套房 =65

■ PRICE/價錢

👤	$ 4,500-5,800
👥	$ 4,500-5,800
Suites/套房	$ 6,500-45,000
☕	$ 248

Marco Polo
馬哥孛羅

First opened in 1969, this waterfront operation is well placed for transport links and the modern lobby opens directly into the adjacent shopping mall. A refurbishment of the hotel is ongoing but do ask for a bedroom on the 14-16th floors as these have been renovated in a classic European style and are considerably more comfortable than the older rooms. A fitness centre is located in the shopping mall next door.

RESTAURANTS/ 餐廳

Recommended/推薦		Also/其他
Cucina	✕✕	Café Marco/ 馬哥孛羅咖啡廳
Yè Shanghai (Kowloon)/		Nishimura/ 西村
夜上海（九龍）	✿ ✕✕✕	

馬可孛羅酒店於1969年開幕，位處維港之旁，新穎的酒店大堂與
毗鄰的購物商場海港城相連，交通和購物都極為便利。酒店正進行
一系列翻新工程，切記選擇14至16樓的客房，它們已翻新成傳統
歐陸風格的客房，顯然較舊式客房舒適。健身中心位於海港城內。

■ ADDRESS/地址
TEL. 2113 0088
FAX. 2113 0011
Harbour City, Canton Road,
Tsim Sha Tsui, Kowloon
九龍尖沙咀廣東道海港城
www.marcopolohotels.com

■ ROOMS AND SUITES/客房及套房
Rooms/客房 ＝615
Suites/套房 ＝49

■ PRICE/價錢

🧍	$ 1,400-4,420
🧍🧍	$ 1,500-4,520
Suites/套房	$ 2,550-11,700
☕	$ 198

Metropark (Causeway Bay)
銅鑼灣維景

Near to Victoria Park, this 31-storey tower offers very good comforts and facilities for business travellers. Most bedrooms have excellent harbour views and all have bathrooms lined with marble. The rooftop swimming pool is very appealing, with its glass walls and underwater music. The Café du Parc offers all-day buffet dining and blends French and Japanese cooking plus other international favourites.

RESTAURANTS/ 餐廳

Recommended/推薦	Also/其他
	Café Du Parc/ 繽紛維苑餐廳

酒店大樓樓高三十一層，鄰近維多利亞公園，為商務旅客提供舒
適環境及設施。大部分客房都坐擁無敵海景及設有大理石浴室。
天台游泳池經過精心設計，玻璃幕牆和水底音樂都別出心裁。繽
紛維苑餐廳（Café du Parc）提供全日自助餐，搜羅法國、日本及
其他國際美食。

■ ADDRESS/地址
TEL. 2600 1000
FAX. 2600 1111
148 Tung Lo Wan Road, Causeway Bay
銅鑼灣道148號
www.metroparkhotel.com

■ ROOMS AND SUITES/客房及套房
Rooms/客房　=243
Suites/套房　=23

■ PRICE/價錢

👤	$ 900-3,500
👥	$ 1,900-3,500
Suites/套房	$ 6,800
⌑	$ 120

Novotel Century
諾富特世紀

Business travellers and tourists alike will find this property convenient as it's located close to the Hong Kong Convention and Exhibition Centre. The last refurbishment ensured it has modern, well-equipped bedrooms in a uniform style, with light wood furniture but quite small bathrooms. Superior rooms are more spacious and have the harbour views. An international buffet is offered at Le Café; Italian food at Pepino.

RESTAURANTS/ 餐廳

Recommended/推薦

Also/其他

Le Café

Pepino

商務客及需求相若的旅客會發覺這家酒店位置方便，吡鄰近香港會議展覽中心。酒店於數年前裝修，客房風格統一為富有現代感、設備完善的設計，輕木傢俱和小巧的浴室。豪華房間則更寬敞，並可觀賞維多利亞港景色。Le Café提供多國自助餐，Pepino則提供義大利餐點。

■ ADDRESS/地址

TEL. 2598 8888

FAX. 2598 8866

238 Jaffe Road, Wan Chai

灣仔謝斐道238號

www.novotel.com/asia

■ ROOMS AND SUITES/客房及套房

Rooms/客房 ＝491

Suites/套房 ＝20

■ PRICE/價錢

👤	$ 1,600-2,000
👥	$ 1,600-2,000
Suites/套房	$ 4,000-5,000
☕	$ 130

Panorama
麗景

This nicely located hotel offers the latest in contemporary design, with its 324 rooms slotting into 3 different bedroom types: silver, gold and platinum. The higher you go, the better the view but the best rooms are on corner sites where you can even enjoy the stunning harbour vista while relaxing in the bathtub. On the 38th floor is the Santa Lucia restaurant that offers a broad range of international dishes in a very modern setting.

RESTAURANTS/ 餐廳

Recommended/推薦

Also/其他

Santa Lucia/ 樂醉西餐廳

位置方便的麗景有324間客房均以當代最新穎的款式，設計出三種不同的房間類型，包括銀賓客房、黃金客房和白金客房。要從更佳位置俯瞰景色，便要更上一層樓；而酒店的最佳客房則位於角位，客人更可以一邊享受浸浴，一邊欣賞迷人的維港景致。位於38樓的樂醉西餐廳佈置時尚，教人心動，各式各樣的各國佳餚正待君細嚐。

■ ADDRESS/地址
TEL. 3550 0388
FAX. 3550 0288
8A Hart Avenue, Tsim Sha Tsui, Kowloon
九龍尖沙咀赫德道8A號
www.hotelpanorama.com

■ ROOMS AND SUITES/客房及套房
Rooms/客房 ＝312
Suites/套房 ＝12

■ PRICE/價錢

👤	$ 1,000-3,900
👥	$ 1,000-3,900
Suites/套房	$ 5,800
🛏	$ 188

Royal Plaza
帝京

The Royal Plaza's impressive marble lobby creates a rather grand ambience for arriving guests. Bedrooms are designed in a range of styles: from sober, classic elegance, via early 19th century French Empire, to the contemporary 'Executive Club' on the top two floors. Whatever your choice, all have city views. There's an outdoor pool with an unexpected Roman décor complete with columns; the solarium area has a particularly relaxing atmosphere.

RESTAURANTS/ 餐廳

Recommended/推薦	Also/其他
	La Scala/ 花月庭
	Royal Plaza/ 帝京軒

帝京酒店的雲石大堂格調相當華麗，造成一種堂皇的格調迎接來賓。客房的風格琳琳總總，包括十九世紀法國帝國的沉實古雅設計、最高兩層「行政樓層」的當代設計等，各適其式，所有客房都可享受「繁華城市景」。酒店的露天羅馬式泳池以圓柱作裝飾，設計風格令人驚喜；而日光浴地區的氣氛則特別輕鬆愜意。

■ ADDRESS/地址
TEL. 2928 8822
FAX. 2606 0088
193 Prince Edward Road West,
Kowloon
九龍太子道西193號
www.royalplaza.com.hk

■ ROOMS AND SUITES/客房及套房
Rooms/客房 =659
Suites/套房 =34

■ PRICE/價錢

👤	$ 2,300-3,700
👥	$ 2,700-4,200
Suites/套房	$ 6,300-26,800
🛏	$ 205

Sheraton
喜來登

  ♿ ← ☞ 🅿 ⚲ 🏋 ⊼ ⚐

One of Hong Kong's biggest hotels is located on the mainland but is a short walk from the Star Ferry Pier, which adds up to great views of Victoria Harbour. These can be best appreciated from the Health Club's rooftop pool, over a plate of oysters in the wine bar, or from a swish sea-facing executive room on the 16th and 17th floors. More down-to-earth but thoroughly pleasant are a cigar room, a wine shop and an international café.

RESTAURANTS/ 餐廳

Recommended/推薦		Also/其他
Celestial Court/ 天寶閣	✕✕	Morton's of Chicago
Unkai/雲海	✕✕	Oyster & Wine Bar
		The Café

這是香港最大的酒店之一，位於九龍半島，只需短短的步行距離便到天星碼頭。客人可盡覽維多利亞港的壯麗景色，最佳位置包括Health Club的天台游泳池、16樓及17樓的高級面海行政室，在蠔酒吧吃蠔時亦可享受美景。較為沉實但完全舒適的有雪茄廊、酒舖和國際咖啡廳。

■ ADDRESS/地址

TEL. 2369 1111

FAX. 2739 8707

20 Nathan Road, Tsim Sha Tsui, Kowloon

九龍尖沙咀彌敦道20號

www.sheraton.com/hongkong

■ ROOMS AND SUITES/客房及套房

Rooms/客房 ＝691

Suites/套房 ＝91

■ PRICE/價錢

👤	$ 1,900-3,500
👥	$ 2,000-3,900
Suites/套房	$ 4,000-13,500
☕	$ 220

The Landmark Mandarin Oriental
置地文華東方

From the personal airport pickup to the endless spa choices, this is the hotel for those after a little pampering. Not only are the cool and smartly designed bedrooms big on luxury and size (ranging from 450 to 600Sq.ft) but they also all have very stylish and impressively laid out bathrooms attached, which all feature either a sunken or a circular bath. MO is the cool ground floor bar for all day dining or night time cocktails.

RESTAURANTS/ 餐廳

Recommended/推薦			Also/其他
Amber	✿✿	🏾🏾🏾	MO Bar

從私人機場迎接服務到應有盡有的水療服務，置地文華東方可讓你盡享尊貴服務。令人讚嘆的不祇是客房面積寬敞（由450呎至600呎），設計型格獨特，還有客房內豪華時尚的浴室設備，包括巨型下沉式或圓形浴缸。地下的MO Bar不論日夜，均是品嘗雞尾酒的好地方。

■ ADDRESS/地址
TEL. 2132 0188
FAX. 2132 0199
15 Queen's Road, Central
中環皇后大道中15號
www.mandarinoriental.com/landmark

■ ROOMS AND SUITES/客房及套房
Rooms/客房 ＝101
Suites/套房 ＝12

■ PRICE/價錢

👤	$5,200-6,800
👥	$5,200-6,800
Suites/套房	$9,300-45,000
🍵	$218

The Langham
朗廷

The clamour of Peking Road is left behind as you enter the hushed surroundings of this elegant establishment. Its impressive lobby, furnished in a classical European style, is luxurious and features some impressive contemporary art and sculptures. Bedrooms are a mix of classic luxury and more attractive contemporary Chinese styling in the Grand rooms. All this charm is underpinned by modern facilities and attentive service.

RESTAURANTS/ 餐廳

Recommended/推薦			Also/其他
T'ang Court/ 唐閣	✿✿	🗙🗙🗙	L'Eclipse
			Main St. Deli
			The Bostonian/ 美岸海鮮廳

進入這棟優雅建築物，讓你立刻忘卻北京道熙來攘往的煩囂。設
計奪目的大堂以傳統歐洲風格裝潢，極盡奢華，更以出色當代藝
術品及雕塑點綴。豪華客房融合經典奢華風格及相當吸引的當代
中國裝潢。一切迷人之處，更見於現代設施及細心服務。

■ ADDRESS/地址
TEL. 2375 1133
FAX. 2375 6611
8 Peking Road, Tsim Sha Tsui,
Kowloon
九龍尖沙咀北京道8號
www.hongkong.langhamhotels.com

■ ROOMS AND SUITES/客房及套房
Rooms/客房 ＝469
Suites/套房 ＝26

■ PRICE/價錢

🧍	$ 1,900-3,350
🧍🧍	$ 1,900-3,350
Suites/套房	$ 3,750-8,550
☕	$ 275

The Luxe Manor
帝樂文娜公館

♿ 🔑 ⚡ 🛗 🚴

Leaving the outside world behind, you enter a stylish jewelbox that somehow manages to jumble up oriental influences with Surrealist furnishings to create plenty of quirky charm. The dramatically lit red and black lobby flings together gilt-edged thrones, scallop-shaped banquettes and baroque armchairs upholstered in cartoon characters. Bedrooms are quite compact, apart from the studio rooms and six individually themed suites.

RESTAURANTS/餐廳

Recommended/推薦	Also/其他
Aspasia ✗✗✗	

踏入珠寶盒般的時尚酒店，彷如脫離現實世界進入了世外桃源。帝樂文娜揉合了東方元素和超現實設計，營造迷人的虛幻氣氛。紅黑色的大堂燈光璀璨，照亮鍍金邊的寶座、印有扇貝圖案的走廊，以及裝上卡通人物坐墊的巴洛克風格扶手椅。除了尊尚豪華客房及六間獨立主題套房外，大部分客房都是精緻小巧。

■ ADDRESS/地址
TEL. 3763 8888
FAX. 3763 8899
39 Kimberley Road, Tsim Sha Tsui, Kowloon
九龍尖沙咀金巴利道39號
www.theluxemanor.com

■ ROOMS AND SUITES/客房及套房
Rooms/客房 ＝153
Suites/套房 ＝6

■ PRICE/價錢

👤	$ 1,200-3,000
👥	$ 1,200-3,000
Suites/套房	$ 10,000
☕	$ 138

The Mira　NEW

Give every room an Arne Jacobsen 'Egg chair'; add a cool, urban aesthetic and all the hi-tech extras you'll ever need, and you have The Mira – an eye-catchingly stylish and vibrant modern hotel. What the rooms may lack in size, they more than make up in design and it's worth asking for one facing Kowloon Park; bathrooms are equally contemporary. Suites are even more spectacular. The sumptuous spa is another great feature.

RESTAURANTS/ 餐廳

Recommended/推薦	Also/其他
Cuisine Cuisine at The Mira/	Yamm
國金軒 (The Mira) ❀❀ ✗✗✗	
Whisk ✗✗	

每個房間都放置一張Arne Jacobsen設計的"蛋椅",配合型格、富現代感的設計,再加上所有你需要的高科技產品,你得到的就是The Mira - 一家極為時尚、充滿活力的摩登酒店。這裡的房間面積可能略小,但設計細節可彌補不足,浴室同樣非常現代化。訂房時值得多花時間要求一個面向九龍公園的客房,套房則更加豪華。舒適豪華的水療設施也值得一讚。

■ ADDRESS/地址
TEL. 2368 1111
FAX. 2369 1788
118 Nathan Road, Tsim Sha Tsui, Kowloon
九龍尖沙咀彌敦道118號
www.themirahotel.com

■ ROOMS AND SUITES/客房及套房
Rooms/客房 ＝446
Suites/套房 ＝46

■ PRICE/價錢

👤	$ 1,500-2,800
👥	$ 1,500-2,800
Suites/套房	$ 2,800-38,400
☕	$ 280

The Park Lane
柏寧

Within easy walking distance of Times Square, this tall block directly faces Victoria Park with its jogging routes and tennis courts, and many of the rooms offer superb views of the park's lush greenery. Accommodation is stylish and understated with the Premier Club rooms proving especially spacious and well equipped. Among the food outlets is Riva (on the top floor) offering European based menus and a buffet a lunch, along with fantastic views.

RESTAURANTS/ 餐廳

Recommended/推薦	Also/其他
	Riva

柏寧酒店高聳而立,座落於銅鑼灣區,距離時代廣場僅咫尺之遙,面向維多利亞公園的緩跑徑和網球場。酒店大部分客房均坐擁綠樹林蔭的維園美景。客房設計時尚,與商務樓層(Premier Club)的房間實為完美配搭,地方特別寬敞,設備亦更齊全。位於頂層的Riva法國餐廳冠絕全酒店的食肆,配上歐陸餐點及絕佳景觀,午市更提供自助餐。

■ ADDRESS/地址
TEL. 2293 8888
FAX. 2576 7853
310 Gloucester Road, Causeway bay
銅鑼灣告士打道310號
www.parklane.com.hk

■ ROOMS AND SUITES/客房及套房
Rooms/客房 ＝793
Suites/套房 ＝12

■ PRICE/價錢
👤	$ 2,000-5,200
👥	$ 2,000-5,200
Suites/套房	$ 6,200-18,000
☕	$ 178

The Peninsula
半島

Opened in 1928, this is the grandee of Hong Kong hotels. Testimony to its niche position is the fleet of Rolls-Royces and the two helipads. The iconic lobby is the place for afternoon tea and the Salon De Ning for intimate cocktails. The superb spa boasts a Roman style pool and a swish terrace. Rooms blend Victorian English with delicate Asian touches; the sumptuous corner suites make the most of their harbour vistas.

RESTAURANTS/ 餐廳

Recommended/推薦		Also/其他
Chesa/ 瑞樵閣	ⅩⅩ	Felix
Gaddi's/ 吉地士	ⅩⅩⅩⅩⅩ	Imasa/ 今佐
Spring Moon/ 嘉麟樓	ⅩⅩⅩ	The Lobby/ 大堂茶座
		Verandah/ 露台餐廳

開幕於1928年的半島酒店是本港酒店業老大哥，一列列的勞斯萊斯和兩個直昇機坪，印證其特殊地位。有代表性的酒店大堂是享用下午茶的好地方，而玲瓏酒廊也是享受雞尾酒的不二之選。一流的水療設施包括羅馬式游泳池和時尚陽台。客房揉合了英國維多利亞風格及雅緻的亞洲風情，位處轉角位的的豪華套房可將廣闊維港景色盡收眼底。

■ ADDRESS/地址
TEL. 2920 2888
FAX. 2722 4170
Salisbury Road, Tsim Sha Tsui, Kowloon
九龍尖沙咀梳士巴利道
www.peninsula.com

■ ROOMS AND SUITES/客房及套房
Rooms/客房 ＝246
Suites/套房 ＝54

■ PRICE/價錢

👤	$4,200-5,800
👥	$4,200-5,800
Suites/套房	$6,800-68,000
🛏	$250

The Royal Garden
帝苑

In a prized position close to Victoria Harbour, the Royal Garden exudes cool class. Its most notable feature is a 110 foot atrium that brims with daylight and its foliage-strewn presence is ubiquitous, as guestrooms are accessible through corridors overlooking it. When booking, ask for one of the renovated rooms as these are more contemporary in style. On the roof is a welcoming surprise: a pleasant swimming pool.

RESTAURANTS/ 餐廳

Recommended/推薦	Also/其他
Dong Lai Shun/ 東來順 🔞 ✕✕	Le Soleil
Inagiku (Tsim Sha Tsui)/ 稻菊 (尖沙咀) ✕✕	The Greenery/ 雅苑座
Sabatini ✕✕✕	The Royal Garden/ 帝苑軒

帝苑酒店毗鄰維多利亞港，地理位置優越，別樹一格。最具特色的是它110呎高的中庭在充沛的陽光下，令人豁然開朗。酒店以葉飾作點綴，從通往客房的走廊向下望，舉目皆是。喜愛現代設計概念的客人訂房時謹記選擇已重新裝潢的房間。頂層設有一個舒適的露天泳池，為住客帶來意想不到的驚喜。

■ ADDRESS/地址
TEL. 2721 5215
FAX. 2369 9976
69 Mody Road, East Tsim Sha Tsui, Kowloon
九龍尖東麼地道69號
www.rghk.com.hk

■ ROOMS AND SUITES/客房及套房
Rooms/客房 =369
Suites/套房 =48

■ PRICE/價錢

🧍	$1,500-4,600
🧍🧍	$1,500-4,600
Suites/套房	$2,500-15,800
☕	$220

The Upper House NEW
奕居

♿ ⋖ 🚗 🅿 ⫽ 🚲

Already on the wish-list of fashionistas everywhere, The Upper House is a discreet and stylishly understated hotel. Art, sculptures and natural materials are used to great effect and help create the feeling of being in a private residence, albeit one with a pervading sense of calm. Bedrooms are airy and uncluttered but with concealed hi-tech extras; they also have yoga mats! Good-sized bathrooms have tubs with views.

RESTAURANTS/ 餐廳

Recommended/推薦	Also/其他
Café Gray Deluxe ❀ ✕✕	

奕居早已成為潮流人士趨之若鶩的住宿熱點。這裏是一家經過精心設計，細緻豪華的時尚酒店。藝術品、雕塑和天然物料帶來非凡效果，更能打造私人居所的感覺，瀰漫著平和氣息。房間通爽而秩序井然，但附有不少隱藏高科技用品。他們甚至提供瑜珈墊！浴室大小適中，安坐浴缸中就能觀賞美妙景色。

■ ADDRESS/地址

TEL. 2918 1838
FAX. 3968 1200
Pacific Place, 88 Queensway,
Admiralty
香港金鐘道88號太古廣場
www.upperhouse.com

■ ROOMS AND SUITES/客房及套房
Rooms/客房 ＝96
Suites/套房 ＝21

■ PRICE/價錢

👤	$3,000-4,200
👤👤	$3,000-4,500
Suites/套房	$5,500-12,000

W

With room categories like 'Wonderful' and 'Fabulous' one can probably guess that the W hotel is a little unconventional. On top of Elements shopping mall, it offers stylish, modern design at every turn, from the bathroom's rainforest showers to the surround sound in every bedroom. It has one of the world's highest outdoor pools on the 76th floor: the 'wet', along with a gym 'sweat' and a spa 'bliss'. Perhaps 'fab far east' sums it up.

RESTAURANTS/ 餐廳

Recommended/推薦	Also/其他
	Fire
	Kitchen

從「奇妙客房」到「絕佳客房」等客房分類，已可感受到W酒店與別不同。W位於圓方購物商場，從浴室的熱帶雨林花灑以致每間臥房的環迴立體聲，每個角落均設計得時尚而現代。它擁有全球最高樓層的室外泳池--- 76樓：'wet'、健身室 'sweat' 及水療設備 'bliss'。也許 'fab far east' 是最為貼切的形容方式。

■ ADDRESS/地址
TEL. 3717 2222
FAX. 3717 2888
1 Austin Road West, Kowloon Station, Kowloon
九龍柯士甸道西1號九龍站
www.whotels.com/hongkong

■ ROOMS AND SUITES/客房及套房
Rooms/客房 ＝351
Suites/套房 ＝42

■ PRICE/價錢

👤	$ 2,000-3,700
👥	$ 2,000-3,700
Suites/套房	$ 8,000-45,000
☕	$ 230

MACAU
澳門

RESTAURANTS
餐廳

STARRED RESTAURANTS

Within this selection, we have highlighted a number of restaurants for their particularly good cooking. When awarding one, two or three Michelin Stars there are a number of factors we consider: the quality and compatibility of the ingredients, the technical skill and flair that goes into their preparation, the clarity and combination of flavours, the value for money and above all, the taste. Equally important is the ability to produce excellent cooking not once but time and time again. Our inspectors make as many visits as necessary, so that you can be sure of the quality and consistency.

A two or three star restaurant has to offer something very special that separates it from the rest. Three stars – our highest award – are given to the very best.

Cuisines in any style of restaurant and of any nationality are eligible for a star. The decoration, service and comfort levels have no bearing on the award.

星級餐廳

在這系列的選擇裡，我們特意指出菜式上佳的餐廳。
給予一、二或三粒米芝蓮星時，我們考慮到以下因
素：材料的質素和相容性、烹調技巧和特色、氣味
濃度和組合、價錢是否相宜，以及味道。同樣重要
的是能夠持續提供美食。我們的評審員會因應需要
而多次到訪，所以讀者可肯定食物品質和一致性。
二或三星餐廳必有獨特之處，比其他餐廳更出眾。
最高評級 - 三星 - 只會給予最好的餐廳。
不論餐廳的風格如何，供應哪個國家的菜式，都可獲
星級。 餐廳陳設、服務及舒適程度亦不會影響評級 。

Exceptional cuisine, worth a special journey.
出類拔萃的菜餚，值得專程到訪。

One always eats here extremely well, sometimes superbly. Distinctive dishes are precisely executed, using superlative ingredients.

食客可在這裡享用美味的菜餚，有時令人更讚不絕口。獨特的菜式以最高級的材料精密地烹調。

Robuchon a Galera 法國餐廳		XxxX	French contemporary 時尚法式	411

Excellent cuisine, worth a detour.
傑出美食，值得繞道前往。

Skilfully and carefully crafted dishes of outstanding quality.

有技巧地精心烹調菜餚，品質優秀。

The Eight 8餐廳	ᵕᵕ	XxxX	Chinese 中式	415
Tim's Kitchen 桃花源小廚	ᵕᵕ	XxX	Cantonese 粵菜	417
Zi Yat Heen 紫逸軒		XxX	Cantonese 粵菜	421

A very good restaurant in its category.
同類別中出眾的餐廳。

A place offering cuisine prepared to a consistently high standard.

持續高水準菜式的地方。

Aurora 奧羅拉		XxX	Italian 意式	386
Il Teatro 帝雅廷	ᵕᵕ	XxxX	Italian 意式	397
Jade Garden 蘇浙匯		XX	Shanghainese 上海菜	400
Lei Garden 利苑酒家		XX	Cantonese 粵菜	403
Wing Lei 永利軒		XxX	Cantonese 粵菜	419

BIB GOURMAND

This symbol indicates our inspector's favourites for good value. Restaurants offering good quality cooking for $ 300 or less (price of a 3 course meal excluding drinks).

這標誌表示評審員認為價錢合理而美味的餐廳。300 元或以下便可享用優質美食（三道菜式的價錢，不包括飲料）。

Luk Kei Noodle 六記粥麵　NEW	🍜	Noodles and Congee 粥麵	405
Lung Wah Tea House 龍華茶樓	🍜	Cantonese 粵菜	406
Noodle & Congee Corner 粥麵莊	🍜	Noodles and Congee 粥麵	408
Oja Sopa De Fita Cheong Kei 祥記	🍜	Noodles and Congee 粥麵	409
Square Eight 食 · 八方	🍴	Chinese 中式	413

RESTAURANTS BY AREA
餐廳 — 以地區分類

Macau/澳門

NEW : New entry in the guide/ 新增推介
🍃 : Restaurant promoted to a Bib Gourmand or Star/ 評級有所晉升的餐廳

RESTAURANTS BY CUISINE TYPE
餐廳 — 以菜式分類

Cantonese/粵菜

Canton 喜粵		✗✗	Taipa 冰仔	392
Chan Kuong Kei (Rua do Dr. Pedro Jose Lobo) 陳光記(羅保博士街) NEW		🍴	Macau 澳門	393
Imperial Court 金殿堂		✗✗✗	Macau 澳門	398
Laurel 丹桂軒		✗✗	Macau 澳門	402
Lei Garden 利苑酒家	❀	✗✗	Taipa 冰仔	403
Lung Wah Tea House 龍華茶樓	☺	🍴	Macau 澳門	406
San Tou Tou 新陶陶 NEW		✗	Taipa 冰仔	412
Tim's Kitchen 桃花源小廚	💱 ❀❀	✗✗✗	Macau 澳門	417
Tou Tou Koi 陶陶居		✗	Macau 澳門	418
Wing Lei 永利軒	❀	✗✗✗	Macau 澳門	419
Ying 帝影樓		✗✗✗	Taipa 冰仔	420
Zi Yat Heen 紫逸軒	❀❀	✗✗✗	Taipa 冰仔	421

Chinese/中式

Beijing Kitchen 滿堂彩 NEW		✗✗	Taipa 冰仔	389
Golden Flower 京花軒 NEW		✗✗✗	Macau 澳門	396
Square Eight 食 · 八方	⊛	✗	Macau 澳門	413
The Eight 8餐廳	💱 ❀❀	✗✗✗✗	Macau 澳門	415

French/法式

Aux Beaux Arts 寶雅座		✗✗	Macau 澳門	387

French contemporary/時尚法式

Robuchon a Galera 法國餐廳	❀❀❀	✗✗✗✗	Macau 澳門	411

International/國際菜

Belcanção 鳴詩		✗✗	Taipa 冰仔	390

NEW : New entry in the guide/ 新增推介
💱 : Restaurant promoted to a Bib Gourmand or Star/ 評級有所晉升的餐廳

Italian 意式

Aurora 奧羅拉		❀	𝟀𝟀𝟀	Taipa 氹仔	386
Don Alfonso 當奧豐素			𝟀𝟀𝟀𝟀	Macau 澳門	395
Il Teatro 帝雅廷	❞	❀	𝟀𝟀𝟀𝟀	Macau 澳門	397

Japanese/日式

Inagiku 稻菊		𝟀𝟀	Macau 澳門	399
Okada 岡田		𝟀𝟀	Macau 澳門	410

Japanese Tempura/日式天婦羅

Tenmasa 天政		𝟀𝟀	Taipa 氹仔	414

Macanese/澳門菜

Café Encore 咖啡廷	NEW	𝟀𝟀	Macau 澳門	391
Litoral 海灣餐廳		𝟀	Macau 澳門	404

Noodles and Congee/粥麵

Luk Kei Noodle 六記粥麵	NEW	☕	🍜	Macau 澳門	405
Ngao Kei Ka Lei Chon 牛記咖喱美食	NEW		🍜	Macau 澳門	407
Noodle & Congee Corner 粥麵莊		☕	🍜	Macau 澳門	408
Oja Sopa De Fita Cheong Kei 祥記		☕	🍜	Macau 澳門	409

Portuguese/葡式

Antonio 安東尼奧		𝟀𝟀	Taipa 氹仔	384
A Petisqueria 葡國美食天地		𝟀	Taipa 氹仔	385
Banza 百姓		𝟀	Taipa 氹仔	388
Clube Militar de Macau 澳門陸軍俱樂部		𝟀𝟀	Macau 澳門	394

Shanghainese/上海菜

Jade Garden 蘇浙匯	❀	𝟀𝟀	Macau 澳門	400

Spanish/西班牙菜

La Paloma 芭朗瑪		𝟀𝟀	Macau 澳門	401

Steakhouse/扒房

The Kitchen 大厨		𝟀𝟀	Macau 澳門	416

PARTICULARLY PLEASANT RESTAURANTS
上佳的餐廳

NEW ：New entry in the guide/ 新增推介
❀ ：Restaurant promoted to a Bib Gourmand or Star/ 評級有所晉升的餐廳

感受澳門
EXPERIENCE MACAU !

3 -5/2	農曆新年 Chinese New Year Holidays
29/4 - 28/5	第二十二屆澳門藝術節 22nd Macau Arts Festival
4 - 6/6	澳門國際龍舟賽 Macau International Dragon Boat Races
24 - 28/8	世界女子排球大獎賽 — 總決賽 FIVB World Grand Prix 2011 Finals in Macau
10, 12, 17, 24/9, 1/10	第二十三屆澳門國際煙花比賽匯演 23rd Macau Int'l Fireworks Display Contest
7/10 - 6/11	第二十五屆澳門國際音樂節 25th Macau Int'l Music Festival
17 - 20/11	第58屆澳門格蘭披治大賽車 58th Macau Grand Prix
4/12	澳門國際馬拉松 Macau International Marathon

繽紛世界，澳門就是與別不同
A World of difference, the difference is Macau

澳門特別行政區政府旅遊局
MACAU GOVERNMENT TOURIST OFFICE
www.macautourism.gov.mo

RESTAURANTS
WITH PRIVATE ROOMS
具備私人房間的餐廳

Aurora 奧羅拉		✿	✗✗✗	capacity 16	386
Aux Beaux Arts 寶雅座			✗✗	capacity 12	387
Beijing Kitchen 滿堂彩	NEW		✗✗	capacity 12	389
Canton 喜粵			✗✗✗	capacity 24	392
Clube Militar de Macau 澳門陸軍俱樂部			✗✗	capacity 32	394
Don Alfonso 當奧豐素			✗✗✗✗	capacity 10	395
Golden Flower 京花軒	NEW		✗✗✗	capacity 10	396
Il Teatro 帝雅廷	✨	✿	✗✗✗✗	capacity 14	397
Imperial Court 金殿堂			✗✗✗	capacity 30	398
Inagiku 稻菊			✗✗	capacity 18	399
Jade Garden 蘇浙匯		✿	✗✗	capacity 24	400
La Paloma 芭朗瑪			✗✗	capacity 30	401
Laurel 丹桂軒			✗✗	capacity 36	402
Lei Garden 利苑酒家		✿	✗✗	capacity 12	403
Litoral 海灣餐廳			✗	capacity 120	404
Okada 岡田			✗✗	capacity 16	410
Robuchon a Galera 法國餐廳		✿✿✿	✗✗✗✗	capacity 10	411
Tenmasa 天政			✗✗	capacity 16	414
The Eight 8餐廳	✨	✿✿	✗✗✗✗	capacity 24	415
The Kitchen 大廚			✗✗	capacity 12	416
Tim's Kitchen 桃花源小廚	✨	✿✿	✗✗✗	capacity 30	417
Tou Tou Koi 陶陶居			✗	capacity 24	418
Wing Lei 永利軒		✿	✗✗✗	capacity 12	419
Ying 帝影樓			✗✗✗	capacity 30	420
Zi Yat Heen 紫逸軒		✿✿	✗✗✗	capacity 12	421

NEW : New entry in the guide/ 新增推介
✨ : Restaurant promoted to a Bib Gourmand or Star/ 評級有所晉升的餐廳

Antonio
安東尼奧

You really feel you're in Portugal when you're in cosy little Antonio's, with its dark wood floor, Portuguese inspired paintings and crisp blue and white tiles. Ask Antonio for his menu recommendations: not only will he tell you his specials, which include gratinated goat's cheese with honey and olive oil as a starter, and monkfish, rice and prawns as a main course; he'll also happily give you the lowdown on how he got from Portugal to Macau.

置身於舒適的安東尼奧餐廳,感覺就像身處葡萄牙一樣:深色木地板、葡式油畫,以及典型的藍白色瓷磚,裝潢甚具風味。安東尼奧的推介相當不錯,他不但會向你推薦他的拿手菜式,包括蜜糖橄欖油烤山羊芝士作前菜,以及鮟鱇魚鮮蝦飯作主菜;同時亦很樂於細説他從葡萄牙來到澳門的故事。

■ ADDRESS/地址

TEL. 2899 9998

3 Rua dos Negociantes, Taipa
氹仔客商街3號
www.antoniomacau.com

■ OPENING HOURS, LAST ORDER
　營業時間,最後點菜時間
Lunch/午膳 12:00-15:00 (L.O.)
Dinner/晚膳 18:00-22:30 (L.O.)

■ PRICE/價錢
à la carte/點菜   MOP400-600

A Petisqueria
葡國美食天地

Don't be put off by the unattractive façade; step through the door here and you could be in a cosy little restaurant in the Portuguese countryside. A tiny bar at the entrance leads you into a simple, rustic dining room with nothing fancy on the menu, just decent Portuguese cuisine served in a friendly, unpretentious atmosphere. Authentic dishes include bacalhau prepared in five different ways, fried clams, and six to seven specials of the day.

不要因餐廳外觀不吸引而卻步，踏入大門你便會感受到這裡舒適的葡國風情。餐廳入口設有小酒吧，而餐室本身設計簡樸，菜式亦毫不花巧，以親切友善的服務奉上不俗的葡國美食。正宗的菜式包括以五種不同方法烹調的馬介休、炒蜆，以及六至七款是日精選。

■ ADDRESS/地址

TEL. 2882 5354

15 Rua S. Joao, Taipa
冰仔生央街15號

■ ANNUAL AND WEEKLY CLOSING
　休息日期
Closed Monday
週一休息

■ OPENING HOURS, LAST ORDER
　營業時間，最後點菜時間
Lunch/午膳 12:30-14:30 (L.O.)
Dinner/晚膳 18:45-22:00 (L.O.)

■ PRICE/價錢
à la carte/點菜   MOP170-340

Aurora
奧羅拉

🐾 🏛 ⟨ ☞ 🅿 ⬚16 🎋

Diners are spoilt for choice at Aurora: there's the option of easy-going Gallic brasserie fare or a more upmarket gastronomic menu based on southern Italian cuisine. You have a choice of where to eat, too: the high tables for tapas, an elegant dining room, or the outside terrace with its great views over Macau. There's a remarkable 500-strong wine list and this is also a great place for cocktails or Sunday brunch. Try the chef's saffron risotto.

這裡菜式選擇之多令食客三心兩意，涵蓋高盧式簡樸餐館的菜式，及以南意大利美食為主的較高價菜式。食客亦可自選用餐的地方，包括無拘束的西班牙小點高桌、高雅餐室、以及坐擁澳門美景的露台。可供選擇的還有五百種烈酒，琳瑯滿目。適合舉行雞尾酒會或星期天早午併餐。試試大廚推介的帶子露荀意大利飯。

■ ADDRESS/地址

TEL. 8803 6622

10F, Altira Hotel,
Avenida de Kwong Tung, Taipa
氹仔廣東大馬路新濠鋒酒店10樓
www.altiramacau.com

■ OPENING HOURS, LAST ORDER
　營業時間，最後點菜時間
Lunch/午膳 12:00-14:30 (L.O.)
Dinner/晚膳 18:00-22:30 (L.O.)

■ PRICE/價錢
Lunch/午膳　set/套餐　　　MOP168-198
　　　　　　à la carte/點菜 MOP200-400
Dinner/晚膳　set/套餐　　　MOP780
　　　　　　à la carte/點菜 MOP500-1,000

Aux Beaux Arts
寶雅座

This elegant Parisian-style brasserie has a true Belle Epoque feel with classic 1930s bubble-glass chandeliers and original French paintings from that period, loaned from a Shanghai museum. There's a beautiful glass-enclosed cellar for private parties, the Russian Room for caviar, and the Ice Bar for champagne. Authentic French classics include 'les cocottes': casserole specialities.

這家巴黎風格的餐廳配置著三十年代的經典氣泡玻璃吊燈，與從上海博物館借回來的法國原畫，交織成美麗時期（Belle Epoque)的優雅品味和純正氣質。漂亮的玻璃牆地適合舉辦私人派對。魚子屋供應魚子醬，香檳庫則提供香檳，美饌佳釀各適其適。經典法國菜式原汁原味，包括公認為砂鍋美食的各種烤肉（les cocottes)。

■ ADDRESS/地址

TEL. 8802 3888
GF, MGM Grand Hotel,
Avenida Dr Sun Yat Sen , Nape
外港新填海區孫逸仙大馬路
美高梅金殿酒店地下
www.mgmgrandmacau.com

■ OPENING HOURS, LAST ORDER
營業時間，最後點菜時間
Dinner/晚膳 18:30-22:30 (L.O.)

■ PRICE/價錢
Dinner/晚膳 set/套餐   MOP588
                à la carte/點菜 MOP360-700

Banza
百姓

Banza is the owner's nickname in Portuguese and he likes to visit the local markets each morning to decide on the chef's frequently-changing daily specials. The restaurant is in Taipa, on the much quieter side of Macau, and is on the ground floor of a huge apartment complex. Inside comes in tones of green and white, with large paintings and a cosy mezzanine seating about six. Banza can also give you advice on his selection of Portuguese wines.

「百姓」原是店主的葡萄牙文別名，他熱愛每天早上前往本地市場，為經常變出新煮意的每日精選作出決定。餐廳座落於氹仔，在澳門較寧靜的一區，位於一幢大型住宅大樓的地下。內部裝潢以白、綠為主色，掛有大型圖畫。洋溢溫暖氣氛的閣樓座位約有六個。百姓（店主）更會為你提供他精選的葡萄牙美酒名單。

■ ADDRESS/地址

TEL. 2882 1519

Avenida de Kwong Tung, n°s 154A e 154B, Edf. Nam San Garden, Bl. 5, r/c "G" e "H", Taipa

氹仔廣東大馬路154A及154B號
南新花園第5座地下G,H座

■ ANNUAL AND WEEKLY CLOSING
　休息日期
Closed Monday
週一休息

■ OPENING HOURS, LAST ORDER
　營業時間，最後點菜時間
Lunch/午膳 12:00-15:00 (L.O.)
Dinner/晚膳 18:30-23:00 (L.O.)

■ PRICE/價錢
à la carte/點菜　　　　MOP200-400

Beijing Kitchen   NEW
滿堂彩

'Dinner and a show' at Beijing Kitchen means one and the same, as the cooking is divided between four lively show kitchens which will hold your attention. There's a dim sum and noodle area; a duck section with two applewood-fired ovens; a wok station and a dessert counter whose bounty is well worth leaving room for. Northern China provides many of the specialities. Ask for one of the tables under the bird-cages suspended from the ceiling.

在滿堂彩，你將能見識「晚餐與表演」如何融合為一體，因為這裡的菜式分別在四個開放式「現場直播」之廚房烹調，絕對能吸引你的視線。開放式廚房分為點心與粉麵區；設兩座掛爐式烤鴨磚爐，以棗木為燒製材料的烤鴨區；另外還有鐵鑊區與讓人垂涎三尺的甜品區。這裡大部分的招牌菜都是北方菜。建議選擇有鳥籠飾於天花上的座位。

■ ADDRESS/地址

TEL. 8868 1930
GF, Grand Hyatt Hotel,
Estrado do Istmo, Cotai
路氹連貫公路君悅酒店地下
www.macau.grand.hyatt.com

■ OPENING HOURS, LAST ORDER
  營業時間，最後點菜時間
10:30-24:00

■ PRICE/價錢
Lunch/午膳   à la carte/點菜 MOP150-600
Dinner/晚膳   à la carte/點菜 MOP250-600

Belcanção
鳴詩

Belcanção is a casual dining restaurant offering a buffet and is ideal for those who can't decide on what to eat. Warm, natural colours of brown and beige decorate the room, while chefs from different countries man the open kitchens. There are stations offering mainly Portuguese, Chinese, Indian and international cuisines and a wide variety of mostly French pastries is also available. Brunch at weekends is from 9:00am -12:30pm.

座落於世上最大室內娛樂場的一角，喜粵擁有時尚的煙灰玻璃外觀，配備玻璃地板的高貴走廊，以及英國喬治風格的經典灰泥天花板，設計別出心裁！餐室呈誘人的深紅色，設計甚具現代感。喜粵的菜單以廣州粵菜為主，亦有提供一系列的餃子。

■ ADDRESS/地址
TEL. 2881 8888
GF, Four Seasons Hotel, Estrada da Baia de N. Senhora de Esperanca, s/n, The Cotai Strip, Taipa
氹仔路氹金光大道-望德聖母灣大馬路
四季酒店地下
www.fourseasons.com/macau/

■ OPENING HOURS, LAST ORDER
營業時間，最後點菜時間
Lunch/午膳 12:00-14:30 (L.O.)
Dinner/晚膳 18:00-22:30 (L.O.)

■ PRICE/價錢
Lunch/午膳   set/套餐   MOP268
Dinner/晚膳   set/套餐   MOP368

Café Encore NEW
咖啡廷

Café Encore is an elegant restaurant on the ground floor of the Encore hotel. The look is that of a classic European café but one with a strong Italian accent. The menu offers a combination of Macanese and Portuguese cuisine, along with a separate menu of Cantonese dishes. But it is the Macanese specialities where the kitchen particularly excels, in such dishes as curried crab and baked African chicken.

咖啡廷位於萬利酒店地下，格調優雅。餐廳的設計以傳統歐洲餐館為藍本，並滲入大量意大利藝術的元素。菜單包括澳門菜與葡國菜，另設粵菜菜單。不過這裡最出色的還是地道澳門菜，例如咖哩蟹與非洲雞。

■ ADDRESS/地址

TEL. 2888 9966

GF, Encore Hotel,
Rua Cicade de Sintra, Nape
外港新填海區仙德麗街萬利酒店地下
www.wynnmacau.com

■ OPENING HOURS, LAST ORDER
　營業時間，最後點菜時間
Open 24 hours
24小時營業

■ PRICE/價錢
à la carte/點菜　　　　　MOP150-500

Canton
喜粵

Located in a corner of the world's biggest indoor gaming floor, Canton is a smart restaurant with a chic smoked glass facade and elegant walkway that has a glass floor and classic English Georgian-style plaster ceiling. The dining room is a deep sensual red in colour, and very modern in design. A Kouan-Chiau (gastronomic) version of Cantonese cooking prevails, though Shanghai steamed dumplings have their own section.

座落於世上最大室內娛樂場的一角，喜粵擁有時尚的煙灰玻璃外觀，配備玻璃地板的高貴走廊，以及英國喬治風格的經典灰泥天花板，設計別出心裁！餐室呈誘人的深紅色，設計甚具現代感。喜粵的菜單以廣州粵菜為主，亦有提供一系列的餃子。

■ ADDRESS/地址

TEL. 8118 9930

Shop 1018, Casino level, The Venetian Resort, Estrada da Baia de N. Senhora de Esperanca, s/n, The Cotai Strip, Taipa

氹仔路氹金光大道-望德聖母灣大馬路威尼斯人酒店娛樂場地下1018號舖

www.venetianmacao.com

■ OPENING HOURS, LAST ORDER
營業時間，最後點菜時間

Lunch/午膳 11:00-15:00 L.O.14:45
Dinner/晚膳 18:00-23:00 L.O.22:45

■ PRICE/價錢

à la carte/點菜 MOP300-700

Chan Kuong Kei (Rua do Dr. Pedro Jose Lobo) NEW
陳光記(羅保博士街)

Red and yellow are the colours of this very clean shop, as well as the uniforms worn by the efficient team of well-organised ladies who run it. Their barbecue meats and noodles attract an eclectic mix of customer, ensuring that it is always crowded and full of life. The roast goose and the barbecue pork are two of the most popular choices but it is also worth trying the double or triple rice plates.

此店非常整潔，主色是紅色和黃色，就連勤快的女店員身上的制服也不例外。這裡的燒味與粉麵吸引了各式各樣的客人，店裡經常客似雲來，充滿生命力。這裡的燒鵝和叉燒最受歡迎，雙拼與三拼飯同樣值得一試。

■ ADDRESS/地址
TEL. 2831 4116
19 Rua do Dr. Pedro Jose Lobo, Centro
澳門羅保博士街19號

■ OPENING HOURS, LAST ORDER
營業時間，最後點菜時間
10:30-22:30 (L.O.)

■ PRICE/價錢
à la carte/點菜   MOP25-60

Clube Militar de Macau
澳門陸軍俱樂部

🍴🍴

♿ 🚊32 ☎🍴

This classic piece of 19th century Portuguese architecture used to be an army mess hall – unfortunately its lovely bar and lounge are only available to club members. Dining – for the public – takes place in a large room with echoing wood floors, potted palms at netted windows, and Colonial ambience. The Portuguese cooking is straightforward, hearty and tasty. Typical dishes are bacalhau and 'Bairrada' style suckling pig.

陸軍俱樂部始建於十九世紀，氣派典雅，原興建以供葡軍的食堂。雖然酒吧及休息室都是會員專用，不過餐廳對外開放，讓食客可盡情大快朵頤。餐廳地方寬敞，採用木地板，窗前擺放棕櫚盆栽，襯托著整幢建築的殖民地色彩。這裡的葡國菜既簡單又充滿心思，味道濃郁，香味十足。經典菜式包括馬介休(鹽醃製深海鱈魚)及葡式烤乳豬。

■ ADDRESS/地址

TEL. 2871 4000
975 Avenida da Praia Grande
南灣大馬路975號
www.clubemilitardemacau.net

■ OPENING HOURS, LAST ORDER
營業時間，最後點菜時間
Lunch/午膳 12:00-15:00 L.O. 14:45
Dinner/晚膳 19:00-23:00 L.O. 22:45

■ PRICE/價錢
set/套餐   MOP128
à la carte/點菜   MOP250-400

Don Alfonso
當奧豐素

This opulent dining room features dozens of red Murano chandeliers and a huge fresco of the Italian coast divided into five parts. The somewhat dated feel and bright lights can detract from the experience but the Italian cuisine uses well-selected ingredients, and flavours are clean and sharp. Service can be almost overly attentive. If you're lucky, you'll be here during one of the owner's quarterly visits when he prepares his tasting menu.

豪華的餐室設有許多紅色的穆拉諾穆玻璃吊燈，以及一幅把意大利海岸分為五部分的巨型壁畫，盡顯其獨特之處。古老的風格和明亮的燈光可能令人分心，不過這裡的意大利菜式選材不俗，清新味美，服務更幾乎是太過周到。如果你運氣不錯，還有機會一試店主每年一季的特備餐單。

■ ADDRESS/地址

TEL. 8803 7722

3F, Grand Lisboa Hotel,
Avenida de Lisboa
葡京路新葡京酒店3樓
www.grandlisboa.com

■ OPENING HOURS, LAST ORDER
　營業時間，最後點菜時間
Lunch/午膳 12:00-14:30 (L.O.)
Dinner/晚膳 18:30-22:30 (L.O.)

■ PRICE/價錢

Lunch/午膳	set/套餐	MOP280-480
	à la carte/點菜	MOP540-1,760
Dinner/晚膳	set/套餐	MOP680-1,590
	à la carte/點菜	MOP540-1,760

Golden Flower NEW
京花軒

Adorned with the colours of gold and orange, this is an elegant and sophisticated restaurant within the Encore hotel. The white leather circular booths are the prized seats but wherever you sit you'll receive charming service from the strikingly attired ladies, including the 'tea sommelier'. The kitchen is noted for its dextrous preparation of three different cuisines: the Sichuan, Lu and Tan specialities are all created using superb ingredients.

京花軒座落於澳門萬利酒店內，以金色和橙色裝潢，既典雅又獨特。設有白色皮質圓形卡位，不管安坐何處，都能享受衣著端莊的女侍應為你提供的惜心服務，包括「調茶師」。廚房最出色之處是能俐落地烹調出三種不同菜系的菜式：川菜、魯菜和譚家菜，採用優質材料自不在話下。

■ ADDRESS/地址

TEL. 8986 3689

GF, Encore Hotel,
Rua Cicade de Sintra, Nape
外港新填海區仙德麗街萬利酒店地下
www.wynnmacau.com

■ ANNUAL AND WEEKLY CLOSING
　休息日期
Closed Monday
週一休息

■ OPENING HOURS, LAST ORDER
　營業時間，最後點菜時間
Dinner/晚膳 18:00-23:00 L.O.22:30

■ PRICE/價錢

set/套餐	MOP888-1,380
à la carte/點菜	MOP450-1,200

Il Teatro
帝雅廷

To recommend a restaurant for something other than its food may seem odd, but at Il Teatro it appears most diners turn up primarily to watch the stunning fountains; these are in a lake and are musically choreographed to change colour and appearance every few minutes. Ask for a table with a view and don't wear sneakers, or you won't get in. The cuisine? Straightforward Italian fare, such as seafood risotto or pasta, served with style and élan.

推薦一家餐廳的菜餚以外的物品聽上來有點奇怪，不過大部分到帝雅廷的食客似乎主要是為了觀賞噴泉美景。餐廳七成以上的座位是面向表演湖噴池，每數分鐘音樂水柱交替、激光穿梭的震撼，在帝雅廷可盡收眼簾。記得預訂面向噴泉的座位！不過要記住穿著波鞋是不准進入的。至於菜餚方面，餐廳提供簡單的意大利菜，例如海鮮意大利飯或意大利粉，菜式風格獨特，服務殷勤周到。

■ ADDRESS/地址

TEL. 8986 3663
GF, Wynn Hotel,
Rua Cidade de Sintra, Nape
外港填海區仙德麗街永利酒店地下
www.wynnmacau.com

■ ANNUAL AND WEEKLY CLOSING
   休息日期
Closed Monday
週一休息

■ OPENING HOURS, LAST ORDER
   營業時間，最後點菜時間
Dinner/晚膳 17:30-23:30 (L.O.)

■ PRICE/價錢
à la carte/點菜   MOP400-700

Imperial Court
金殿堂

This is an elegant and contemporary restaurant, found on the same floor as the VIP lobby. The Grand Imperial Court upstairs has a more classical and comfortable setting. The focus of attention in the main room is its massive marble pillar with a carved dragon. The kitchen prepares Cantonese cuisine, served by attentive staff. However, if you just want a quick bite then simply visit the Noodle House.

與貴賓大堂位於同一樓層的金殿堂，集優雅與現代感於一身。上層的金殿堂貴賓廳設計更見經典舒適。主餐廳最吸引人的地方要算是雕龍大型雲石柱。餐廳主要供應廣東菜，職員服務細心。但如你只想趕快吃飽，大可直接到「麵店」。

■ ADDRESS/地址
TEL. 8802 3888
GF, MGM Grand Hotel,
Avenida Dr. Sun Yat Sen, Nape
外港新填海區孫逸仙大馬路
美高梅金殿酒店地下
www.mgmgrandmacau.com

■ OPENING HOURS, LAST ORDER
　營業時間，最後點菜時間
Lunch/午膳 12:00-14:30 L.O. 14:00
Dinner/晚膳 18:00-23:00 L.O. 22:30

■ PRICE/價錢
Lunch/午膳　à la carte/點菜 MOP300-1,000
Dinner/晚膳　à la carte/點菜 MOP500-1,000

Inagiku
稻菊

Gamblers, fashionistas and foodies make this a destination of choice in Macau. A serious and well-run Japanese restaurant, Inagiku has a laid-back, relaxing aura, which balances contemporary style, Japanese culture and clubby vibes. You can select a table, or sit at the sushi bar, tempura area or teppanyaki counter. The set lunches and the teppanyaki are always a favourite at Inagiku.

稻菊是一家成功的日本餐廳，營運認真，娛樂場玩家、追捧潮流者和食家紛紛到此朝聖。這裡的輕鬆悠閒氣氛，與現代風格、日本文化及夜店感覺相映成趣。食客可以選擇在餐桌、壽司吧、天婦羅區或鐵板燒檯用餐。稻菊的午市套餐及鐵板燒套餐最受歡迎。

■ ADDRESS/地址
TEL. 8290 8668
5F, StarWorld Hotel,
Avenida da Amizade
友誼大馬路星際酒店5樓
www.starworldmacau.com

■ OPENING HOURS, LAST ORDER
　營業時間，最後點菜時間
Lunch/午膳 12:00-14:30 (L.O.)
Dinner/晚膳 18:00-22:30 (L.O.)

■ PRICE/價錢
Lunch/午膳　set/套餐　　　MOP88-988
　　　　　　à la carte/點菜 MOP300-600
Dinner/晚膳　set/套餐　　　MOP750-988
　　　　　　à la carte/點菜 MOP300-600

Jade Garden
蘇浙匯

⌁ 🔑   🍽24

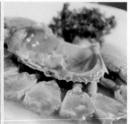

Its location at the heart of the peninsula makes it a suitable place for a business lunch or for high-rollers wanting a quick bite. There are private rooms at the entrance and within the restaurant and booth seating along one side. It's part of a popular group from Shanghai, offering fine Shanghainese dining with a blend of the traditional and the modern. Specialities include sautéed river shrimps and Jade Garden tea-smoked duck.

蘇浙匯位於半島的中心地帶，非常適合商務午餐或想趕快隨意進食的賭場高手。入口及整間餐廳內都設有貴賓房，其中一邊設有卡位雅座。餐廳屬於著名上海集團旗下，提供精緻上海菜，融和傳統與現代。著名菜式包括清炒河蝦仁及蘇浙樟茶鴨。

■ ADDRESS/地址

TEL. 8290 8638

6F, StarWorld Hotel,
Avenida da Amizade
友誼大馬路星際酒店6樓
www.starworldmacau.com

■ OPENING HOURS, LAST ORDER
    營業時間，最後點菜時間
Lunch/午膳 11:00-15:00 (L.O.)
Dinner/晚膳 17:00-22:45 (L.O.)

■ PRICE/價錢
Lunch/午膳 à la carte/點菜 MOP150-600
Dinner/晚膳 à la carte/點菜 MOP250-600

La Paloma
芭朗瑪

Secluded like hidden treasure from the rest of the city, La Paloma is a very appealing restaurant and bar, enhanced by a charming terrace, floor-to-ceiling glass and stone walls, which are part of the original 17th century fortress foundations. A bold nouveau riche style of furniture lends it a casual chic; it's wonderfully intimate and romantic at night. The refined Spanish cuisine offers a great assortment of tapas and exquisite paellas.

芭朗瑪餐廳及酒吧，位於一座十七世紀舊城堡改建而成的酒店，遠離城市的煩囂。迷人的露台、落地玻璃和古堡原來的石牆，構成芭朗瑪的獨特風采。傢具陳設高尚優雅，氣派舒適時尚，晚上更是浪漫醉人。餐廳的西班牙菜精緻優雅，涵蓋多種西班牙前菜（tapas）及精美的西班牙海鮮飯（paella）。

■ ADDRESS/地址

TEL. 2837 8111

2F, Pousada de São Tiago Hotel, Avenida da República, Fortaleza de São Tiago da Barra

西灣民國大馬路聖地牙哥古堡酒店2樓

www.saotiago.com.ma

■ OPENING HOURS, LAST ORDER

營業時間，最後點菜時間

Lunch/午膳 12:00-14:30 (L.O.)
Dinner/晚膳 18:30-22:30 (L.O.)

■ PRICE/價錢

Lunch/午膳	set/套餐	MOP198-258
	à la carte/點菜	MOP500-900
Dinner/晚膳	set/套餐	MOP1,380
	à la carte/點菜	MOP500-900

Laurel
丹桂軒

Part of a famous restaurant chain from Shenzhen and popular because of its reasonable prices. The chef serves authentic Cantonese food, delicious dim sum and a variety of soups. Some of the locals' favourites include roast pigeon, pan-fried beef fillet with sweetened pineapple and deep-fried steamed bean curd. The setting is elegant yet simple, mixing east and west and using whites and greens. There is also a large glass-enclosed wine cellar.

丹桂軒乃深圳著名連鎖餐廳集團的一員，因價格合理而廣受歡迎。大廚炮製正宗廣東菜，美味點心和一系列湯羹。部份本地人最愛菜式包括脆皮燒乳鴿、蜜餞鳳梨牛柳以及煎琵琶豆腐。餐廳佈置高雅簡約，混合了中西色彩，以白、綠為主色。餐廳內更有大型玻璃餐酒庫。

■ ADDRESS/地址

TEL. 8290 8628

2F, StarWorld Hotel,
Avenida da Amizade
友誼大馬路星際酒店2樓
www.starworldmacau.com

■ OPENING HOURS, LAST ORDER
　營業時間，最後點菜時間
11:00-23:00 (L.O.)

■ PRICE/價錢
Lunch/午膳　à la carte/點菜 MOP150-750
Dinner/晚膳　à la carte/點菜 MOP350-750

Lei Garden
利苑酒家

Smart restaurant set amongst the canals of this vast hotel's third floor - arrive on a gondola if you wish...Venetian guests predominate here; gamblers mostly give it a miss as it's too far from the gaming tables. Walls of marble provide the backdrop to a comprehensive range of traditional Cantonese dishes served at breakneck speed by an efficient team of waiters. The best place to be seated is in one of the cosy booths.

餐廳設於三樓，佔據此巨型酒店的運河旁位置，雄據地利。有興趣不妨乘坐貢朵拉前往餐廳。這裡的顧客以酒店住客為主；因為離博彩桌太遠，娛樂場玩家通常會選擇其他餐廳。雲石的牆壁與清一色的傳統廣東菜配合得天衣無縫。侍應生服務速度簡直快如閃電，極有效率！這裡最好的座位是靠近前門的舒適卡位。

■ ADDRESS/地址
TEL. 2882 8689
Shop 2130, 3F Grand Canal Shoppes,
The Venetian Resort, Estrada da Baia
de N. Senhora de Esperança, Taipa
氹仔路望德聖母灣大馬路威尼斯人酒店
大運河購物中心3樓2130號舖
www.venetianmacao.com

■ OPENING HOURS, LAST ORDER
營業時間，最後點菜時間
Lunch/午膳 11:30-15:00 L.O. 14:30
Dinner/晚膳 18:00-23:00 L.O. 22:15

■ PRICE/價錢
Lunch/午膳 à la carte/點菜 MOP150-450
Dinner/晚膳 à la carte/點菜 MOP250-450

Litoral
海灣餐廳

🍽 120

The neat and tidy façade of Litoral compensates for the charmless street in which it's located. The small exterior is deceiving: the interior goes over two floors and 250 diners can be accommodated – though this can prove a bit of a challenge to the waiting staff. The rustic atmosphere is courtesy of Portuguese nuance, which also influences the menus, along with local dishes. Try the curry shrimp with crabmeat and baked Portuguese chicken.

雖然餐廳所處的街道稍欠魅力，但整潔的正門令人留下好印象。看似狹窄的外觀頗有誤導成份：內裡共分為兩層，可以容納約250位顧客—不過這對餐廳員工來説可能是個挑戰！樸素的氣氛極具葡萄牙特色，這亦反映在餐廳菜式及本地菜式中。特別推介咖喱蟹肉蝦及焗葡國雞。

■ ADDRESS/地址

TEL. 2896 7878

261A Rua do Almirante Sérgio

河邊新街261A舖

http://restaurante-litoral.com

■ OPENING HOURS, LAST ORDER

　　營業時間，最後點菜時間

Lunch/午膳 12:00-15:00 (L.O.)

Dinner/晚膳 17:30-22:30 (L.O.)

■ PRICE/價錢

à la carte/點菜　　　　MOP250-450

Luk Kei Noodle   NEW
六記粥麵

The second generation owner-chef insists on making his very popular noodles the traditional way: with a bamboo stick. This is a very clean and popular shop, found on a lively street. The small menu provides photos of the specialities which include noodles with dried prawn roe; crunchy deep-fried wontons; crispy fish balls with soft centres served with either oyster or soy sauce; and the filling congee with crab.

第二代店主兼大廚堅持以傳統手法，炮製極受歡迎的 "竹昇麵" 。此店既清潔又受歡迎，座落在充滿活力的街道上。小小的餐牌上附有特色食品的照片，包括蝦子撈麵、炸鴛鴦（炸雲吞及米通綾魚球），還有水蟹粥。

■ ADDRESS/地址

TEL. 2855 9627
1-D Travessa da Saudade
沙梨頭仁慕巷1號D

■ ANNUAL AND WEEKLY CLOSING
   休息日期
Closed 4 days Lunar New Year
and Public Holidays
農曆新年4天及公眾假期休息

■ OPENING HOURS, LAST ORDER
   營業時間，最後點菜時間
Dinner/晚膳 18:30-02:30 (L.O.)

■ PRICE/價錢
à la carte/點菜   MOP40-70

Lung Wah Tea House
龍華茶樓

Little has changed from when this old-style Cantonese tea house, up a flight of stairs, opened in the 1960s: the large clock still works, the boss still uses an abacus to add the bill and you still have to refill your own pot of tea at the boiler. The owner buys fresh produce, including their popular chicken dish, from the market across the road. Their stir-fried noodles with beef is another speciality. Get here early for the fresh dim sum.

這家有一列樓梯的傳統廣東茶樓自一九六零年代開業以來，變化不大——古老大鐘依然不停擺動，老闆依然用算盤算帳單，你依然要自行到熱水器沖茶。店主從對面街市選購新鮮食材，包括茶樓名菜油雞。此外，此處的干炒牛河亦是一絕。建議預早前來享用新鮮點心。

■ ADDRESS/地址

TEL. 2857 4456

3 Rua Norte do Mercado Aim-Lacerda
提督市北街3號

■ ANNUAL AND WEEKLY CLOSING
   休息日期
Closed 4 days Lunar New Year,
4 days May and 4 days October
農曆新年、五月及十月各休息 4 天

■ OPENING HOURS, LAST ORDER
   營業時間，最後點菜時間
07:00-14:00 (L.O.)

■ PRICE/價錢
à la carte/點菜   MOP25-80

Ngao Kei Ka Lei Chon   NEW
牛記咖喱美食

Set at the corner of a main road and a narrow street full of industrious little shops; with regulars popping in and out throughout the day. The broken neon lights outside may make it seem less appealing but this is a friendly, well-run and well-staffed little noodle shop. Bestsellers are the crab noodles and the crab congee but it's also worth trying the clear soup with beef flank and the spicy chicken or beef curry with noodles.

此店位於大街的一角的小巷內，座落其中的都是客似雲來的小店，常客每天往來不絕。店外破落的霓虹燈看似減弱了餐廳的吸引力，但無損這家小麵店職員的態度友善、管理有序，服務令人滿意。最暢銷的美食要算是水蟹、蟹黃炆伊麵和蟹粥，清湯牛腩和椰汁咖哩雞、牛跟麵也值得一試。

■ ADDRESS/地址
TEL. 2895 6129
GF, 1 Rua de Cinco de Outubro
十月初五街1號地下

■ OPENING HOURS, LAST ORDER
  營業時間, 最後點菜時間
08:00-02:00 (L.O.)

■ PRICE/價錢
à la carte/點菜   MOP60-100

Noodle & Congee Corner
粥麵莊

This simple, good value eatery is located – incongruously – on a gallery that opens onto the casino. It's really a cafeteria, or even 'tea-eria', as one wall is full of teapots. What's special for diners is the view they have of chefs from different parts of the country preparing a noodle speciality from their home region using fresh, tasty produce. These can be combined with various soups and ingredients: the menus, handily, include photos.

這家簡樸的餐廳提供價錢合宜的美食，位於娛樂場上層樓上，彼此風格迥然不同。粥麵莊的確是一家餐館，而其中一道牆更放滿茶壺，洋溢著「茶檔」的感覺。特別的是食客更可在晚餐時觀賞來自五湖四海的廚師，採用新鮮味美的食材，分別炮製出家鄉的特色麵食的烹飪過程！餐廳亦提供不同款式的湯類和其他菜式；菜單附有圖片，便於瀏覽。

■ ADDRESS/地址

TEL. 8803 7755
1F, Grand Lisboa Hotel,
Avenida de Lisboa
葡京路新葡京酒店1樓
www.grandlisboa.com

■ OPENING HOURS, LAST ORDER
　營業時間，最後點菜時間
Open 24 hours
24小時營業

■ PRICE/價錢
à la carte/點菜　　　　　MOP50-200

Oja Sopa De Fita Cheong Kei
祥記

Although handily placed on Rua da Felicidade, you'll need to weave round shoppers and stalls to get to Cheong Kei. A family business since the '70s, this tiny noodle shop sticks to its roots and their thin, fine noodles are pressed by bamboo shoots in their own little factory nearby. Their soup uses dried prawns and bonito and is cooked for 8 hours. The wontons with noodles are clearly a must but also try the dried prawn roe with stewed noodles.

雖然祥記位於福隆新街，選址便利，但還是得花一番功夫繞過購物的人潮及攤販。這家小麵店是七十年代開業的家族生意，鄰近自設小型廠房製造幼細竹昇麵。麵湯以蝦乾和柴魚熬製八小時，雲吞麵當然不能缺少，煆籽撈麵亦不容錯過。

■ ADDRESS/地址

TEL. 2857 4310
68 Rua de Felicidade
福隆新街68號

■ ANNUAL AND WEEKLY CLOSING
休息日期
Closed 3 days each month
每月休息3天

■ OPENING HOURS, LAST ORDER
營業時間，最後點菜時間
12:00-01:00 (L.O.)

■ PRICE/價錢
à la carte/點菜 MOP16-50

Okada
岡田

Situated alongside the casino, there are no prizes for guessing the clientele of this attractive restaurant whose pale, dry-stone walls are its most appealing feature, its garden views obscured by a wall of bamboo. Apart from the main room, there's a sushi counter and grill bar. The menu delivers a large Japanese menu – sushi, sashimi, tempura, teppanyaki, grilled fish – but authenticity can be sacrificed in the desire to 'refuel' gamblers.

這間日式料理毗鄰娛樂場，不用猜想都知食客固然也是娛樂場的顧客。餐廳的淺色石牆魅力獨特，十分迷人；而竹林的排列則使園林景致若隱若現。餐廳設有主餐室、壽司吧和燒烤吧。菜單涵蓋大量日本菜式，包括壽司、天婦羅、鐵板燒、烤魚等等。味道可能不夠正宗，不過可以為食客「充電」，然後繼續到娛樂場大展身手。

■ ADDRESS/地址

TEL. 8986 3663

GF, Wynn Hotel,
Rua Cidade de Sintra, Nape
外港新填海區仙德麗街永利酒店地下
www.wynnmacau.com

■ ANNUAL AND WEEKLY CLOSING
　休息日期
Closed Tuesday
週二休息

■ OPENING HOURS, LAST ORDER
　營業時間，最後點菜時間
Dinner/晚膳 17:30-23:30 (L.O.)

■ PRICE/價錢

set/套餐	MOP888
à la carte/點菜	MOP250-1,000

Robuchon a Galera
法國餐廳

✿ ✿ ✿   ✗✗✗✗

♿ ☞ 🅿 📺10 📞🍴 🎐

Joël Robuchon's restaurant is a lavishly adorned and stylish location in which to dine. The early 19th century ambience has a warm, soft feel, accentuated by elegant and expensive fabrics. Excellent fresh ingredients underpin the contemporary Gallic cuisine and it's well worth leaving room for the impressive selection of homemade pastries on the dessert trolley. The wine list, too, is superb, with over 3,400 wines from around the world.

Joël Robuchon的餐廳裝潢得非常奢華時尚，供食客享受美食。溫暖柔和的感覺營造自十九世紀早期的氣氛，再飾以昂貴的布料，更顯感覺高雅。用優質新鮮的食材炮製出一道道當代法國菜，甜品車上的的家鄉酥餅充滿魅力，值得留肚品嚐。酒牌亦不遑多讓，提供超過3400款來自全球的美酒。

■ ADDRESS/地址
TEL. 2888 3888
3F, Hotel Lisboa,
2-4 Avenida de Lisboa
葡京路2-4號葡京酒店3樓
www.hotelisboa.com

■ OPENING HOURS, LAST ORDER
營業時間，最後點菜時間
Lunch/午膳 12:00-14:30 (L.O.)
Dinner/晚膳 18:30-22:30 (L.O.)

■ PRICE/價錢
Lunch/午膳 set/套餐   MOP400-638
            à la carte/點菜 MOP400-2,100
Dinner/晚膳 set/套餐   MOP1,588-2,100
            à la carte/點菜 MOP1,100-2,100

San Tou Tou　NEW
新陶陶

Found on a narrow street in the centre of Taipa is this Cantonese restaurant, run by the same family for three generations and now supervised by two brothers. The cooking is very traditional and the chicken soup with served in very hot clay pots is what attracts so many. But there are plenty of other, more affordable, specialities. The restaurant is spread over two floors and the air conditioning is most efficient!

此廣東菜餐廳位於冰仔中心的小巷上，家族經營了三代，現時由兩兄弟主理。煮法非常傳統，這裡的燉雞湯是用砂煲盛載，吸引大量食客。除此之外，這裡也提供很多其他價錢相宜的選擇。餐廳雖分為兩層，但並不影響其冷氣系統的流通！

■ ADDRESS/地址
TEL. 2882 7065
26 Rua Correia da Silva, Taipa
冰仔告利雅施利華街26號

■ ANNUAL AND WEEKLY CLOSING
　休息日期
Closed 1 week Lunar New Year, 2 days early May and 2 days early October
農曆新年7天、五月初及十月初各休息2天

■ OPENING HOURS, LAST ORDER
　營業時間，最後點菜時間
Lunch/午膳　11:30-15:00 (L.O.)
Dinner/晚膳　17:30-22:00 (L.O.)

■ PRICE/價錢
Lunch/午膳　à la carte/點菜 MOP100-300
Dinner/晚膳　à la carte/點菜 MOP300-600

Square Eight
食・八方

Square Eight is a large, informal, western-style eatery that never closes its doors. It's vibrant and busy, and its cuisine covers large swathes of Asia, from China to Thailand to Korea. You're given a large sheet of paper with all the dishes, and you just tick the ones you'd like. Service is fast and furious, but staff are engaging and attentive. A long, open-plan kitchen adds to the hustle and bustle of the place.

食・八方二十四小時開放，地方寬敞，環境輕鬆時尚。餐廳人氣旺盛，生氣勃勃，美食超越中西界限，涵蓋中菜、泰國菜、韓國菜等。點菜單上羅列出全部菜式，食客可以自行打剔點選。環境時而喧鬧，不過服務快捷周到。長形的開放式廚房為餐廳更添一份忙碌氣氛。

■ ADDRESS/地址

TEL. 8802 3888
GF, MGM Grand Hotel,
Avenida Dr. Sun Yat Sen, Nape
外港新填海區孫逸仙大馬路
美高梅金殿酒店地下
www.mgmgrandmacau.com

■ OPENING HOURS, LAST ORDER
營業時間，最後點菜時間
Open 24 hours
24小時營業

■ PRICE/價錢
à la carte/點菜　　　　　MOP60-250

Tenmasa
天政

An utterly charming restaurant named after the original Tenmasa, which opened in Tokyo in 1937 and is still going strong. Taipa's version boasts a sushi bar, a tempura counter, tatami floor and decked walkways leading across golden pebble ponds to private rooms. Here you can sit and watch the chef at work, admiring his precise light frying of superb ingredients and wonderfully well-balanced dishes. Attentive waitresses wear smart kimonos.

譽滿東京的天政早於1937年開業，至今仍廣受歡迎，更把料理帶到澳門皇冠。澳門的天政設有壽司吧、榻榻米地板、鋪板走廊、金石水池、私人餐室，以及天婦羅檯。食客可安坐在天婦羅檯，觀看廚師大顯身手，將優質食材炮製成美味菜式。服務員穿著整潔的和服，服務周到。

■ ADDRESS/地址

TEL. 8803 6611

11F, Altira Hotel,
Avenida de Kwong Tung, Taipa
氹仔廣東大馬路新濠鋒酒店11樓
www.altiramacau.com

■ OPENING HOURS, LAST ORDER
　營業時間，最後點菜時間
Lunch/午膳　12:00-14:30 (L.O.)
Dinner/晚膳　18:00-22:30 (L.O.)

■ PRICE/價錢
Lunch/午膳　set/套餐　　　MOP160-850
　　　　　à la carte/點菜 MOP400-1,200
Dinner/晚膳　set/套餐　　　MOP380-2,000
　　　　　à la carte/點菜 MOP400-1,200

The Eight
8餐廳

The Eight's stylish appearance can't fail to impress: water cascades down walls, images are projected onto the floor... and that's just the entrance corridor. Even the goldfish on the walls inside the restaurant are hand-sewn. The menu includes some very innovative Cantonese dishes which includes dim sum like deep-fried abalone puff stuffed with black mushroom and asparagus and the baked tartelette with crabmeat in curry sauce.

8餐廳的時尚設計令人印象深刻：流水沿著牆壁潺潺而下，地板上更投射著粼粼影像⋯這只是入口走廊而已！餐廳牆上的金魚也都是人手繡成的!餐牌包括部分非常創新的廣東菜，點心類如特式鮑魚酥及葡香焗蟹撻。

■ ADDRESS/地址
TEL. 2828 3838
2F, Grand Lisboa Hotel,
Avenida de Lisboa
葡京路新葡京酒店2樓
www.grandlisboa.com

■ OPENING HOURS, LAST ORDER
營業時間，最後點菜時間
Lunch/午膳 12:00-14:30 (L.O.)
Dinner/晚膳 18:30-22:30 (L.O.)

■ PRICE/價錢
Lunch/午膳 à la carte/點菜 MOP160-1,000
Dinner/晚膳 à la carte/點菜 MOP400-1,000

The Kitchen
大厨

You can tell this is somewhere slightly different when you enter via a beautiful wooden screen and gain access to a bar in the shape of a golden cow. The restaurant itself is intimate and stylish, with shiny metal rods suspended from the ceiling and a wall of water behind the sushi counter. Cuisine is mix of Western steakhouse and Japanese dishes. There's also live fish from the tank and a superb wine list. For the gentlemen, don't forget to check out the floating money in the bathroom.

踏進餐廳，經過美麗的木製屏風，看到金牛形的酒吧，你便會意識到這裡的非凡之處。餐廳時尚愜意，天花板懸掛著閃閃生輝的金屬棒，壽司吧後方更設有一道水牆。菜式揉合西式扒房風格和日本菜餚而成。餐廳亦設有游水魚魚缸，並提供優質美酒。男士們，不要忘記一睹男廁內的飄浮紙幣！

■ ADDRESS/地址
TEL. 8803 7777
3F, Grand Lisboa Hotel,
Avenida de Lisboa
葡京路新葡京酒店3樓
www.grandlisboa.com

■ OPENING HOURS, LAST ORDER
營業時間，最後點菜時間
Lunch/午膳 12:00-14:30 (L.O.)
Dinner/晚膳 18:30-22:30 (L.O.)

■ PRICE/價錢
Lunch/午膳 set/套餐 MOP208-398
à la carte/點菜 MOP680-1,500
Dinner/晚膳 à la carte/點菜 MOP680-1,500

Tim's Kitchen
桃花源小廚

One for the connoisseurs – Hong Kong foodies make special pilgrimages here. This restaurant is filled with opera photos and costumes. The Cantonese dishes may look simple, but they are well prepared. These may include steamed pork slices with eggplant & preserved vegetables and sweet & sour pork ribs. Make sure you try the crystal prawn; while in winter there is always the snake ragout - a joy for the taste buds!

桃花源是行家的必然之選，香港食家也少不免到此朝聖。餐廳放滿歌劇照片和戲服裝飾。粵菜餐牌看似簡單，其實經過精心炮製。菜式包括梅菜肉片蒸茄瓜及京都骨。萬勿錯過玻璃蝦球，冬天的重頭戲則離不開蛇羹。實在能「感動味蕾」！

■ ADDRESS/地址
TEL. 8803 3682
Shop F25, GF, Hotel Lisboa,
East Wing, 2-4 Avenida de Lisboa
葡京路2-4號葡京酒店東翼地下F25號鋪
www.hotelisboa.com

■ OPENING HOURS, LAST ORDER
營業時間，最後點菜時間
Lunch/午膳 12:00-15:00 L.O. 14:30
Dinner/晚膳 18:30-23:00 L.O. 22:00

■ PRICE/價錢
Lunch/午膳 à la carte/點菜 MOP170-500
Dinner/晚膳 à la carte/點菜 MOP350-1,200

Tou Tou Koi
陶陶居

🚋24 ◎🍴

As this 80 year old restaurant is simply always packed it's vital to make a reservation; you can then also pre-order the duck. It's dim sum during the day and Cantonese cuisine at night. The roast barbeque corner is next to the entrance; the seafood is found at the front of the shop in large tanks. Service is extremely swift to accommodate the non-stop flow of customers. Other favourites include deep-fried crab and chicken soup.

陶陶居總是賓客如雲，必須訂座，你亦可順道預訂八寶鴨。日間以點心為主，晚上則提供粵菜。燒味櫃面位於入口附近，店面前方的大水缸放滿海鮮。服務非常具效率，以應付絡繹不絕的人流。其它著名菜式包括金錢蟹盒和古法雞煲。

■ ADDRESS/地址

TEL. 2857 2629

6-8 Travessa do Mastro
爐石塘巷6-8號

■ OPENING HOURS, LAST ORDER
　營業時間，最後點菜時間
Lunch/午膳　08:00-15:00 (L.O.)
Dinner/晚膳　17:00-24:00 L.O. 23:30

■ PRICE/價錢
Lunch/午膳　à la carte/點菜 MOP90-150
Dinner/晚膳　à la carte/點菜 MOP200-400

Wing Lei
永利軒

 12

An opulent restaurant in vibrant red, characterised by vast lanterns at the entrance and a superb three-dimensional dragon made of ninety thousand pieces of crystal. The comfy red dining chairs add to a feeling of well-being. The décor may be excellent, but the service can occasionally be somewhat lacklustre. Gamblers and a large number of families create a noisy ambience as they tuck in to a big menu of classical Cantonese dishes.

這家紅當當的餐廳入口掛著一些大型燈籠，襯托一條以九千片水晶製成的立體龍，盡展豪華氣派；而舒適的紅色座椅讓人更添好感。餐廳的裝潢實屬一流，不過相比之下，服務態度有時略嫌失色。食客多是一家大小或娛樂場玩家，環境熱鬧非常。餐廳供應傳統粵菜，菜式選擇良多。

■ ADDRESS/地址
TEL. 8986 3663
GF, Wynn Hotel,
Rua Cidade de Sintra, Nape
外港新填海區仙德麗街永利酒店地下
www.wynnmacau.com

■ OPENING HOURS, LAST ORDER
營業時間，最後點菜時間
Lunch/午膳　11:30-15:00 (L.O.)
Dinner/晚膳　18:00-23:00 (L.O.)

■ PRICE/價錢
Lunch/午膳　à la carte/點菜 MOP150-300
Dinner/晚膳　à la carte/點菜 MOP200-920

Ying
帝影樓

♿ ◁ ☞ 🅿 🍽30 ❀

This is a terrific restaurant with breathtaking views looking north to Macau. The beautifully styled interior has been designed with real taste and quality; even the beaded curtains – featuring gold cranes and crystal trees – are striking. The Cantonese dishes on offer are prepared with contemporary twists and great flair, and are served by charmingly professional staff. The place to come for some of the best Cantonese cooking in the region.

帝影樓坐擁澳門北部的壯麗景致，扣人心弦。餐廳內部設計品味獨特，風格絢麗；甚至珠簾亦配有金鶴和水晶樹，使裝潢更添神采。餐廳的粵菜融入了當代元素，烹調技藝精湛。服務專業，態度令人賓至如歸。這裡的一些粵菜菜式可謂冠絕全城。

■ ADDRESS/地址
TEL. 8803 6600
11F, Altira Hotel,
Avenida de Kwong Tung, Taipa
氹仔廣東大馬路新濠鋒酒店11樓
www.altiramacau.com

■ OPENING HOURS, LAST ORDER
　營業時間，最後點菜時間
Lunch/午膳 11:00-14:30 (L.O.)
Dinner/晚膳 18:00-22:30 (L.O.)

■ PRICE/價錢
Lunch/午膳　à la carte/點菜 MOP150-900
Dinner/晚膳　à la carte/點菜 MOP300-900

Zi Yat Heen
紫逸軒

✿✿   ✕✕✕

    ♿ ☝ 🅿 ⛶12 ⚓

Conveniently located on the 1st floor of the Four Seasons Hotel Macao, Zi Yat Heen is an elegant and spacious restaurant, with a large glass-encased wine cellar at its centre. Chef Mak has created a traditional Cantonese menu but with a lighter, fresher taste by using premium ingredients and minimal seasonings. Interesting creations include the baked lamb chops with coffee sauce, while a more authentic choice would be the pigeon with Yunnan ham.

紫逸軒位於澳門四季酒店一樓，格調高雅，地方寬敞，正中位置更有大型玻璃櫃餐酒庫。大廚麥先生烹製傳統粵菜時採用最新鮮的食材與最少的調味料，帶來更鮮味清新的粵菜。有趣創作菜式包括咖啡汁焗羊排，而更傳統的選擇有酥香雲腿伴鴿脯。

■ ADDRESS/地址

TEL. 2881 8888

GF, Four Seasons Hotel, Estrada da
Baia de N. Senhora de Esperanca, s/n,
The Cotai Strip, Taipa
氹仔路氹金光大道-望德聖母灣大馬路
四季酒店地下
www.fourseasons.com/macau

■ OPENING HOURS, LAST ORDER
   營業時間，最後點菜時間
Lunch/午膳 12:00-14:30 (L.O.)
Dinner/晚膳 18:30-22:30 (L.O.)

■ PRICE/價錢
Lunch/午膳 set/套餐   MOP1,288
       à la carte/點菜 MOP200-900
Dinner/晚膳 set/套餐   MOP1,288
       à la carte/點菜 MOP300-900

HOTELS
酒店

HOTELS BY ORDER OF COMFORT
酒店 — 以舒適程度分類

Altira
新濠鋒

High quality design, a serene atmosphere and wondrous peninsula views produce something jaw-droppingly spectacular here. Guests arrive at the stylish lobby on the 38th floor; the luxury penthouse feel is enhanced by a superb lounge and terrace on the same level. Rooms, all on a lower floor, face the sea and merge tranquil tones with sheer contemporary style. As if this weren't enough, there's also a sumptuous spa boasting a pool-with-a-view.

RESTAURANTS/ 餐廳

Recommended/推薦			Also/其他
Aurora/ 奧羅拉	✿	✗✗✗	Kira/ 吉良
Tenmasa/ 天政		✗✗	
Ying/ 帝影樓		✗✗✗	

新濠鋒酒店設計獨特，舒適典雅，位處優越地段，讓澳門半島的環迴美景盡入眼簾，令人讚嘆不已。時尚尊貴的大堂位於38樓，同層的「天宮」酒廊備有室內酒廊及露天陽台高雅舒適，散發著豪華瑰麗的味道。客房位於其他較低樓層，海景一望無際，寧靜感覺和現代設計相互交織，氣派超凡。此外，酒店設有豪華的水療設施，享用服務的同時更可飽覽美景。

■ ADDRESS/地址
TEL. 2886 8888
FAX. 2886 8666
Avenida de Kwong Tung, Taipa
氹仔廣東大馬路
www.altiramacau.com

■ ROOMS AND SUITES/客房及套房
Rooms/客房 ＝184
Suites/套房 ＝32

■ PRICE/價錢

🧍	MOP1,800-5,380
🧍🧍	MOP1,800-5,380
Suites/套房	MOP8,880-12,800
☕	MOP128

Encore
萬利

For VIPs who want an even more exclusive resort experience than the Wynn, there is Encore – their luxury brand. The word 'standard' certainly does not apply here as the choice is between a suite or a villa, all of which are lavishly decorated in reds and golds. You also get an exceptional spa which offers bespoke treatments and Bar Cristal, as small as a jewel box and just as precious. Even the casino is largely made up of VIP game rooms.

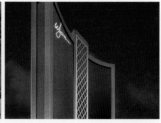

RESTAURANTS/ 餐廳

Recommended/推薦		Also/其他
Café Encore/ 咖啡廷	✗✗	99 Noodles/ 99 麵
Golden Flower/ 京花軒	✗✗✗	

尊貴如你，如欲享受比永利更獨特尊貴的度假體驗，大可選擇萬利——永利旗下的帝皇級品牌。「標準」一詞絕對不適用於萬利，你可選擇入住萬利豪華套房或尊貴豪華套房，兩者均以紅色與金色裝潢，更顯富麗堂皇。你亦可於貴賓級水療中心盡情享受度身訂造的療程，酒店內的Bar Cristal酒吧更一如其名——如珠寶盒一般嬌小而高貴。附設賭場內，絕大部分均為貴賓遊樂房。

■ ADDRESS/地址
TEL. 2888 9966
FAX. 2832 9966
Rua Cidade de Sintra, Nape
外港新填海區仙德麗街
www.wynnmacau.com

■ ROOMS AND SUITES/客房及套房
Suites/套房 =414

■ PRICE/價錢
Suites/套房　MOP9,000-16,000
☕　　　　　MOP168

Four Seasons
四季

Opened in the summer of 2008, Four Seasons fuses East and West by blending together Colonial Portuguese and Chinese traditions. The lobby functions like a living room, with its fireplace, Portuguese lanterns and Chinese lacquer screens. The hotel also has a luxury shopping mall and connects to The Venetian and gaming at the Plaza Casino. If you want respite from the buzz and the glitz, then escape to the spa or relax by one of five pools.

RESTAURANTS/ 餐廳

Recommended/推薦			Also/其他
Belcanção/ 鳴詩		XX	Splash/ 撲滿
Zi Yat Heen/ 紫逸軒	✿✿	XXX	Windows

2008年夏季開幕的四季融合了東方和西方元素，將殖民地時代葡萄牙與中國傳統元素融為一體。大堂有如客廳，設有壁爐、葡國燈籠和中國雕漆屏風。酒店亦設有豪華購物商場，直通威尼斯人酒店及百利沙娛樂場。如果你想從五光十色中喘息一下，可享用水療設備和五個泳池的池畔酒吧。

■ ADDRESS/地址

TEL. 2881 8888
FAX. 2881 8899
Estrada da Baia de N. Senhora de Esperanca, s/n, The Cotai Strip, Taipa
氹仔路氹金光大道-望德聖母灣大馬路
www.fourseasons.com/macau

■ ROOMS AND SUITES/客房及套房

Rooms/客房 =276
Suites/套房 =84

■ PRICE/價錢

🚹	MOP2,700-4,600
🚹🚹	MOP2,700-4,600
Suites/套房	MOP5,100-40,000
☕	MOP198

Grand Hyatt NEW
君悅

The hotel forms part of the 'City of Dreams' urban resort, which includes a casino, shopping mall and a number of restaurants and hotels, and shares the same 'water' theme. The lobby sets the tone, with its striking 22m ceiling and fabulous artwork, with drops appearing to fall from a cloud. The stylish, contemporary bedrooms are split between the two towers. Mezza9 opens onto a terrace and offers nine different dining options.

RESTAURANTS/ 餐廳

Recommended/推薦		Also/其他
Beijing Kitchen/ 滿堂彩	✗✗	Mezza9

君悅酒店是「新濠天地」城市度假村的一部份，度假村內設有賭場、商場及一系列餐廳與酒店，以「水」為共同主題。大堂已可見酒店格調——足有22米高的天花與出色的藝術品，配搭彷似要從天上雲層落下的水點。富當代時尚感的房間分布於兩棟大樓中。延伸成室外庭園的Mezza9為顧客提供九種不同餐點，任君選擇。

■ ADDRESS/地址
TEL. 8868 1234
FAX. 8867 1234
City of Dreams,
Estrada do Istmo, Cotai
路氹連貫公路
www.macau.grand.hyatt.com

■ ROOMS AND SUITES/客房及套房
Rooms/客房 ＝503
Suites/套房 ＝288

■ PRICE/價錢

👤	MOP1,300-3,200
👥	MOP1,300-3,200
Suites/套房	MOP2,300-13,000

Grand Lisboa
新葡京

㤿 ⬱ ☝ 🚗 ⬳ 🏄 🤿 🅢🅟🅐 👣 ⬭⬭⬭

Impossible to miss, the Grand Lisboa, opened in December 2008, can be seen from miles away with its eye-popping, brightly-lit lotus design atop a shining diamond. Opulent soundproofed bedrooms typically feature brown walls, red armchairs and Asian paintings, and offer grand sea or city vistas. If you have a corner room or a suite, you'll get the added bonus of a sauna; if you have neither, you can at least make use of a sumptuous spa.

434

RESTAURANTS/ 餐廳

Recommended/推薦		Also/其他

Don Alfonso/ 當奧豐素   🍴🍴🍴🍴

Noodle & Congee Corner/
粥麵莊   🍴 🍜

The Eight/ 8餐廳   ❀❀ 🍴🍴🍴🍴

The Kitchen/ 大廚   🍴🍴

2008年12月開幕的新葡京外形像一片耀目的黃蓮葉，座落於一顆
閃爍的鑽石之上，遠處可見，實在不容錯過！客房非常隔音，擁有
典型的棕色牆壁、紅色扶手椅和亞洲油畫，並坐擁豪華海景或澳門
的秀麗風光。角位客房及套房更設有桑拿設施，其他客房亦可享用
豪華的水療設施。

■ ADDRESS/地址

TEL. 2828 3838
FAX. 2888 2828
Avenida de Lisboa
葡京路
www.grandlisboa.com

■ ROOMS AND SUITES/客房及套房
Rooms/客房 ＝381
Suites/套房 ＝50

■ PRICE/價錢

🧍	MOP3,800-5,700
🧍🧍	MOP3,800-5,700
Suites/套房	MOP7,800-48,000
☕	MOP150

Lisboa
葡京

The Lisboa is one of the city's more 'traditional' hotels with its 1970s style façade providing a stark contrast to the brand new Grand Lisboa. There are 10 types of guestroom available; ask for a Tower room, as these are more luxurious and larger in size than the rooms in the east wing. You won't find a swimming pool, but, rather handily, you can nip over to the Grand Lisboa and use theirs.

RESTAURANTS/ 餐廳

Recommended/推薦

Robuchon a Galera/
法國餐廳 ✿✿✿ ✕✕✕✕
Tim's Kitchen/ 桃花源小廚 ✿✿ ✕✕✕

Also/其他

New Furusato/ 新故鄉
Portas do Sol/ 葡京日麗

葡京酒店是澳門的「傳統」酒店之一，保留著七十年代的外觀，與新落成的新葡京相映成趣。酒店共有十種客房，尊尚客房比東翼的客房更大更豪華，物有所值。雖然葡京沒有泳池，不過走到新葡京那邊使用泳池，亦十分方便快捷。

■ ADDRESS/地址
TEL. 2888 3888
FAX. 2888 3838
2-4 Avenida de Lisboa
葡京路 2-4 號
www.hotelisboa.com

■ ROOMS AND SUITES/客房及套房
Rooms/客房 ＝876
Suites/套房 ＝50

■ PRICE/價錢

👤	MOP1,850-3,400
👥	MOP1,850-3,400
Suites/套房	MOP4,400-18,000
🛏	MOP78

MGM Grand
美高梅金殿

This stunning glass sky-scraper with Taipa view is one of the jewels of Macau. The 35 floors have three distinct horizontal layers designed in chic curves – bronze, silver and gold – gold signifying the best rooms, although all are luxurious, built in a well-judged modern style with very fine materials, the huge windows proffering wow-factor views. A Chihuly glass display dominates the vast lobby and the superb spa boasts infinity pool.

RESTAURANTS/ 餐廳

Recommended/推薦		Also/其他
Aux Beaux Arts/ 寶雅座	ⅩⅩ	Rossio/ 盛事
Imperial Court/ 金殿堂	ⅩⅩⅩ	
Square Eight/ 食 · 八方	☺ Ⅹ	

美高梅金殿是澳門的一顆璀璨明珠。這幢摩天大樓擁有玻璃外牆，坐擁冰仔景色。樓高35層的酒店設計獨特，以波浪曲線由三種不同顏色（黃金色、白金色及玫瑰金色）的玻璃舖設外牆。黃金色部分標示著最佳的客房，但事實上所有客房都極盡奢華，以精細的物料塑造悅目的時尚風格。透過寬闊的窗戶，更將動人美景盡收眼底，令人讚嘆不已。宏偉的大堂展示著國際玻璃藝術大師Dale Chihuly的作品，星級的水療設施包括無邊際泳池 。

■ ADDRESS/地址
TEL. 8802 8888
FAX. 8802 3333
Avenida Dr. Sun Yat Sen, Nape
外港新填海區孫逸仙大馬路
www.mgmgrandmacau.com

■ ROOMS AND SUITES/客房及套房
Rooms/客房 ＝468
Suites/套房 ＝125

■ PRICE/價錢

👤	MOP3,200-3,800
👥	MOP3,200-3,800
Suites/套房	MOP7,800-9,800
☕	MOP150

Pousada de Mong-Há
望廈賓館

A very good value hotel with a distinct difference...it's run by the Institute for Tourism Studies, and is in a guaranteed peaceful environment away from the casinos. It's surrounded by a lovely garden, while inside, students learning their trade welcome you at the reception desk. Bedrooms are not big (especially singles), but they're quiet and feature some nice Asian touches. The restaurant offers a good opportunity to enjoy Macanese cuisine.

RESTAURANTS/ 餐廳

Also/其他

IFT Educational Restaurant/
旅遊學院教學餐廳

這家超值的賓館由旅遊學院營運，位處寧靜的望廈山半山腰，
遠離娛樂場的煩囂，確是與眾不同。賓館被一個可愛的花園環繞
著，而接待處的學院學生則隨時為你服務。客房地方不大，尤其
是單人房，不過環境寧靜，並擁有亞洲設計風格。賓館的餐廳是
體驗澳門菜的好去處。

■ ADDRESS/地址
TEL. 2851 5222
FAX. 2855 6925
Colina de Mong-Há,
Rampe do Forte de Mong-Há
望廈山
www.iftedu.mo

■ ROOMS AND SUITES/客房及套房
Rooms/客房 ＝16
Suites/套房 ＝4

■ PRICE/價錢

👤	MOP480-680
👥	MOP640-960
Suites/套房	MOP960-1,360
⛢	MOP120

Pousada de São Tiago
聖地牙哥古堡

Exquisite boutique hotel, built into the hillside on the foundations of a 17th century fort alongside traditional Portuguese villas. Atmospheric old steps lead from the entrance up to reception. By contrast, the interior is modern, chic and very stylish, with subdued taste the key. Guestrooms boast cool marble floors and rich colours and fabrics; all look onto the Straits of Macau. Discover the pool amongst charming little hillside terraces.

RESTAURANTS/ 餐廳

Recommended/推薦		Also/其他
La Paloma/ 芭朗瑪	✕✕	

這家座落於山腰的精品酒店，精緻優雅。由一座十七世紀的舊城堡改建而成，毗鄰傳統的葡式住宅。古樸的石階別具風情，拾級而上便可由入口到達接待處。酒店內部與外觀形成鮮明的對比，設計十分現代時尚，獨樹一格，卻不浮誇造作。客房採用大理石地板、鮮明的顏色和布質材料，品味非凡；所有客房都坐擁澳門內港的醉人景色。迷人的山腰陽台設有一個戶外泳池。

■ ADDRESS/地址
TEL. 2837 8111
FAX. 2855 2170
Avenida da República,
Fortaleza de São Tiago da Barra
西灣民國大馬路聖地牙哥大炮台
www.saotiago.com

■ ROOMS AND SUITES/客房及套房
Suites/套房 ＝12

■ PRICE/價錢
Suites/套房　MOP3,200-3,500
🍵　　　　　MOP120

Rocks
萊斯

Being part of the Fisherman's Wharf, this interesting seaside hotel's ambience is inspired by the Victorian era and has a lobby full of Victorian-style décor and furnishings including a fireplace, paintings and a large white marble staircase. A cosy terrace overlooks the bay, while relaxing bedrooms have a balcony and sea views. Of particular note...unlike most hotels, there's no casino here – just right for those who prefer the quieter side of Macau.

RESTAURANTS/ 餐廳

Recommended/推薦	Also/其他
	Vic's Café/ 怡景

萊斯酒店座落於澳門漁人碼頭，海邊的醉人環境靈感來自維多利亞時期。酒店大堂佈滿富維多利亞風格的裝飾及傢俱，包括火爐、掛畫及大型白色雲石樓梯。舒適怡人的花園可盡收海灣醉人景致，設有海景露臺的臥室可讓你盡情放鬆身心。注意，和大部分酒店不同，這裡不設賭場，專為嚮往澳門寧靜一面的人士而設。

■ ADDRESS/地址

TEL. 2878 2782
FAX. 2870 8800
Macau Fisherman's Wharf
澳門漁人碼頭
www.rockshotel.com.mo

■ ROOMS AND SUITES/客房及套房
Rooms/客房 = 66
Suites/套房 = 6

■ PRICE/價錢

👤	MOP1,880-2,880
👥	MOP1,880-2,880
Suites/套房	MOP4,080-6,660

Sands
金沙

This huge, bright gold building has a vast 'Sands' logo –
prime Las Vegas real estate relocated in Asia. The hotel,
with its own entrance and areas, is separate from the
casino, though dining on the mezzanine, overlooking three
vast gaming areas, resembles peering down onto a stock
exchange trading floor. The spacious lobby is of western
style, as are the bedrooms, which are all large and luxurious
suites; each has a sea or city view.

RESTAURANTS/ 餐廳

Recommended/推薦	Also/其他
	Copa/ 高雅
	Golden Court/ 金沙閣
	Perola/ 金帆船

這家龐大的金沙酒店,金色外牆閃閃發亮,並擁有巨型的「金沙」霓虹燈招牌,是拉斯維加斯博彩業鉅頭於亞洲營運的娛樂場酒店。酒店與娛樂場分開,設有獨立的入口和範圍,不過在夾樓用餐時,卻可俯瞰三個大型博彩廳,恰似觀看股交所會場一般!寬敞的大堂和客房均以西式設計,所有客房都是寬闊的豪華套房,更坐擁海景或城市美景。

■ ADDRESS/地址

TEL. 2888 3388

FAX. 2888 3377

203 Largo de Monte Carlo

蒙地卡羅前地203號

www.sands.com.mo

■ ROOMS AND SUITES/客房及套房

Rooms/客房 =204

Suites/套房 =34

■ PRICE/價錢

👤	MOP2,088-2,788
👥	MOP2,088-2,788
Suites/套房	MOP3,588-4,588
☕	MOP200

StarWorld
星際

You will be impressed with the hotel's attractive glass façade and glittery night lighting. Those who stick with StarWorld will find supremely luxurious rooms, full of every mod con. They're named after the view – City, Sea or Lake – with Lake View rooms offering the best vista while the StarWorld suite provides all you can imagine. The hotel also has a good selection of restaurants with Asian cuisines.

RESTAURANTS/ 餐廳

Recommended/推薦			Also/其他
Inagiku/ 稻菊		XX	Temptations/ 品味坊
Jade Garden/ 蘇浙匯	✿	XX	
Laurel/ 丹桂軒		XX	

你會被酒店極為吸引的玻璃正門和閃爍晚間燈飾迷倒。留宿星際的貴客可享用美輪美奐的豪華套房，配備所有現代生活所需。套房根據所享景色命名——都會景、海景或湖景，提供最佳景致。星際將你的無限想像變成可能。酒店內設有一系列精選餐廳，提供亞洲名菜。

■ ADDRESS/地址

TEL. 2838 3838

Avenida da Amizade

友誼大馬路

www.starworldmacau.com

■ ROOMS AND SUITES/客房及套房

Rooms/客房 =423

Suites/套房 =42

■ PRICE/價錢

🚹	MOP2,300-2,800
🚹🚹	MOP2,300-2,800
Suites/套房	MOP4,600-7,800

The Venetian
威尼斯人

You need a map to find your way round the largest integrated resort in Asia. It's based on Venice: third floor canals with singing gondoliers! Identikit luxury is assured in a towering bedroom skyscraper that has 3,000 capacious rooms. Opulent fakes are everywhere: frescoes, colonnades, sculptures. It's impossible to stay here without being swept along by hoards of gamblers. The Cirque de Soleil show, ZAIA, will be sure to take your breath away.

RESTAURANTS/ 餐廳

Recommended/推薦		Also/其他
Canton/ 喜粵	🍴🍴🍴	Morton's of Chicago
Lei Garden/ 利苑酒家	❀ 🍴🍴	Portofino

你需要一張地圖才能環遊全亞洲最大型的綜合度假酒店！概念源自威尼斯，三樓運河上的貢多拉船夫更會一邊掌船一邊唱歌！高聳而立的摩天大樓擁有三千間寬敞客房，同樣極盡奢華。壁畫、列柱、雕塑等均仿照原物而製，展露豪華氣派。置身於威尼斯人難免會到娛樂場一展身手。Cirque du Soleil®(太陽劇團™)ZAiA™肯定會讓你屏息。

■ ADDRESS/地址
TEL. 2882 8888
FAX. 2882 8889
Estrada da Baia de N. Senhora de Esperanca, s/n, The Cotai Strip, Taipa
氹仔路氹金光大道-望德聖母灣大馬路
www.venetianmacao.com

■ ROOMS AND SUITES/客房及套房
Rooms/客房 ＝2900
Suites/套房 ＝100

■ PRICE/價錢

🧍	MOP1,500-2,100
🧍🧍	MOP1,500-2,100
Suites/套房	MOP2,500-3,500
☕	MOP200

Wynn
永利

The Wynn's easy-on-the-eye curving glass façade is enhanced with a lake and dancing fountains, while the classically luxurious interior includes Murano glass chandeliers, plush carpets and ubiquitous marble. An attractively landscaped oasis pool forms the centrepiece to corridors lined with the top retail names. Bedrooms – classical but contemporary – display a considerable degree of taste. The Prosperity tree, meanwhile, is not easily forgotten...

RESTAURANTS/ 餐廳

Recommended/推薦

Il Teatro/ 帝雅廷	✿	✗✗✗✗
Okada/ 岡田		✗✗
Wing Lei/ 永利軒	✿	✗✗✗

Also/其他

Café Esplanada/ 咖啡苑
Red 8/ 紅8

永利的弧形玻璃外觀十分奪目，更設有表演湖及噴池。至於酒店內部則散發著經典的豪華氣息：穆拉諾穆玻璃吊燈、豪華的地毯，且觸目所及皆是大理石。走廊中心設有一個造形迷人的綠洲池，而兩旁則置滿名店。客房融合了經典和當代的風格設計，盡顯優越品味。此外，永利的吉祥樹更會令你印象深刻。

■ ADDRESS/地址

TEL. 2888 9966
FAX. 2832 9966
Rua Cidade de Sintra, Nape
外港新填海區仙德麗街
www.wynnmacau.com

■ ROOMS AND SUITES/客房及套房
Rooms/客房 ＝460
Suites/套房 ＝140

■ PRICE/價錢

👤	MOP3,500-3,700
👥	MOP3,500-3,700
Suites/套房	MOP7,800-35,000
☐	MOP168

MAPS
地圖

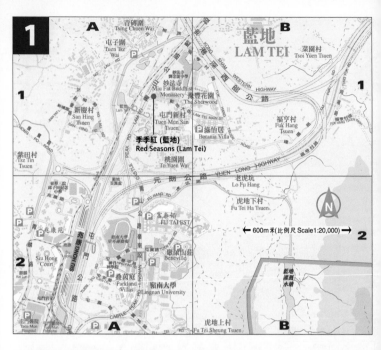

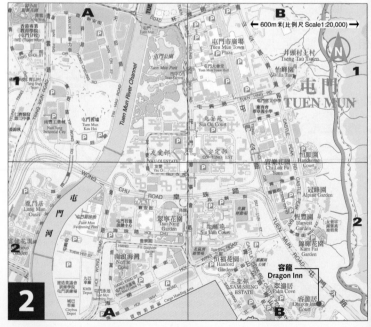

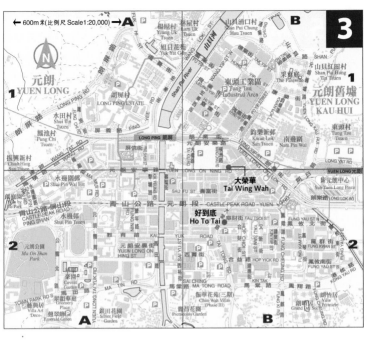

← 600m米(比例尺 Scale1:20,000) →A

B

楊屋村
Yeung Uk
Tsuen

林屋村
Lam Uk
Tsuen

山貝涌口村
Shan Pui Chung
Hau Tsuen

山貝紅田村
Shan Pui Hung
Tin Tsuen

採葉庭
The Parcville

元朗
YUEN LONG

旭日花苑
Yuk Yat Garden

元朗舊墟
YUEN LONG
KAU HUI

朗屏村
LONG PING ESTATE

水田村
Shui Tin
Tsuen

鳳池村
Fung Chi
Tsuen

東頭工業區
Tung Tau
Industrial Area

東頭村
Tung Tau
Tsuen

屏信街

釣樂新邨
Kwan Lok
San Tsuen

南邊圍
Nam Pin Wai

新元朗中心
Sun Yuen Long Plaza

振興新村
Chun Hing
Tsuen

水邊圍邨
Shui Pin Wai Est

大榮華
Tai Wing Wah

好到底
Ho To Tai

元朗公園
Ma On Shan
Park

元朗安寧街
YUEN LONG ON
HING ST

西菁街
SAI CHING

振華花苑(三期)
Chun Wah Villas
(Phase III)

銀田花園
Silver Field
Garden

翠田花園
Greenery
Place

A

B

深井
SHAM TSENG

深井新村
Sham Tseng
San Tsuen

深井舊村
Sham Tseng
Kau Tsuen

9

裕記
Yue Kee

海韻花園
Rhine Garden

海韻臺
Rhine
Terrace

深井村
Sham Tseng
Tsuen

青山公路
CASTLE PEAK RD

碧堤半島
Bellagio

屯門公路
TUEN MUN ROAD

第一期
浪翠園 Phase 1
Sea Crest Villa

海逸軒
Angler's Bay

麗都花園
Lido Garden

海韻居
Ocean
Pointe

第二期
Phase 2

浪翠園
Sea Crest Villa

釣魚灣
Anglers' Beach

黃金花園
Golden Villa

第三期
Phase 3

青山公路
CASTLE PEAK RD

← 527m米(比例尺 Scale1:17,574) →

A

B

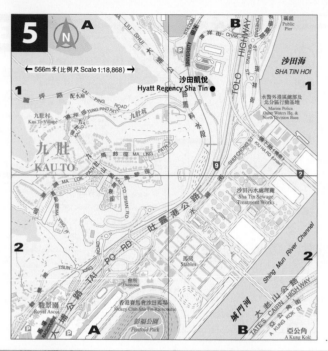

5

N A B

← 566米(比例尺 Scale 1:18,868) →

公帑外水坑大 LIU SHUI ST

大學 UNIVERSITY

翔祥街 CHAK

TOLO HIGHWAY

碼頭 Public Pier

沙田海 SHA TIN HOI

1

麗坪路 LAI PING ROAD 配水庫

TUNG PING PATH

沙田凱悅 Hyatt Regency Sha Tin ●

水警外港區總部及北分區行動基地 Marine Police Outer Waters Hq. & North Division Base

1

九肚村 Kau To Village

棄坪 TUNG PING PATH

九肚城

九肚

KAU TO

馬嶺徑 MA LING PATH

沙田正街 SHA CHENG ST

九肚路 KU HA RD

9

2

MA LOK

九肚山路 KAU TO SHAN RD

吐露港公路 TAI PO RD

排水口 水

沙田污水處理廠 Sha Tin Sewage Treatment Works

2

TSUEN KING

會所 Clubhouse

馬房 Stables

城門河 Shing Mun River Channel

駿景園 Royal Ascot

香港賽馬會沙田馬場 Jockey Club Sha Tin Racecourse

彭福公園 Penfold Park

大老山公路 TATES CAIRN HIGHWAY

亞公角街 A KUNG KOK ST

亞公角 A Kung Kok

A

B

茶灣花園 Allway Gardens

A

荃 TSUEN

潮江春(荃灣) Chiu Chow Garden (Tsuen Wan)

B

白田壩 Pak Tin Pa

象鼻山路

茶果嶺花園 TSUEN KING GARDEN

茶果花園 TSUEN TAK GARDENS

ROUTE TWISK

柴灣角 Chai Wan Kok

青山公路 CASTLE PEAK RD

象鼻山路 PEI SHAN RD

荃灣 TSUEN WAN

石圍角邨 SHEK WAI KOK EST

1

福來邨 FUK LOI ESTATE

綠楊新邨 LUK YEUNG SUN CHUEN

1

福滿樓 Serenade Cove

荃灣 TSUEN WAN

大窩口 TAI WO HAU

大河道 TSUEN WAN RD

荃灣西 TSUEN WAN WEST

Luna Garden

TSUEN WAN

如心廣場 Nina Tower

大窩口邨 TAI WO HAU EST

5

Chelsea Court

葵涌 KWAI SHING

葵盛西邨 Kwai Shing W. Est

2

N

← 740m米(比例尺 Scale 1:24,655) →

TSUEN WAN ROAD

TEXACO RD

海濱花園 Riviera Gardens

6

A

B

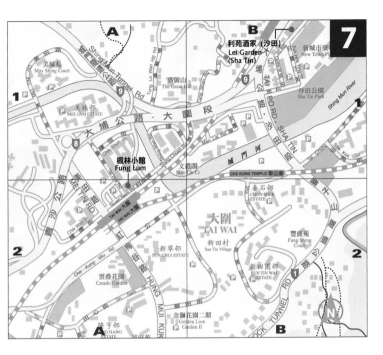

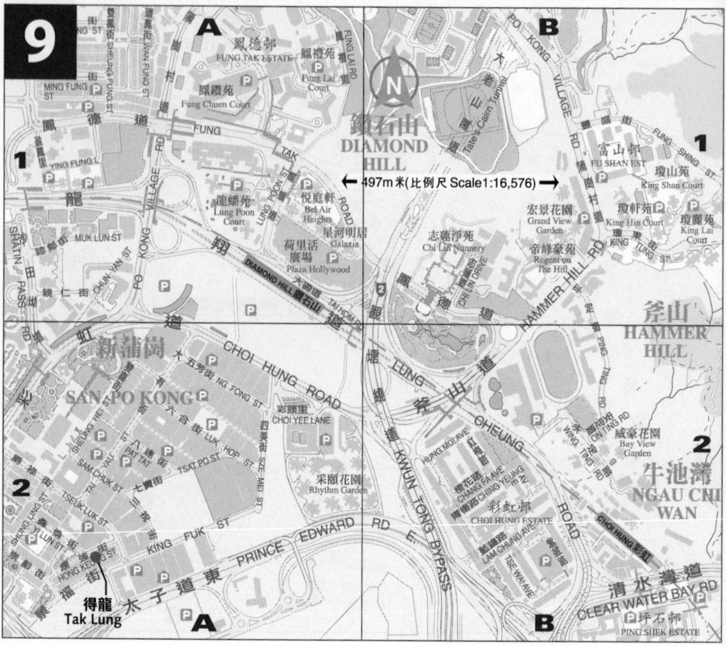
9
A
B
1
2
鳳德邨
FUNG TAK ESTATE
鳳禮苑
Fung Lai Court
FUNG LAI RD
鳳鑽苑
Fung Chuen Court
MING FUNG ST
YING FUNG L
MUK LUN ST
CHUN YAN ST
SHATIN PASS RD
PO KONG VILLAGE RD
FUNG
TAK
LUNG POON ST
龍蟠苑
Lung Poon Court
悅庭軒
Bel Air Heights
星河明居
Galaxia
荷里活廣場
Plaza Hollywood
DIAMOND HILL 鑽石山
TAI HOM RD
鑽石山
DIAMOND HILL
大老山隧道
Tate's Cairn Tunnel
← 497m米(比例尺 Scale1:16,576) →
PO KONG VILLAGE RD
富山邨
FU SHAN EST
FUNG SHING ST
瓊山苑
King Shan Court
宏景花園
Grand View Garden
瓊軒苑
King Hin Court
瓊麗苑
King Lai Court
KING TUNG ST
志蓮淨苑
Chi Lin Nunnery
CHI LIN DRIVE
帝峰豪苑
Regent on The Hill
HAMMER HILL RD
斧山
HAMMER HILL
PING TING RD
新蒲崗
SAN PO KONG
CHOI HUNG ROAD
NG FONG ST
LUK HOP ST
SZE MEI ST
彩頤里
CHOI YEE LANE
采頤花園
Rhythm Garden
SHEUNG HEI ST
TAI YAU ST
PAT TAT
SAM CHUK ST
TSAT PO ST
TSEUK LUK ST
SHUNG LING ST
YI LUN ST
HONG KEUNG ST
KING FUK ST
PRINCE EDWARD RD E.
太子道東
得龍
Tak Lung
KWUN TONG BYPASS
LUNG CHEUNG ROAD
HUNG MUI AVE
CHANG FA AVE
CHING YEUNG AVE
彩虹邨
CHOI HUNG ESTATE
LAM CHUNG AVE
TSE WAI AVE
ON TING RD
WING TING RD
威豪花園
Bay View Garden
牛池灣
NGAU CHI WAN
CHOI HUNG 彩虹
清水灣道
CLEAR WATER BAY RD
坪石邨
PING SHEK ESTATE

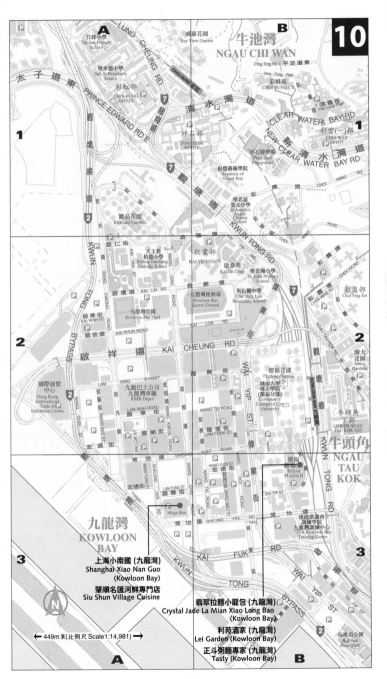

上海小南國 (九龍灣)
Shanghai Xiao Nan Guo
(Kowloon Bay)

肇順名匯河鮮專門店
Siu Shun Village Cuisine

翡翠拉麵小籠包 (九龍灣)
Crystal Jade La Mian Xiao Long Bao
(Kowloon Bay)

利苑酒家 (九龍灣)
Lei Garden (Kowloon Bay)

正斗粥麵專家 (九龍灣)
Tasty (Kowloon Bay)

← 449m 米(比例尺 Scale1:14,981) →

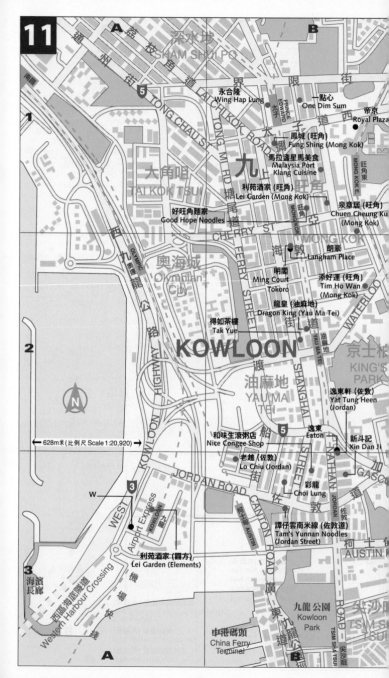

11

深水埗 SHAM SHUI PO

A B

太子道 PRINCE EDWARD 水坪街

界限街

欽州街 LAI CHI KOK ROAD

荔枝角道 LAI CHI KOK RD

通州街 TONG CHAU ST

5

永合隆
Wing Hap Lung

一點心
One Dim Sum

帝京
Royal Plaza

旺角 MONG KOK

旺角東 MONG KOK

九龍

大角咀
TAI KOK TSUI

鳳城 (旺角)
Fung Shing (Mong Kok)

馬拉盞星馬美食
Malaysia Port
Klang Cuisine

利苑酒家 (旺角)
Lei Garden (Mong Kok)

旺角 MONG KOK

旺角 MONG KOK

泉章居 (旺角)
Chuen Cheung Ku
(Mong Kok)

好旺角麵家
Good Hope Noodles

塘尾道

櫻桃街 CHERRY ST

奧運 OLYMPIC

九龍 KOWLOON

奧海城
Olympian
City

海壇街

FERRY STREET

渡船街

新填地街 SHANGHAI STREET

海敦

朗豪
Langham Place

明閣
Ming Court
Tokoro

添好運 (旺角)
Tim Ho Wan
(Mong Kok)

龍皇 (油麻地)
Dragon King (Yau Ma Tei)

得如茶樓
Tak Yue

廟街

油麻地

KOWLOON

渡船

WATERLOO

京士柏
KING'S
PARK

油麻地
YAU MA
TEI

N

← 628m米 (比例尺 Scale 1:20,920) →

九龍公路 KOWLOON HIGHWAY

油麻地 YAU MA TEI

逸東軒 (佐敦)
Yat Tung Heen
(Jordan)

和味生滾粥店
Nice Congee Shop

逸東
Eaton

新斗記
Xin Dan Ji

老趙 (佐敦)
Lo Chiu (Jordan)

彩龍
Choi Lung

加士居 GASCO

JORDAN ROAD

佐敦道 JORDAN ROAD

佐敦道 CANTON ROAD

彌敦道 NATHAN JORDAN 佐敦道

佐敦道 AUSTIN

3

W

機場快線 Airport Express

圓方 KOWLOON

譚仔雲南米線 (佐敦道)
Tam's Yunnan Noodles
(Jordan Street)

柯士甸道 AUSTIN

利苑酒家 (圓方)
Lei Garden (Elements)

3

海濱長廊

西區海底隧道
Western Harbour Crossing

機場快線

九龍公園
Kowloon
Park

尖沙咀 TSIM SHA TSUI

中港碼頭
China Ferry
Terminal

廣東道 CANTON ROAD

柯士甸道 ROAD

尖沙咀 TSIM SHA TSUI

A B

BOUNDARY STREET
PRINCE EDWARD ROAD WEST
ARGYLE STREET
馬頭圍
MA TAU WAI
九龍醫院

8度海逸
Harbour Plaza 8 Degrees

土瓜灣
TO KWA WAN

MA TAU WAI RD

KOWLOON CITY RD

TO KWA WAN RD

5

馬頭圍
MA TAU WAI RD

何文田
HO MAN TIN

PRINCESS MARGARET ROAD

KWONG STREET

2

利沙伯
醫院
E Hosp

GNE ROAD

紅磡
HUNG HOM

香港
理工大學
Hong Kong
Polytechnic
University

HUNG HOM ROAD

正斗粥麵專家 (紅磡)
Tasty (Hung Hom)

黃埔花園
Whampoa
Garden

九龍海逸君綽
Harbour Grand Kowloon

CHATHAM ROAD

香港科學館
Hong Kong
Science Museum

香港體育館
Hong Kong Coliseum

Harbour Grill

海逸軒
Hoi Yat Heen

3

維多利亞港
VICTORIA HARBOUR

SALISBURY RD

C　1　　　　D

13

避風塘興記
Hing Kee

老趙 (尖沙咀)
Lo Chiu
(Tsim Sha Tsui)

富豪 (尖沙咀)
Fu Ho (Tsim Sha Tsui)

新同樂
Sun Tung Lok

國金軒 (The Mira)
Cuisine Cuisine at The Mira

Whisk

The Mira

翡翠拉麵小龍包 (尖沙咀)
Crystal Jade La Mian
Xiao Long Bao (TST)

鼎泰豐 (尖沙咀)
Din Tai Fung (Tsim Sha Tsui)

爵樂
Gaylord

唐閣
T'ang Court

朗廷
The Langham

南海一號
Nanhai No.1

馬哥孛羅
Marco Polo

胡同
Hutong

Hullett House

隆濤院
Loong Toh Yuen
St. George

半島
The Peninsula

BLT Steak

Cucina

夜上海 (九龍)
Yè Shanghai (Kowloon)

北京樓 (九龍)
Peking Garden
(Kowloon)

瑞樵閣
Chesa

吉地士
Gaddi's

嘉麟樓
Spring Moon

尖沙咀
TSIM SHA TSUI

← 250m米 (比例尺 Scale 1:8,333) →

TAK SHING ST

Kowloon
Cricket Club
先施草地滾球場
Kowloon Bowling
Green Cliub

C

D

香港理工大學
The Hong Kong
Polytechnic University

14

ROAD 柯士甸道

松山道

AUSTIN AVE.

HILLWOOD RD

香港天文台
HK Observatory

CHEONG WAN ROAD

香港歷史
博物館
HK Museum
of History

1

百利商業

CHATHAM C 漆咸道

福臨門 (九龍)
Fook Lam Moon
(Kowloon)

Conococia Plaza

梳士巴利

帝樂文娜公館
The Luxe Manor

OBSERVATORY

KNUTSFORD TERR

諾士佛臺

Aspasia

諾士佛臺

KIMBERLEY

CARNARVON ROAD 加拿分道

金巴利道 利園

KIMBERLEY STREET

君怡閣
Kimberley Chinese Restaurant

KIMBERLEY RD

加連威老道 GRANVILLE RD

香港科學館
Hong Kong
Science Museum

SCIENCE MUSEUM

新文華中心
New Mandarin Plaza

科學館道

星光行

金巴利道

CAMERON ROAD

厚福街 BAU FOOK ST

金巴利利園

利苑酒家 (尖沙咀)
Lei Garden (Tsim Sha Tsui)

PRAT AVE.

麗景
Panorama

帝苑
The Royal
Garden

海景嘉福
Intercontinental
Grand Stanford

尖沙咀凱悅
Hyatt Regency
Tsim Sha Tsui

九龍香格里拉大
Kowloon Shangri-La

MODY ROAD

海景軒
Hoi King Heen

海風餐廳
The Mistral

2

SALISBURY

希戈
Hugo's

凱悅軒
The Chinese Restaurant
Steik World Meats

Angelini

香宮
Shang Palace

東來順
Dong Lai Shun

稻菊 (尖沙咀)
Inagiku (Tsim Sha Tsui)

Sabatini

喜來登
Sheraton

EAST TSIM SHA TSUI 尖東

新世界中心
New World Centre

洲際
Intercontinental

天寶閣
Celestial Court

雲海
Unkai

Avenue of Stars

Nobu
Spoon by Alain Ducasse
The Steak House

欣圖軒
Yan Toh Heen

維多利亞港
VICTORIA HARBOUR

3

C

D

469

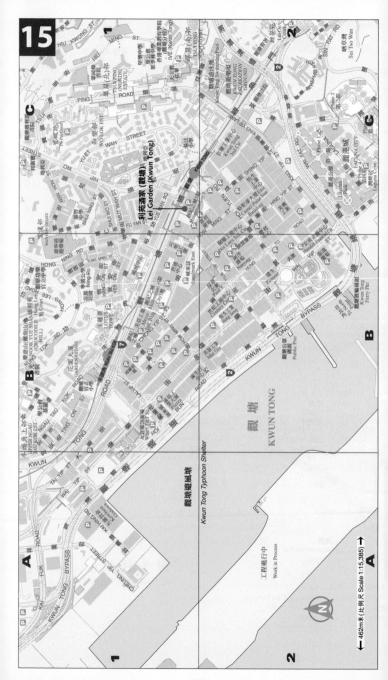

利苑酒家（觀塘）
Lei Garden (Kwun Tong)

觀塘遊風塘
Kwun Tong Typhoon Shelter

觀塘
KWUN TONG

工程進行中
Work in Process

462米 (比例尺 Scale 1:15,385)

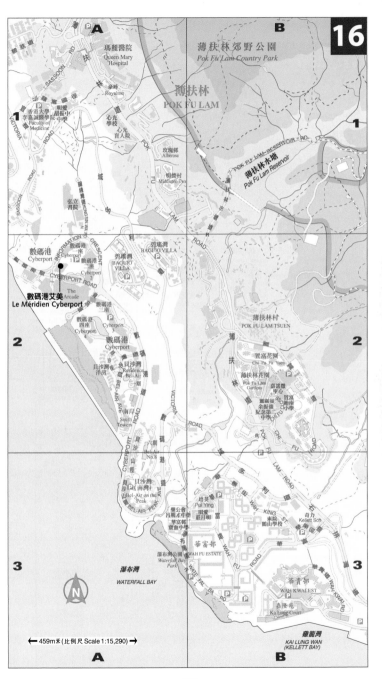

瑪麗醫院
Queen Mary Hospital

薄扶林郊野公園
Pok Fu Lam Country Park

薄扶林
POK FU LAM

豪峰
Royalton

香港大學
李嘉誠醫學院
Faculty of
Medicine

明愛胡振中
中學

心光樓
心光盲人院

玫瑰邨
Alberose

胡應村
Middleton Twn

SASSOON RD

弘立書院

POK FU LAM RESERVOIR RD.

薄扶林水塘
Pok Fu Lam Reservoir

數碼港
Cyberport

碧瑤灣
BAGUIO VILLA

數碼港一座
Cyberport

數碼港二座
Cyberport

數碼港艾美
Le Méridien Cyberport

The
Arcade

數碼港三座
Cyberport

數碼港四座
Cyberport

數碼港
Cyberport

薄扶林村
POK FU LAM TSUEN

貝沙灣洋房
Residence
Bel-Air

南灣
South
Towers

賈富花園
Chi Fu Fa Yuen

海扶林花園
Pok Fu Lam
Gardens

富裕閣

余振強
紀念第二
中學

六期
南灣
No.8

貝沙灣
Bel-Air

貝沙灣(南灣)
Bel-Air

山頂
Bel-Air at
the Peak

培英
Pui Ying

樂善堂
梁銶琚學校
華富邨
寶血會小學

明愛莊月明

鄧肇堅學校

奇力
Kellett Sch

東華三院鄺錫坤伉儷中學

華富邨
WAH FU ESTATE

華貴邨
WAH KWAI EST

瀑布灣公園
Waterfall Bay
Park

瀑布灣
WATERFALL BAY

嘉隆苑
Ka Lung Court

雞龍灣
KAI LUNG WAN
(KELLETT BAY)

← 459m米 (比例尺 Scale 1:15,290) →

A   B

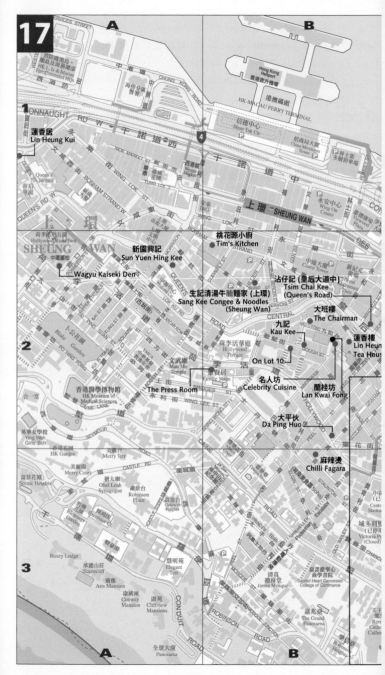

A

B

SERVICES STREET

西消防
港消防處、滅島及海務總部
HK 1, 2 & Marine
Fire Command HQs
西消防

中港道
CHUNG KONG ROAD

海傍分區警署

Hong Kong Helipad
香港直升機場

港澳碼頭
HK-MACAU FERRY TERMINAL

1

CONNAUGHT RD W 干諾道西

信德中心
Shun Tak Ctr

招商局大廈
China Merchants
Tower

林士街多層停車場

蓮香居
Lin Heung Kui

NEW MARKET ST

干諾道西

BONHAM STRAND W

永安中心
Wing On
Centre

Queen's
Terrace
帝后華庭

WING LOK ST

上環 SHEUNG WAN

QUEEN'S RD C

上 環

DES

荷李活道公園
Hollywood Road Park

SHEUNG WAN

中國置地

桃花源小廚
Tim's Kitchen

Cosco Tower
中遠大廈

新紀元廣場

新園興記
Sun Yuen Hing Kee

QUEEN'S

沾仔記 (皇后大道中)
Tsim Chai Kee
(Queen's Road)

Wagyu Kaiseki Den

生記清湯牛腩麵家 (上環)
Sang Kee Congee & Noodles
(Sheung Wan)

大班樓
The Chairman

WELLINGTON 九記

九記
Kau Kee

蓮香樓
Lin Heun
Tea Hous

2

Blake
Garden
卜公花園

荷李活華庭
Hollywood
Terrace

On Lot 10

香港醫學博物館
HK Museum of
Medical Sciences

文武廟
Man Mo
Temple

李寶店
Centre Stage

名人坊
Celebrity Cuisine

蘭桂坊
Lan Kwai Fong

合一堂

The Press Room

永利街 WING LEE ST

HOLLYWOOD

英華女學校
Ying Wan
Girls Sch

SEYMOUR

大平伙
Da Ping Huo

花 街

香港花園
HK Garden

CASTLE RD

麻辣燙
Chilli Fagara

芙蓉街
Merry Terr

衛城道

美輪閣
Merry Court

碧太廟
Ohel Leah
Synagogue

羅便臣道
Robinson
Place

中環
(已
Centr
Station

富景花園
Scenic Heights

豪園

卑利士
Bickleys
Gardens

金堆台
Goldwin
Hill

清真
Jamia

域多利
(已拆除)
Victoria P
(Closed)

3

Buxey Lodge

慧雅
Arts Mansion

慧明苑
Elegant Terr

康威園
Conway
Mansion

康苑
Cliffview
Mansions

CONDUIT

清真禮拜堂
Jamia Mosque

嘉諾撒聖心
商學書院
Sacred Heart Canossian
College of Commerce

天主
Rom
Cathe
Cathe

全景大廈
Panorama

ROBINSON

ROAD

嘉富
The Grand
Panorama

羅便臣
Robinson
Heights

A

B

472

C

Caprice
稻菊 (國際金融中心)
Inagiku (IFC)
龍景軒
Lung King Heen
The Lounge

1號碼頭 Pier 1

3號碼頭 Pier 3

2號碼頭 Pier 2

4號碼頭 Pier 4

5號碼頭 Pier 5

6號碼頭 Pier 6

7號碼頭 Pier 7

Agnès b. Le Pain Grillé (Central)
H One
利苑酒家 (國際金融中心)
Lei Garden (IFC)
正斗粥麵專家 (國際金融中心)
Tasty (IFC)

四季
Four Seasons

Watermark

麥奀記(忠記)麵家 (永吉街)
Mak An Kee Noodle
(Wing Kut Street)

19

洞庭樓 (中環)
Hunan Garden
(Central)

翠玉軒
The Square

文華扒房+酒吧
Mandarin Grill + Bar
文華廳
Man Wah
Pierre

文華東方
Mandarin Oriental

Harvey Nichols
Zuma

8½ Otto e Mezzo
北京樓 (中環)
Peking Garden (Central)

L'Atelier de
Joël Robuchon

Amber

置地文華東方
The Landmark
Mandarin Oriental

港島廳
Island Tang

473

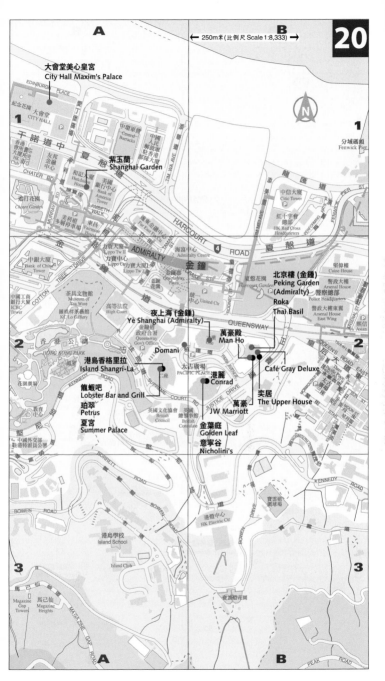

← 250m米 (比例尺 Scale 1:8,333) →

A

大會堂美心皇宮
City Hall Maxim's Palace

EDINBURGH PLACE

記念花園

大會堂
CITY HALL

中環軍營
Central
Barracks

中國人民東
中國人民解放軍
駐香港部隊

B

干諾道中
CHATER RD

香港
會所
HK
Club

淀打花園
Chater Garden

紫玉蘭
Shanghai Garden

和記大廈
Hutchison
House

美國
銀行中心
Bank of
America

LAMBETH
WALK

東昌
Farmfield

分域碼頭
Fenwick Pier

菲
顯利道

中信大廈
Citic Tower

紅十字會
總部
HK Red Cross
Headquarters

HARCOURT

ROAD

夏慤道

ADMIRALTY

海富中心
Admiralty
Centre

金鐘

力寶大廈II
Lippo Tw II
力寶中心
Lippo Ctr
力寶大廈I
Lippo Tw I

金鐘
花園
Queensway
Plaza

力寶中心
United Ctr

北京樓 (金鐘)
Peking Garden
(Admiralty)

Roka

Thai Basil

中銀大廈
Bank of China
Tower

中國工商
銀行亞洲
ICBC
Tower

茶具文物館
Museum of
Tea Ware

羅桂祥茶藝館
K.C. Lo Gallery

高等法院
High Court

夏慤花園
Harcourt Garden

警政大樓
Arsenal House

警政大樓東翼
Arsenal House
East Wing

夜上海 (金鐘)
Yè Shanghai (Admiralty)

金鐘道
政府合署
Queensway
Gov's Offices

2

香港公園
HONG KONG PARK

花園廣場

港島香格里拉
Island Shangri-La

龍蝦吧
Lobster Bar and Grill

珀翠
Petrus

夏宮
Summer Palace

中國外交部
駐港特派員公署

Domani

太古廣場
PACIFIC PLACE

二座

英國文化協會
British
Council

英國
總領事館
British
Consulate

萬豪殿
Man Ho

港麗
Conrad

Café Gray Deluxe

奕居
The Upper House

萬豪
JW Marriott

金葉庭
Golden Leaf

意寧谷
Nicholini's

BOWEN

ROAD

3

港島學校
Island School

Island Club

Magazine
Gap Towers

馬己仙
Magazine
Heights

寶雲徑
遊樂場

港燈中心
HK Electric Ctr

寶雲道花園

PEAK

ROAD

A

B

475

A

B

N

← 236米 (比例尺 Scale 1:7,851) →

博覽海濱花園
Expo Promenade

金紫荊
Golden Bauhinia

香港會議展覽中心新翼
HKCEC New Wing

貿易發展局
易購資訊 IPo
TDC Business InfoCentre

Grissini
港灣壹號
One Harbour Road

君悅
Grand Hyatt

滿福樓 (灣仔)
Dynasty (Wan Chai)

CONVENTION AV

分域碼頭
Fenwick Pier

LUNG KING ST.

香港會議展覽中心
HK Convention &
Exhibition Centre
(往會場A出口)

分域碼頭街

香港演藝學院
HK Academy
for Performing Arts

香港
藝術中心
Art Centre

瑞安中心
Shui On Centre

灣仔政府大樓
Wanchai
Tower

港灣
消防局

中信大廈
Citic Tower

電訊大廈
Telecom House

稅務大樓
Revenue
Tower

入境事
務大樓
Immigration
Tower

中環廣場
Central Plaza

紅十字會總部
HK Red Cross
Headquarters

夏慤道

車氏尊菜軒
Che's

GLOUC

堅偉樓
Caine House

美國高通大廈
Men Minal Tower

夏慤大廈
Harcourt House

留園雅敍
Liu Yuan Pavilion

祥記飯店
Cheung Kee

夏慤花園
Harcourt Garden

警政總部
Arsenal House

警察總部
Police Headquarters

莎巴
Sabah

QUEENSWAY

軍械大廈東翼
Arsenal House
East Wing

熙信樓
Asian

Uno Más

生記
Sang Kee

永華雲吞麵家
Wing Wah

灣仔 WAN CHAI

囍宴 甜·藝
Xi Yan Sweets

福臨門 (灣仔)
Fook Lam Moon (Wan Chai)

Bo Innovation

Cépage

一碗麵 (聖佛蘭士街)
Olala (St. Francis Street)

St. Francis Canossian

新九記粥麵
Sun Kau Kee Noodle Shop

帝后殿
Queen's Palace

KENNEDY

BOWER DRIVE

寶雲道
網球場

BOWEN ROAD

胡忠大廈
Wu Chung Hse

1

2

3

A

B

476

逸東軒 (灣仔)
Yat Tung Heen (Wan Chai)

富聲 (灣仔)
Fu Sing (Wan Chai)

諾富特世紀
Novotel Century

利苑酒家 (灣仔)
Lei Garden (Wan Chai)

楊記麵家
Yeung's Noodle

再興
Joi Hing

靠得住
Trusty Congee King

明
Wooloomooloo Steakhouse
(Wan Chai)

杭州酒家
Hong Zhou

翡翠拉麵小籠包 (灣仔)
Crystal Jade La Mian Xiao
Long Bao (Wan Chai)

麗悅
Cosmo

麗都
Cosmopolitan

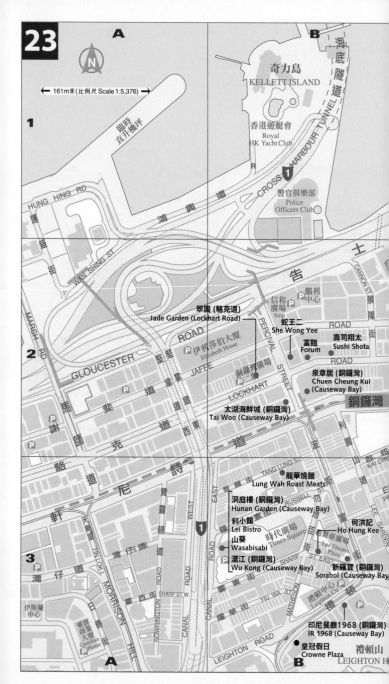

23

A　　　　　　　B

N

← 161m米 (比例尺 Scale 1:5,376) →

臨時直升機坪

奇力島
KELLETT ISLAND

海底隧道

香港遊艇會
Royal HK Yacht Club

CROSS HARBOUR TUNNEL

警官俱樂部
Police Officers Club

HUNG HING RD
鴻興道

蓮　街

WAN SHING ST

告士

CANNON ST景隆街

MARSH RD

信和廣場
Sino

勝利中心

翠園 (駱克道)
Jade Garden (Lockhart Road)

蛇王二
She Wong Yee

壽司翔太
Sushi Shota

GLOUCESTER

ROAD

PERCIVAL STREET

伊利莎伯大廈
Elizabeth House

銅鑼灣廣場

富臨
Forum

堅拿道

JAFFE

泉章居 (銅鑼灣)
Chuen Cheung Kui
(Causeway Bay)

馬師道

謝斐道

LOCKHART

銅鑼灣

太湖海鮮城 (銅鑼灣)
Tai Woo (Causeway Bay)

駱克道

軒尼詩道

WEST

TANG LUNG ST

龍華燒臘
Lung Wah Roast Meats

洞庭樓 (銅鑼灣)
Hunan Garden (Causeway Bay)

利小館
Lei Bistro

山葵
Wasabisabi

滬江 (銅鑼灣)
Wu Kong (Causeway Bay)

RUSSELL

時代廣場
Times Square

ST EAST

和舞臺廣場
Ece Theatre Plaza

何洪記
Ho Hung Kee

新羅寶 (銅鑼灣)
Sorabol (Causeway Bay)

TIN LOK LANE

MORRISON HILL

灣仔道

BOWRINGTON ROAD

SHARP ST W

CANAL ROAD

YIU WA ST

MATHESON ROAD

SHARP

伊斯蘭中心

駿群商業大廈
Guardian House

LEIGHTON ROAD

YIU WA STREET

禮頓中心
Leighton Ctr

印尼餐廳1968 (銅鑼灣)
IR 1968 (Causeway Bay)

皇冠假日
Crowne Plaza

禮頓山
LEIGHTON H

A　　　　　　　B

478

銅鑼灣避風塘
Causeway Bay
Typhoon Shelter

維多利亞公園
VICTORIA PARK

銅鑼灣
CAUSEWAY BAY

VICTORIA PARK ROAD

告士打道

PATERSON ST

LELAND ST

HOUSTON ST

KINGSTON STREET

京士頓街

百德大廈
Pearl City Mansion

三珠城大廈

柏寧
The Park Lane

東角中心
East Point Ctr

社貿易場中心
Ce Ctr

GREAT GEORGE ST

記利佐治街

CAUSEWAY BAY

香港大廈

皇室大廈
Windsor House

恒隆中心
Hang Lung

GLOUCESTER RD

CAUSEWAY 威道

怡和街

YEE WO ST

JARDINE'S BAZAAR

嘉蘭中心

記利佐治街

樂聲大廈

鼎泰豐 (銅鑼灣)
Din Tai Fung
(Causeway Bay)

伊榮街
Palibury

富聲 (銅鑼灣)
Fu Sing (Causeway Bay)

銅鑼灣道

TUNG LO WAN RD

聖馬利亞堂

何東中學

LAN FONG RD

JARDINE'S CRESCENT

The Drawing Room

Jia

伊榮街
IRVING

PENNINGTON ST

敬誠街

富豪金殿
Regal Palace
聖保祿學校
St. Paul's Convent
School

Lanson Place

Caroline Centre

HYSAN AVE

SUNNING RD

新寧大廈

新寧道

YUN PING RD

LEIGHTON

渣甸坊

何東分校

Mist

飯堂
Fan Tang

HOI PING RD

HAVEN ST

聖保祿醫院
St Paul's Hospital

KA NING PATH

農圃
Farm House
雪園 (銅鑼灣)
Snow Garden (Causeway Bay)

郵政署
港島區

路政署
港島區

聖保祿修院

COTTON PATH

保良局
Po Leung Kuk

連出道

棉花路

紀律人員體育
及康樂會

25

A | B

北角
NORTH POINT

北角渡輪碼頭
North Point Ferry Pier
往九龍城．紅磡
To Kowloon City, Hung Hom

1

← 313m米 (比例尺 Scale 1:10,417) →

WEST EMBANKMENT

HARBOUR PARADE
北角渡輪碼頭

維 多 利 亞 港
VICTORIA HARBOUR

銀幕中心
Silvercord Centre

阿鴻小吃
Hung's Delicacies

NORTH POINT ROAD

加藤喬司
Sushi Kato

KAM PING ST

KING'S

利苑酒家 (北角)
Lei Garden (North Point)

城市花園
City Garden

PEACOCK RD

港島海逸君綽
Harbour
Grand Hong Kong

電燈中心
The Electric
Centre

厚天大廈
Sky Scraper 雲峰大廈
Summit Court

2

君綽軒
Kwan Cheuk Heen
Le 188°

夏慤臺 Coral Court
Harbour View 珊瑚閣
Terr
Hanking 仁豪閣
Court
Clementi

富豪園 Beverly
富欣園 Height
Flora Garden 峰景大廈
Hilltop

海峰園
Harbour Heights

香港樹仁大學
Shue Yan
University

宏利保險中心
Manulife
Tower

海天
峰
Sky
Horizon

Orkney・Shelland
Braemer
Heights

海景台
Sea View Est

WATSON RD

威景台
Evian Villas

裕景台
Seaview
Garden

繁榮台
Evelyn
Towers

香港
日本人
學校

鰂魚涌
Quarry B
Schoo

WING HING ST

庇理羅士女子
Belilios Pub.Sch

東霆李潤田
Lee Ching Dea
Mem.Col.

基督教路德會
Concordia
Lutheran Sch

漢國際
學校
Chinese
International
School

VICTORIA PARK RD

留家廚房
Kin's Kitchen

3

荔園游泳池
Victoria Park
Swimming Pool

桔景景
Park Towers

維 多 利 亞 公 園
VICTORIA PARK

銅鑼灣維景 (銅鑼灣)
Metropark (Causeway Bay)

金龍大廈
Dragon
Court

A | B

480

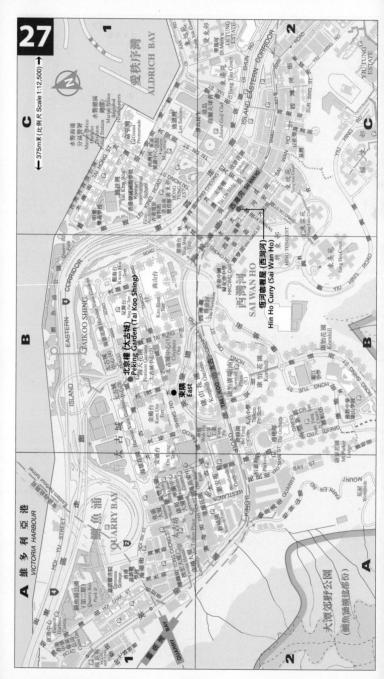

28

香港海防博物館

魚類批發市場
Fish Wholesale Market

筲箕灣避風塘
Shau Kei Wan Typhoon Shelter

愛秩序灣
ALDRICH BAY

筲箕灣避風塘海濱花園

Aldrich Bay Promenade

愛秩序灣官立中學

東旭苑
Tung Yuk Court

愛東邨
OI TUNG ESTATE

聖馬可
St.Mark's

愛蝶灣
Aldrich Garden

阿公岩
A Kung Ngam

筲箕灣官立

安利
On Lee

恆河咖喱屋（筲箕灣）
Hin Ho Curry (Shau Kei Wan)

明華大廈

ISLAND   EASTERN

CORRIDOR   筲箕灣   SHAU KEI WAN

南安街   NAM ON ST

愛秩序灣遊樂場

鯉魚門花園
Perfect Mount

寶文街 PO MAN ST

金華街 KAM WA ST

MING WAH DAI HA

筲箕灣 H.S.

柴灣道   CHAI   WAN   ROAD

南康街 NAM HONG ST

聖十字徑
Holy Cross Path

工廠街 FACTORY ST

教堂里
CHURCH

耀東邨
YIU TUNG ESTATE

SHAU KEI   WAN

筲箕灣遊樂場

工廠街遊樂場

Elsa High Sch Kellett

筲箕灣道

街民街 NGOI MAN ST

勵志會梁李秀娛
Siu Ming Court

東盛苑
Tung Shing Court

慈幼會修院
Salesian School

筲箕灣
SHAU KEI WAN

慈幼會修院

聖馬可
St. Mark's

← 242m米(比例尺 Scale 1:8,064) →

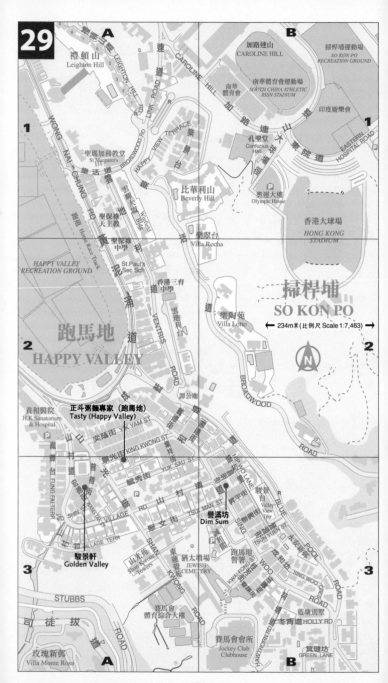

禮頓山
Leighton Hill

加路連山
CAROLINE HILL

掃桿埔運動場
SO KON PO
RECREATION GROUND

連

道

CAROLINE HILL ROAD

加

路

南華體育會運動場
SOUTH CHINA ATHLETIC
ASSN STADIUM

連

印度遊樂會
EASTERN HOSPITAL ROAD

WONG NAI CHUNG ROAD

LEIGHTON HILL ROAD

BROADWOOD RD

HAPPY VIEW TERRACE

樂

活

道

樂

景

台

南華
體育會

山

孔聖堂
Confucius
Hall

東院道

東

院

道

聖瑪加利教堂
St Margaret's

藥

黃

比華利山
Beverly Hill

奧運大樓
Olympic House

P

聖保祿
天主教

聖保祿
中學

藍塘道 Horse Race Track

Winfield
Bldg

樂翠台
Villa Rocha

泥

黃

泥

涌

道

HAPPY VALLEY
RECREATION GROUND

St.Paul's
Sec Sch

香港三育
中學

香港大球場
HONG KONG
STADIUM

VENTRIS ROAD

樂地利台

掃桿埔
SO KON PO

道

樂陶苑
Villa Lotto

涌

道

跑馬地
HAPPY VALLEY

←234m米(比例尺 Scale 1:7,463)→

BROADWOOD ROAD

ⒷN

源公廟

養和醫院
H.K. Sanatorium
& Hospital

P

正斗粥麵專家 (跑馬地)
Tasty (Happy Valley)

山光道

YAK YAM ST

景光街 KING KWONG ST

毓秀街 YUK SAU ST

聯興街

奕廕街

P

毓成街

奕蔭街

蟠龍道

VILLAGE

SHAN KWONG RD

成和道

藍塘道

黃泥涌道

骏景台
Valley
View
Terr

BLUE

晉源街 TSUI MAN ST

譽滿坊
Dim Sum

成和道

昌明街

POOL

村屋街

TSUN YUEN ST

永豐街

富明街

鳳輝台 FUNG FAI TERR

醫院道

光明街

桂芳街

奕廕街 SHING WOO RD

駿景軒
Golden Valley

VILLAGE TERR

山光苑
Shan Kwong
Towers

東蓮
覺苑

猶太墳場
JEWISH
CEMETERY

跑馬地
警署

P

成和道

KWAI FONG ST

桂芳街

和益街

SING WOO ROAD

黃泥涌道

永豐街

ROAD

STUBBS ROAD

SHAN KWONG ROAD

體育綜合大樓

賽馬會會所
Jockey Club
Clubhouse

HAWTHORN ROAD

藍塘別墅

冬青道 HOLLY RD

菎璉坊
GREEN LANE

司徒拔道

玫瑰新邨
Villa Monte Rosa

Ⓐ

Ⓑ

484

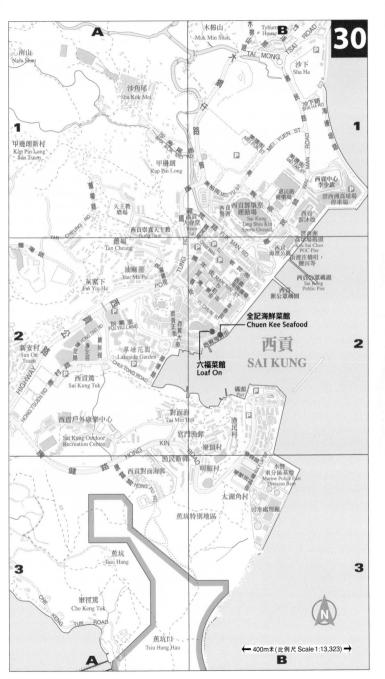

MACAU
澳門

31

A   B

珠海市
Zhuhai Shi

1

ESTRADA MARGINAL DA

美麗
花園

青洲
青洲山
55.6
Ilha Verde

Fok Tak
Sun Chun

澳門新福利公共
汽車有限公司

紀念孫中山市政公園
Sun Yat Sen
Park

台山
Toi San

李寶樁街

燒灰花園
Jardim Iat Lai

AVENIDA DO CONSELHEIRO

跑狗場
Greyhound
Races

澳門賽狗
有限公司

RUA DO GENERAL IVENS FERRAZ

槟榔基
北灣

2

Fai Chi Kei

AVENIDA MARGINAL DO LAM MAU

紅街市

龍華茶樓
Lung Wah
Tea House

新橋
San Kiu

RUA DA RIBEIRA DO PATANE

六記粥麵
Luk Kei Noodle

沙梨頭
Patane

白鴿巢賈梅士公園
Camoes Park

牛記咖喱美食
Ngao Kei Ka Lei Chon

聖味基墳場
Cemiterio S.
Miguel
Arcanjo

消防博物館

鏡湖醫院
Kiang Wu
Hospital

3

內港
Inner
Harbour

天主教藝術
博物館
Museum of
Sacred Art

澳門博物館
Museum
of Macau

大三巴
牌坊
Ruins of
St Paul's

大炮台
Monte
Fort

哪吒廟

祥記
Oja Sopa
De Fita Cheong Kei

東方基金會
East Asia

保良廟

新馬路 AVENIDA DE ALMEIDA RIBEIRO

典當業
展示館

陶陶居
Tou Tou Koi

大堂
Se

玫瑰堂

大堂
Cathedral

A   B

488

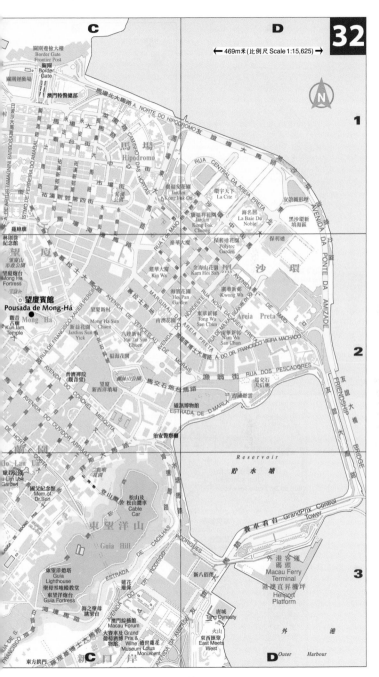

← 469m米 (比例尺 Scale 1:15,625) →

N

關閘邊檢大樓
Border Gate
Frontier Post

關閘
Border
Gate

澳門特警總部

廣場北大馬路 A. NORTE DO HIPODROMO 友誼橋大馬路

馬場
Hipodromo

ISTMO DE FERREIRA DO AMARAL

RUA CENTRAL DA AREIA PRETA

廣福安花園
Jardim
Kong Fok On

環宇天下
La Cité

海名居
La Baie Du
Noble

友漁圍鄰埠

黑沙環新
填海區

AVENIDA DA PONTE DA AMIZADE

蓮峰廟

林則徐
紀念館

望
廈

望廈山
市政公園

望廈炮台
Mong Ha
Fortress

望廈賓館
Pousada de Mong-Há

觀音
古廟
Kun Iam
Temple

Mong Ha

RUA DE FRANCISCO PEREIRA

AVENIDA DE VENCESLAU

AVENIDA DO COELHO DO AMARAL

AVENIDA DO OUVIDOR ARRIAGA

DE HORTA

望廈新村
Mong Ha Sun
Chuen

新益花園
Jardins Sun
Yick

八建新村
Pai Tat Sun
Chuen

福寧花園

RUA DO MARGINAL DA AREIA PRETA

廣福祥花園隅
Jardim
Kong Fok
Cheong

保利達花園
Polytec
Garden

金海山花園
Kam Hoi San

海暉花園
Hoi Pan
Garden

南灣花園

東華新村
Tong Wa
San Chuen

留華新村
Nam Wa
San Chuen

門 沙 環

廣華新邨
Kwong Wa

AVENIDA DE

NORDESTE

AVENIDA NOVA DE SALFETE BM

A. DO DR. FRANCISCO VIEIRA MACHADO

Areia Preta

保利達

AVENIDA DE

DA PONTE DA AMIZADE

DE MORAIS

肯讀挎院
(醫靈堂)

望廈
新西洋墳場

望廈山公園

馬交石炮台馬路

ESTRADA DE D.MARIA

ESTRADA DE

治安警察廳

渔翁街 RUA DOS PESCADORES

馬交石
天后廟

導流燈塔

FRIENDSHIP

友誼大馬路

BRIDGE

Ho Lam
Lin ...

東望洋
Ho Lim Lei
Garden

國父紀念館
Mem.of
Dr.Sun

松山廣場

松山及
松山纜車
Cable
Car

賽車看台 GrandPrix Control
Tower

Reservoir
貯 水 塘

AVENIDA DE

SIDÓNIO PAIS

DE

RODRIGUES

東望洋山
Guia Hill

東望洋燈塔
Guia
Lighthouse

聖母雪地殿教堂

東望洋炮台
Guia Fortress

海之聖母
瞭望台

ESTRADA

DE

CACILHAS

ESTRADA DO

ESTRADA DO

RUA DE

DE S.

新八佰伴

唐城
Tang Dynasty

外港客運
碼頭
Macau Ferry
Terminal

港澳直昇機坪
Heliport
Platform

外 港

澳門綜藝館
Macau Forum

大賽車及
葡萄酒博
物館
Grand
Prix &
Wine
Museum

澳世蓮花
Lotus
Monument

火山
東西匯聚
East Meets
West

D Outer Harbour

東方拱門

新口岸

C

C

1

2

3

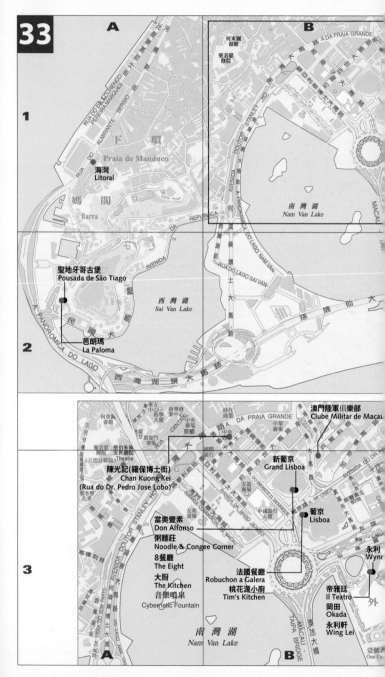

A B

1

RUA DO PE. ANTÓNIO
RUA DO ALMIRANTE SÉRGIO
RUA DE S. LOURENÇO
何東圖書館
聖若瑟修院
A. DA PRAIA GRANDE
亞美利士比盧大馬路
AVENIDA DA REPÚBLICA
RUA DO DOUTOR STANLEY HO

下環

Praia de Manduco

海灣
Litoral

媽閣
Barra

南灣湖
Nam Van Lake

MACAU

2

聖地牙哥古堡
Pousada de São Tiago

芭朗瑪
La Paloma

西灣湖
Sai Van Lake

湖南灣
RUA DO LAGO SAI VAN
RUA DO LAGO NAM VAN
仙鴻德珠

A. PANORÂMICA DO LAGO

西灣湖景大馬路

3

何東圖書館
聖伯多祿
五世廟院
(三巴仔修院)
聖老楞佐
教堂
Theatre

A. DA PRAIA GRANDE

陳光記(羅保博士街)
Chan Kuong Kei
(Rua do Dr. Pedro Jose Lobo)

當奧豐素
Don Alfonso
粥麵莊
Noodle & Congee Corner
8餐廳
The Eight
大廚
The Kitchen
音樂噴泉
Cybernetic Fountain

澳門陸軍俱樂部
Clube Militar de Macau

新葡京
Grand Lisboa

葡京
Lisboa

法國餐廳
Robuchon a Galera
桃花源小廚
Tim's Kitchen

永利
Wynn

帝雅廷
Il Teatro
岡田
Okada
永利軒
Wing Lei

外

南灣湖
Nam Van Lake

TAIPA BRIDGE
澳氹大橋

One Ce

新口岸
Outer Habour
Reclamation Area 市

外 港 新 項
N A P E 海

文化中心
廣場

Legend Wharf
澳 阿索館

菜斯
Rocks

1

美高梅金殿
MGM Grand

壹號湖畔
One Central

參考下面
See below

寶雅座
Aux Beaux Arts

金殿堂
Imperial Court

食·八方
Square Eight

2

← 469m米 (比例尺 Scale 1:15,625) →

新口岸
Outer Habour
Reclamation Area

漁人碼頭
Fisherman's Wharf

稻菊
Inagiku

蘇浙匯
Jade Garden

丹桂軒
Laurel

星際
StarWorld

金沙
Sands

澳門
回歸賀禮
陳列館 文化中心
Macau 廣場
Handover
Pavilion

澳門文化中心
Macao Cultural Centre

澳門藝術博物館
Museum of Art

萬利
Encore

3

咖啡廷
Café Encore

京花軒
Golden Flower

港 新 項
N A P E 海

觀音像
Statue of
Kuh Iam

C

D

← 356m米 (比例尺 Scale 1:11,856) →

←627m米(比例尺 Scale 1:20,909)→

A   B

澳氹大橋 Macau-Taipa Bridge

西灣大橋 Sai Van Bridge

1

海洋大馬路

洋花園本馬路

史伯泰海軍馬路 Est dos Sete Tanques

海洋花園 海洋會所

氹仔東

奧羅拉 Aurora

天政 Tenmasa

帝影樓 Ying

觀音岩 澳門大學 University of M

氹仔雕塑 Taipa Monument

110.8

小潭山

新濠鋒 Altira

將軍馬路

菩提禪院 Pou Tai Un Monastery

百姓 Banza

玫瑰山莊

柯維納馬路 Est Governador Albano Oliveira

氹仔炮壘

澳門賽馬會 Macau Jockey Club

賽馬場 Macau Jockey Club

四面佛 Four-Faces Buddha

Avenida de Kwong Tung

Estrada Nordeste

Estrada Est Lou Lim Ieok

澳門運動場 Stadium & Aquatic Centre

2

東亞運大馬路

Avenida dos Jogos da Asia Oriental

奧林匹克 游泳館 Stadium & Aquatic Centre

安東尼奧 Antonio

葡國美食天地 A Petisqueira

氹仔 Taipa Village

新陶陶 San Tou Tou

Hous

珠海市 ZHU HAI CITY

望德聖母灣大馬路 Estrada da Baia de N

蓮花大馬路

A MARGINAL FLOR DE LOTUS

西堤馬路

Avenida de Cotai

路

人工濕地

3

通往珠海市，橫琴 To Zhu Hai City

蓮花大橋 Lotus Bridge

蓮

ESTRADA FLOR DE

路氹 邊檢 Border (

A   B

友誼大橋
Friendship Bridge

馬路

北安永業街
Estrada de Pac On
嘉豐街
拍順樂街
順業街

永福街

信安馬路
Avenida Son On

氹仔臨時客運碼頭
（北安碼頭）
Taipa Temporary Ferry Terminal

1

Estrada da Ponta da Cabrita

氹

嘉
亞
街

仔

159.2
大潭山

天文台科技路

Tai pa

客運大樓
Terminal Building

Avenida Wai Long

羅
頭
馬路

澳門國際機場
Macau International Airport

嘉樂庇
物館
住宅式
ipa
Museum

Avenida Dr Sun

大潭山
壹號

澳門
科技大學
Macau University of
Science &
Technology

2

Senhora da Esperanca

路氹連貫公路
（金光大道）

君悦
Grand Hyatt
滿堂彩
Beijing Kitchen

城

威尼斯人
enetian

四季
Four Seasons
鳴詩
Belcanção
紫逸軒
i Yat Heen

氹

喜薈
Canton
利苑酒家
Lei Garden

星麗門
Cotai

ESTRADA DO ISTMO

十二生肖雕像

澳門東亞運動會
體育館(澳門蛋)
Macau East
Asian
Games
Dome

3

路

蓮花路

C   D

You know
the MICHELIN guide

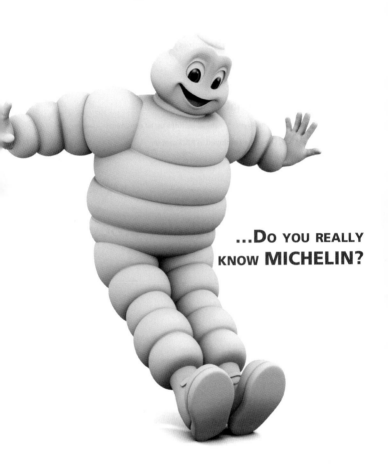

...Do you really
know MICHELIN?

Data 31/12/2009

The world No.1 in tires with 16.3% of the market

A business presence in over **170 countries**

A manufacturing footprint
at the heart of markets

In 2009 **72** industrial sites in **19** countries produced:

- **150** million tires
- **10** million maps and guides

Highly international teams

Over **109 200** employees* from all cultures on all continents

including **6 000** people employed in R&D centers in Europe, the US and Asia.

*102,692 full-time equivalent staff

The Michelin Group at a glance

Michelin competes

At the end of 2009

Le Mans 24-hour race
12 consecutive years of victories

Endurance 2008
- 6 victories on 6 stages in Le Mans Series
- 12 victories on 12 stages in American Le Mans Series

Paris-Dakar
Since the beginning of the event, the Michelin group has won in all categories

Moto Endurance
2009 World Champion

Trial
Every World Champion title since 1981 (except 1992)

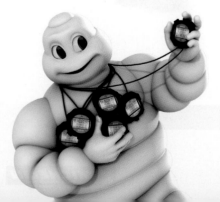

Michelin, established close to its customers

68 plants in 19 countries

- Algeria
- Brazil
- Canada
- China
- Colombia
- France
- Germany
- Hungary
- Italy
- Japan
- Mexico
- Poland
- Romania
- Russia
- Serbia
- Spain
- Thailand
- UK
- USA

A Technology Center spread over 3 continents

- Asia
- Europe
- North America

2 Natural rubber plantations

- Brazil

Our mission

To make a sustainable contribution to progress in the mobility of goods and people by enhancing freedom of movement, safety, efficiency and pleasure when on the move.

ENERGY SAVER

Michelin committed to environmental-friendliness

Michelin, world leader in low rolling resistance tires, actively reduces fuel consumption and vehicle gas emission.

For its products, Michelin develops state-of-the-art technologies in order to:
- Reduce fuel consumption, while improving overall tire performance.
- Increase life cycle to reduce the number of tires to be processed at the end of their useful lives;
- Use raw materials which have a low impact on the environment.

Furthermore, at the end of 2008, 99.5% of tire production in volume was carried out in ISO 14001* certified plants.

Michelin is committed to implementing recycling channels for end-of-life tires.

*environmental certification

**Passenger Car
Light Truck**

Truck

Michelin
a key mobility enabler

Earthmover

Aircraft

Agricultural

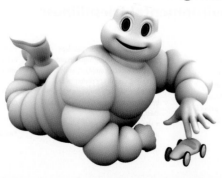

Two-wheel

Distribution

Partnered with vehicle manufacturers, in tune with users, active in competition and in all the distribution channels, Michelinis continually innovating to promote mobility today and to invent that of tomorrow.

Maps and Guides

ViaMichelin, travel assistance services

Michelin Lifestyle, for your travel accessories

MICHELIN
plays on balanced performance

● **Long tire life**

◐ **Fuel savings**

○ **Safety on the road**

... MICHELIN tires provide you with the best performance, without making a single sacrifice.

The MICHELIN tire pure technology

1 Tread
A thick layer of rubber
provides contact with the ground.
It has to channel water away
and last as long as possible.

2 Crown plies
This double or triple reinforced belt
has both vertical flexibility
and high lateral rigidity.
It provides the steering capacity.

3 Sidewalls
These cover and protect the textile casing
whose role is to attach the tire tread
to the wheel rim.

4 Bead area for attachment to the rim
Its internal bead wire
clamps the tire firmly
against the wheel rim.

5 Inner liner
This makes the tire
almost totally impermeable
and maintains the correct inflation pressure.

ENERGY

Heed
the MICHELIN Man's advice

To improve safety:

- I drive with the correct tire pressure
- I check the tire pressure every month
- I have my car regularly serviced
- I regularly check the appearance of my tires (wear, deformation)
- I am responsive behind the wheel
- change my tires according to the season

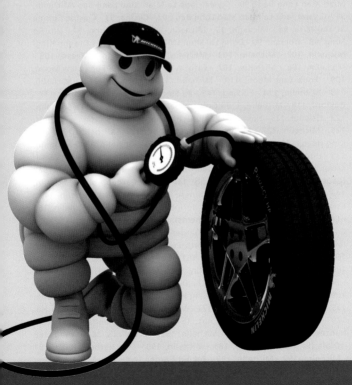

www.michelin.com
www.michelin.(your country extension – e.g. .fr for France)

PICTURE COPYRIGHT
圖片版權

Agnès b. Le Pain Grillé (Central), 66 - Amber, 67 - Angelini, 68 - Aspasia, 69 - BLT Steak, 70 - Bo Innovation, 71 - Bombay Dreams, 72 - Café Gray Deluxe, 73 - Café Siam, 74 - Caprice, 75 - Casa Lisboa, 76 - Celebrity Cuisine, 77 - Celestial Court, 78 - Cépage/Michelin, 79 - Michelin, 80 - Chesa, 81 - Michelin, 82 - Chilli Fagara, 83 - Chiu Chow Garden (Tsuen Wan), 84 - Michelin, 85 - Michelin, 86 - Chuen Cheung Kui (Mong Kok), 87 - Michelin, 88 - City Hall Maxim's Palace/Michelin, 89 - Crystal Jade La Mian Xiao Long Bao , 90 - Crystal Jade La Mian Xiao Long Bao /Michelin, 91 - Crystal Jade La Mian Xiao Long Bao , 92 - Cucina, 93 - Cuisine Cuisine at The Mira, 94 - Michelin, 95 - Michelin, 96 - Din Tai Fung, 97 - Din Tai Fung, 98 - Domani, 99 - Dong Lai Shun, 100 - Michelin, 101 - Dragon King/ Michelin, 102 - Michelin, 103 - Michelin, 104 - 8½ Otto e Mezzo, 105 - Michelin, 106 - Michelin, 107 - Fofo by el Willy, 108 - Fook Lam Moon, 109 - Fook Lam Moon, 110 - Michelin, 111 - Michelin, 112 - Michelin, 113 - Michelin, 114 - Fu Sing, 115 - Fu Sing/Michelin, 116 - Gaddi's, 117 - Gaylord, 118 - Michelin, 119 - Golden Leaf, 120 - Michelin, 121 - Michelin, 122 - Grissini, 123 - Hakka Yé Yé, 124 - Harbour Grill, 125 - Harvey Nichols, 126 - Michelin, 127 - Michelin, 128 - Michelin, 129 - Michelin, 130 - Hoi King Heen, 131 - Hoi Yat Heen, 132 - H One, 133 - Michelin, 134 - Michelin, 135 - Hugo's, 136 - Hunan Garden, 137 - Hunan Garden, 138 - Hung's Delicacies/Michelin, 139 - Hutong, 140 - Inagiku, 141 - Inagiku, 142 - IR1968 (Causeway Bay), 143 - Island Tang, 144 - Jade Garden, 145 - Michelin, 146 - Michelin, 147 - Kimberley Chinese Restaurant, 148 - Michelin, 149 - Kwan Cheuk Heen, 150 - L'Atelier de Joël Robuchon, 151 - Michelin, 152 - Lei Bistro, 153 - Lei Garden (Elements), 154 - Lei Garden (IFC), 155 - Lei Garden (Kowloon Bay), 156 - Lei Garden (Kwun Tong), 157 - Lei Garden (Mong Kok), 158 - Lei Garden (North Point), 159 - Lei Garden (Sha Tin), 160 - Lei Garden (Tsim Sha Tsui), 161 - Lei Garden (Wanchai), 162 - Le 188°, 163 - Michelin, 164 - Michelin, 165 - Michelin, 166 - Michelin, 167 - Lobster Bar and Grill, 168 - Michelin, 169 - Michelin, 170 - Loong Toh Yuen, 171 - Michelin, 172 - Lung King Heen, 173 - Michelin, 174 - Michelin, 175 - Michelin, 176 - Michelin, 177 - Mandarin Grill + Bar, 178 - Man Ho, 179 - Man Wah, 180 - Ming Court, 181 - Mist, 182 - Nanhai No.1, 183 - Naozen, 184 - Michelin, 185 - Michelin, 186 - Nicholini's, 187 - Nobu, 188 - Olala (St. Francis Street), 189 - Michelin, 190 - One Harbour Road, 191 - Michelin, 192 - Michelin, 193 - Peking Garden (Admiralty), 194 - Peking Garden (Central), 195 - Peking Garden (Kowloon), 196 - Peking Garden

NOTES
備註

....

....

....

....

....

....

....

....

....

....

....

....

....

....

....

....

....

....

....

Manufacture française des pneumatiques Michelin
Société en commandite par actions au capital de 304 000 000 EUR
Place des Carmes-Déchaux – 63000 Clermont-Ferrand (France)
R.C.S. Clermont-Fd B 855 200 507

© **Michelin et Cie, Propriétaires-éditeurs**
Dépot légal Novembre 2010

Made in Japan

Published in 2010

E-mail : michelinguide.hongkong-macau@cn.michelin.com

Maps : (C) 2010 Cartographic data Universal Publications, Ltd / Michelin
Design : Akita Design Kan Inc. Tokyo, Japan
Pre-Press: Nord Compo, Villeneuve-d'Ascq, France
Printing and Binding: Toppan, Tokyo, Japan